REELING THROUGH
HOLLYWOOD

Maybe I should have opted for a career in music?

REELINGTHROUGH
HOLLYWOOD

Dan Bessie

How I Spent 40 Fabulous Years
in Film and Never Made a Nickel

Blue Lupin Press

BLUE LUPIN PRESS
bluelupinpress.com
info@bluelupinpress.com

Library of Congress Catalogue Number - 2006901200

ISBN 978-0-9777768-0-1

Copyright © 2006 by Dan Bessie

All rights reserved. No part of this book may be reproduced without prior written consent of the author, except in the case of brief quotations embodied in critical articles and reviews.

Printed in the United States of America by Walch Publishing, Portland, Maine

Frontispiece: the author on his 1st birthday, Vermont, 1932

Acknowledgements: George McManus photo courtesy of Ruth Florea; estate of John Florea. Bringing Up Father © King Features Syndicate. Wallybird image © Delta Air Lines. JELL-O ® "Chinese Baby" © Kraft Foods. Dallas Williams photo courtesy of Gaye Williams. Culligan stills © Culligan International Company. Linus the Lionhearted © Kraft Foods. The Incredible Hulk and The Amazing Spiderman © Marvel Enterprises Inc. *Salt of the Earth* images © 1999 Organa, LLC. *Executive Action* photos and Learning Garden advertisement courtesy of Severo Perez. Roy Rogers and Dale Evans photo used by permission of the Roy Rogers-Dale Evans Museum, Branson, Mo. Harlem Globetrotters image courtesy of The Harlem Globetrotters. "Family Ties" article from *American Film* © 1985, used by permission of the American Film Institute and Robert Aaronson. Bill Ballantine drawings used by courtesy of Roberta Ballentine. Cover reels by photos. com.

Design and Layout: Jannetje Anita Thomas, Binding Plus
information@bindingplus.com

For Jeanne

Contents

CAVEAT	ix
BOOK ONE	1
1. montage	3
2. cartoonery	19
BOOK TWO	25
3. signs by smith	27
4. nibbling on the big apple	39
5. befuddled	46
BOOK THREE	55
6. down the rabbit hole	57
7. faking it	70
8. tent show	85
9. hustlers	92
10. hey culligan man!	98
11. ups and downs	105
12. it's plastic, it's fantastic	114
BOOK FOUR	123
13. flashback: salt of the earth	125
14. mogul fever	133
15. look ma, I'm makin' movies	140
16. executive foreplay	149
17. just desserts	156
18. fumbling along in the land of enchantment	161
19. executive action	169
20. henry who?	191

Contents

BOOK FIVE		195
21.	the graveyard of good ideas	197
22.	wordsmithing	204
23.	flashback: director's book camp	209
24.	remember to wash your hands	215
25.	meadowlark lemon and the king of the cowboys	222
26.	cutting the cord	231
BOOK SIX		239
27.	movies in the shire	241
28.	peter and the wolf	245
29.	a duck, a jabberwock, and uncle milty	266
30.	hard traveling	279
31.	hard traveling II the agony and the ecstasy	302
32.	the littlest movie makers	320
BOOK SEVEN		327
33.	turnabout	329
34.	moving on	346

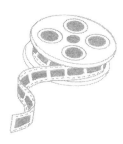

caveat

- **DON'T BUY THIS BOOK** *if the price leaves you without enough for a frappuchino at Starbucks.*

- **DON'T BUY THIS BOOK** *to discover who slept with whom, who beat up his lover, or other tidbits of juicy gossip.*

- **DON'T BUY THIS BOOK** *expecting to discover the secret of finding an agent, selling a screenplay, or landing a starring role in the next Quentin Tarantino flick.*

- **DO BUY THIS BOOK** *because you think it might provide fresh insight into survival in a wonderful but crazy industry, because you enjoy finding out about how someone else made it, and because it looks like it might be a good read.*

Something about me: first, the sub-title. That's a bit of a humbug; I did make a nickel. I went from starvation wages in 1956 to more than $1000 a week for most of 1974.[1] But it didn't last; there were also long dry spells, with paychecks as scarce as wombats in Wal-Mart. During the lean years I lugged water heaters around the stockroom of a swimming pool supply company, snoozed through insulting pitches about how any simpleton could get rich in vacuum cleaner sales, and borrowed my way into outlandish debt with a friendly credit union. Most of you have never heard of me. But I've had my fifteen minutes in the sun, been involved in three features, and have churned out more than a hundred short films, writing,

---

[1] $1000 a week in 1974 might be the equivalent of $6000 in today's dollars.

Reeling Through Hollywood

directing and financing most of them. And I've relished almost every moment. On balance, it's been a great life.

Those folks on the cover? I've had an encounter with each one; some, a mere handshake or a quick hello. Others I knew well. But I've tried to do more than name-drop, mentioning them only when my association related to a project I was involved in.

Names aside, I think you'll like the book. For those curious about the odd and famous, it's filled with enough filmic foolishness to keep you turning pages. There's a pinch of sex, along with a smidgen of politics, and a bit about the tribulations of family; all part of the great carnival of life. On the other hand, if non-stop libido, larceny, and nose powder are your turn-ons, read no further; go pilfer a copy of Julia Phillips' wonderfully glib, rarely insightful, and ultimately sad disgourgarama of Hollywood angst and nastiness, *You'll Never Eat Lunch in This Town Again.*

Metaphorically, yearning to work in film can make you feel like you're on a carousel; every time your horse comes around and you reach out to snatch the brass ring, it eludes you. Or you bubble with jealousy when the guy or gal ahead of you grabs it. In Hollywood, tens of thousands lust for the brass ring. Most eventually end up selling insurance, painting sets for junior college theatricals, get into software to earn their BMWs or become pastry chefs. Nothing wrong with that, the world can always use a superior lemon chiffon pie.

Still, as with any art form, good movie making takes dedication and persistence and above all an immense passion. Mastering the skills that result in lasting or memorable work involves time and patience. Creativity is a stern mistress and the apprenticeship can be long and frustrating. Though even if you fall on your face you still stand a chance of slipping into a quirky kind of fame. Witness Ed Wood, and *Plan 9 From Outer Space.*[2]

---

[2] Often considered the worst director of all time, Edward D. Wood Jr.'s career has been celebrated in the wonderful, loosely fictionalized biopic, *Ed Wood*, starring Johnny Depp, and directed by Tim Burton.

Caveat

Movies, music, sports, publishing, television, and politics: these are the romantic magnets of our day. And they are enormously influential. The stars, singers, sluggers, authors, producers and senators who populate these arenas are held up as icons, glittering examples of the success we should all struggle to emulate. Many earn megabucks. By comparison, most teachers, who play a vastly more important role in molding the character of our future citizens, are penniless beggars. We're encouraged to believe that the new SUV, a bulging wallet, Britney Spears on one arm, or waking up next to Ben Affleck is a truer measure of greatness than is a steady competence, the smile of a handicapped kid we've helped complete some task, or seeing to it that a lonely elder has someone to talk to. Or simply being a decent human being.

Sure, altruism is rewarded; we get a minute and a half of it every three days on News at Eleven. But stack that up against *Who Wants to be a Millionaire*, and what have you got? Like constantly reaching for the brass ring, too many fall for the media hype. And I don't mean to put down sweating hard to catch the ring. But instead of giving up, maybe those who never catch it need to measure success in a different way.

That's why I wrote the book. By reading about how I managed to survive forty years inside a rarely profitable, sometimes maddening, but often deliciously rewarding profession, I hope you'll learn to recognize success in the way I've come to: by enjoying the process. Once you can do that, even if you're never able to send your daughter to Harvard or watch a neighbor's jaw drop when he spots the glitzy new SUV in your drive, you've caught the brass ring.

a word to wannabes

Reeling Through Hollywood was also written with you in mind, all you brave souls who keep trying to wedge your way into the movie business; especially those of you who've had your asses bitten more times than you can count. You're the folks who mortgaged your Toyotas, Grandma's cameo collection (with her permission, I hope), or your bungalow in Wahpeton, North Dakota, to finance your first film. Or your girlfriend has dumped you for a guy who pulls in six figures at Microsoft while you deliver pizzas or sizzle fries at McDonalds, then pop No-Doze until 4 a.m. as you sweat over your new high concept screenplay. Or your boyfriend is pissed because you slog through fourteen-hour days as a free production assistant on *Revenge of the Zombie Dentists,* when you could be home wrestling up a nouvelle chicken provençal and giving him a full body massage. Even your cat has run off because that sixty-five-cent canned tuna at Safeway doesn't cut it.

Still, you hound Aunt Trudy and Uncle Mort for a loan so you can buy one more roll of film, or you bus dishes for the Beautiful People at Ma Maison so you can chunk down $250 bucks for the next fabulous conference where the inside dope on how to break into the biz will be revealed. And why do you do it? For love, of course, like Diana Morales in *A Chorus Line.* That's why I did it. That's why we all do it. We have to. We're following a dream.

The movie business is risky and unforgiving. Today's super giant is often tomorrow's white dwarf. Negotiating the yellow-brick road on the way to the Emerald City may not be as treacherous for you as it was for Dorothy, but neither is anyone likely to strew rose petals in your path.

I wrote the book with all that in mind, confident that reading about my sometimes disjointed journey will help you avoid the dead ends I often ran into along the way; help you focus more clearly, recognize real opportunities when they're presented and convince you to develop both short term and long term goals, so that whatever it is you seek as a creative person won't dribble down

Caveat

the lack-of-foresight drain. While no "how to" manual, my book will, I hope, be a cautionary tale. Perhaps you'll discover films, events and personalities you may not have known about. Maybe the opinionated comments I toss in now and then will get you to look at things a bit differently than you had before. Most of all, I hope that understanding my experience helps you to chart a more rewarding and thoughtful journey of your own. And maybe you'll feel inspired to pass on what you learn along the way to the next generation.

And no matter how many times I tell you how difficult it is to succeed in film, you're probably not going to listen anyway. I don't blame you. Like me, you've got to follow the dream. But what if you don't get there? What if, in spite of working your ass off, you don't "make it" on Hollywood's terms? What if your name never pops up next to Nicholas Cage or Nora Ephron in *People*? If so, will you decide that you're to blame? Will you spend long unhappy years trying to figure out why? Will you allow into your consciousness that tiny pipsqueak voice, the one our society so often uses to put people down, the one that says "loser?"

Don't do it. Don't fall for that mind set. Don't be a slave to your pride, or make the business into some kind of a god. But do go for the dream.

If your film career brings you riches and fame, more power to you. But be realistic; understand that in spite of all your hard work, there's no guarantee. "Making it" is sometimes just plain dumb luck, like being in the right place at the right time. Also, be thankful that the odds against making it big are not as unlikely as winning the lottery. Know that there's a shiny side to the coin. You *can* make films. You can even make decent ones. And with immense determination you might even make a living at it, as I did. (Most of the time.)

Mainly, focus on the process. Enjoy the writing of your screenplay, the trying out for the role, raising the money to make your film. In the movie business your name on the screen before the main title comes on can be a kind of pink smoke, a smoke that dissolves as soon as the crowds you were sure would break box office records stay away in droves. Remember, to put food in your belly or keep little Charlie in diapers, you can always pump gas or wait tables. (Hey, these are honorable ways to make a living.) And if you finally decide, "Screw Hollywood, I'm going back to Oshkosh" to become the greatest lemon-chiffon pie-maker in the world, please zip me an e-mail; lemon-chiffon is my favorite.

But if you're determined to help create movies, know that as you learn to dodge the hot oil poured down over you by the gatekeepers of Fortress Hollywood, you've mainly got to figure out how to appreciate the process of doing. And that simply means being a creative person. As I suggested in the intro, by learning to appreciate the process you'll be nourishing your creative soul. That's my message.

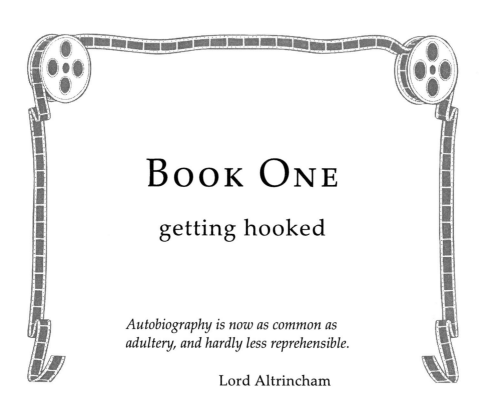

BOOK ONE
getting hooked

Autobiography is now as common as adultery, and hardly less reprehensible.

Lord Altrincham

ONE

montage

FADE IN

INT. RIALTO THEATER. POUGHKEEPSIE, NEW YORK, 1946

"The Rat Hole," locals dub this abandoned picture palace. The label is generous: urine-stained seats, a screen in tatters, and gaping holes in the roof admitting bats and pigeons that roost in the rafters.

Two thirteen-year-old boys jimmy open a rusting exit door and race along an aisle toward the lobby.

PIMPLES, curly haired, and wearing an ill-fitting Eisenhower jacket, edges up a rickety stairwell.

FRECKLES, a hyperactive redhead, discovers an art deco frosted glass partition separating the lobby from the orchestra. Previous miscreants have left it intact, so Freckles assaults the partition with chunks of broken concrete and a crazy laugh.

INT. PROJECTION BOOTH

Pimples enters and looks around.

A battered projector, its glazed eye fixed on the floor, droops like a rejected lover. A box of dusty glass advertising slides sits on a broken chair. In one corner, a five-foot stack of cardboard posters rests against the wall. Pimples turns one over.

INSERT:

Beau Geste, announces the poster. Then another is uncovered.

Modern Times, says the next.

BACK TO SCENE

Intrigued, Pimples slowly inspects the pile of lobby cards advertising every movie the Rialto has featured for the past umpteen years.

Then he runs to the tiny window through which once flickered giant images of Katherine Hepburn and Cary Grant.

PIMPLES
Hey, get up here, I found some stuff!

In a flash, Freckles is in the booth. Pimples displays a *Casablanca* poster.

PIMPLES
Waddya think we ought'a do with this junk?

Freckles hefts an armload of cards and charges out of the booth.

FRECKLES
I got an idea, grab some . . .

Pimples scoops up a stack and chugs after his buddy.

INT. THE RIALTO – BALCONY

Taking turns, our delinquent heroes skim lobby cards from the edge of the balcony down into the orchestra. Testosterone racing, they outdo one another, sailing the posters through a gaping hole in the screen and against the brick wall beyond.

FRECKLES
I got *The Informer* . . .

And away it flies, landing in the third row. [$9500 from a future eBay sale, down the drain.]

PIMPLES
I got *Animal Crackers* . . .

4

MONTAGE

Off it flies, bouncing across a seat and skidding to a stop out of sight on the floor. [There goes another $5000.]

>FRECKLES
>I got *King Kong!*

[$25,000 sails directly across the stage and through the hole in the screen.]

>FRECKLES (CONT'D)
>Bull's eye!

And so it goes, for half an hour, until adolescent boredom sets in and Freckles says —

>FRECKLES (CONT'D)
>This is gettin' to be a **drag. Let's** go downtown and score some chicks

FADE OUT

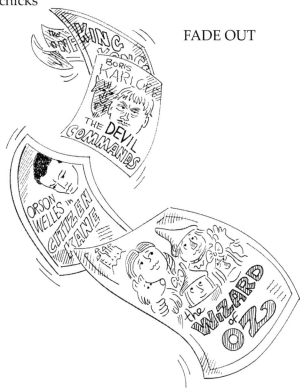

As I sit here in my cozy Sierra foothills home, looking out at the deer munching my wife Jeanne's recently planted hydrangeas, and dredging up that spring of 1946 – with freckle-faced Eddie and me checking to see if we've been spotted as we sneak out of The Rat Hole – my few remaining hairs turn white. Why didn't I, at thirteen, flash on the future value of those now classic movie posters? How come I didn't realize that my future son Joe could have had a free ride through college instead of washing dishes to pay his way? And couldn't I have imagined that I might someday be tooting around in a sleek new Mercedes, instead of the battered 1987 Jeep Cherokee now sitting in our drive?

Well, water over the dam; what does a thirteen-year old know? And anyhow, the Jeep is loved and dependable and gets Jeanne and me to places any self respecting Mercedes would be petrified to navigate.

If, in 1946, I never flashed on the future value of those posters, I also had no clue that the Rialto would not be my last encounter with the magic of the movies. It certainly wasn't my first. But for that we need a long

FLASHBACK:

To 1937. Mom, David and I are living in Brooklyn Heights. I don't even know what a movie *is*. So when my gentle mother leads me into a cavernous space with wall to wall seats and a huge rococo chandelier hanging high above, I'm not sure what to expect. Sure, I know it has something to do with *Snow White and the Seven Dwarfs*, because Mom has read us the story from a picture book.

The lights go down. Pitch black. "Mommy . . ." I whimper. She squeezes my hand, so I feel safe. Then suddenly, magic: music, along with multicolored drawings like those in the picture book, except that they *move*. I quickly find myself pulled along by some mysterious force, captive to the flickering frames, until Snow White's wicked stepmother, in her "old crone" permutation, suddenly fills the screen. Then I freeze, bug-eyed, as she cackles "poison, poison!" with fiendish delight, readying the deadly apple for that rosy-cheeked, animated innocent.

I cower on my seat and scrunch into a ball. Then, as an approaching female someone mumbles "excuse me, excuse me," I uncoil two fingers from the hand covering my eyes and gaze up at a gigantic wavering tush about to land on me. And it does! Fortunately for the forty years in film that lie ahead, the ponderous posterior doesn't crush me. Alerted by a muffled "Help!" beneath her and realizing that she's landed on a tiny person, the Ample One quickly stands, blurts out "Oh gracious, I'm so sorry, dear," and shifts to the next (thankfully unoccupied) seat.

Think of the films that might have been inspired by this cheeky experience had I the foresight to create them: movies featuring a squishy, plush-bottomed serial killer gleefully suffocating small boys in the impersonal darkness of gaudy picture palaces. A unique thriller genre; maybe it could have worked. I might have become another Wes Craven![1]

Everything about those Brooklyn years is rainbow-colored, and my brain is a blotter, sopping experiences into visual memory. A fundraising party for refugees displaced by the Spanish Civil War, held on a huge ship at the waterfront – where, on a big newsprint pad, a cartoonist materializes Mickey Mouse, and Macy's Thanksgiving Day parade, where giant Pluto and Popeye balloons float down New York's Fifth Avenue. Plus the fantasy of Ringling Brothers and

---

[1] Wes Craven: director of horror films such as *A Nightmare on Elm Street, Swamp Thing, Scream,* etc

Barnum and Bailey's Circus, with the great clown Emmett Kelly creeping into the center ring to sweep a spotlight into a dustpan. A midget car chugs to center ring and seventeen clowns – I count them – pile out and scramble aboard a rocket ship. It blasts off. A cloud of smoke obliterates the scene. As it clears, tiny parachutes with tiny clowns float down from the ceiling. Not scary like *Snow White*, and far more thrilling.

But thankfully, neither the giant tush nor the evil stepmother sour me on movies. In rural Pennsylvania, where David and I move with Mom in 1939, we hitch into town one soft summer night with Harold, the barely educated but caring hired man that Mom has recently married, to gawk at Charlie Chaplin dining on his shoe, laces and all, in *The Gold Rush*. Harold turns to me with his crooked, toothy grin and whispers, "It ain't a real shoe, Danny boy, hear tell it was made out'n lic'rish candy."[2]

Evenings, the creative juices in my small brain bubble as I sit, transfixed, listening to Harold describe outlandish exploits he claims to have taken part in but never has, or hang on Mom's dramatized reading of the next chapter from *The Wizard of Oz*, *The Hollow Tree Book*, *The Wind in the Willows*, or *Through the Looking Glass*. All of these construct a marvelous mental jungle gym that becomes a playground of imagination.

Returning to New York from Pennsylvania, I find myself in an after school program at a community center, mesmerized by a short animated film about the "Sunshine Vitamin." How, I wonder, do they get those pictures to move?

Later, Saturday morning movie serials invade my dreams. In Danbury, Connecticut, in 1943, a bunged-up aluminum pot donated for the war effort gets kids in free to see *Bataan* or *Action in the North Atlantic* at the Palace. I not only show up with a handful of dented cookware, but for weeks, neighborhood buddies and I drag broken

---

2 At eight years old, of course, I had no Idea that over forty years later I'd be writing and directing a movie about Harold and Mom, a tragic drama that played itself out in Pennsylvania. (See Chapters 30 and 31, "*Hard Traveling*"; and my memoir, *Rare Birds, an American Family*; University Press of Kentucky, 2000.)

water pipes, rusty boilers and whatever scrap iron we can find, pile it eight feet high on a vacant lot and take turns guarding it at night (from Nazi spies, I suppose). An excited little man claiming to be a reporter appears one afternoon and grinds away with a 16mm camera. "You boys will all be in the movies," he promises. I catch every newsreel for months, but our scrap pile never stars.

Radio too keeps me swinging on the inner jungle gym. Nights, I fight sleep while Orson Welles as *The Shadow* clouds men's minds so he can trap a psychotic killer. I get all goose-bumpy as Raymond creaks open *The Creaking Door*, and am glued to our static-ridden Philco as Jack, Doc and Reggie set off on some terrifying new adventure in *I Love a Mystery*, an adventure deliberately calculated to make half a million kids pee their pants.

> Announcer: "Seven o'clock in the dusk of a hot, tropical evening in the expedition's camp where the beach rises to the jungle on the Island of Skulls."
>
> Doc: "Woo... Listen t' that. An' if you ask me it is going to be darker than the inside of a coal miner's esophagus in a couple of shakes, and then what?"

Tame stuff compared to *A Nightmare on Elm Street*, but even without the visuals it has me cowering under the covers. Awesome

sound effects, edgy writing, foreboding voices and I'm sucked into Wonderland. Years before TV displaces the Philco, I hang on every hackneyed twist of every ridiculous plot.

But soon, fantasy collides with reality.

Poughkeepsie, 1943.

"Hey Eddie," I brag to "Freckles," my new best friend, the smart-alecky redhead with whom I'd later invade the Rialto, "Guess what?

"You farted."

"No, you jerk. My father's in Hollywood. He's writing for the movies."[3]

"What a liar," replies Eddie.

There's raucous laughter from other classmates, who have over-heard. But when the glossy photo signed "to Dan and Dave, from Bud Abbott and Lou Costello" arrives in the big Warner Brothers envelope, presto-changeo, I'm hot stuff. Except with Eddie. "Bet'cha can't score Bette Davis, Bob Hope and Jimmy Durante," he scoffs.

I scribble off a note to Pop. Bette Davis he comes through with.

What I don't tell anyone is that Pop is a Red. And that in order to take the Warner assignment, after a year fighting with American volunteers in Spain against the fascist General Franco, he's quit his thirty-dollar-a-week job as drama critic for the Communist Party's cultural magazine, *New Masses*. I don't tell anyone because to me it's of little consequence. And because at the time I have only the foggiest notion of what communism is. (Doesn't matter, they'll find out four years later when Pop and a group of associates are hauled before the House Committee on Un-American Activities where they refuse to discuss their political affiliations and are front page news as the subversive "Hollywood Ten.")

---

[3] My father, Alvah Bessie (1904-1985), received screenplay or original story credit on ten films, including *Northern Pursuit* (1943), *Objective Burma* and *Hotel Berlin* (both 1945), and *The Sex Symbol* (1974).

MONTAGE

More important to me back in 1943 is that the following summer train tickets arrive from Pop. Tickets on the Santa Fe *Chief*. David and I are going to "the coast" for a visit.

Los Angeles' Union Station, massive and marble, is straight out of movies in which I've seen it featured. And my dream of spotting stars stroll the streets quickly comes true. As we drive along Hollywood Boulevard Pop shouts, "There's Monty Woolley." The fine, bearded character actor, who ran away with stage and film versions of *The Man Who Came to Dinner*[4] is, says Pop, "trolling for boys." I have no idea what he's talking about.

No freeways. No smog. Orange blossoms scent the air. The San Fernando Valley, where Pop, his wife Helen and my half-sister Eva live, is carpeted with walnut groves and chicken ranches.

We visit Warner's, shake hands with Bette Davis ("Alvah, dahling, how ahh you? And these are your sons? Delighted, chahmed.") and with Eleanor Parker, plucked from Ohio obscurity to co-star in *The Very Thought of You*, a film that Pop has recently written. In the years ahead she'll pull in three Oscar nominations before mainly being relegated to minor roles. In the commissary we meet Dane Clark, one of Eleanor's co-stars in the film, who also stars in *Pride of the Marines* and *Destination Tokyo*.

"Dane, This is my older son, Dan. His kid brother says he doesn't want to meet any movie stars. He's outside, being shy."

"Well, shit on him!"

This stuns me. Movie stars are akin to gods; how can one of them put down a nine-year-old like that? Welcome to the real Hollywood, kid!

Even so, the summer is a Technicolor extravaganza, and I return to Poughkeepsie stuffed with images: driving in Pop's 1940 Hudson as we track searchlights slicing through the California night – searchlights that we're sure are announcing a world

---

[4] *The Man Who Came to Dinner* (1942). If you've never seen it, go rent the DVD or a video.

REELING THROUGH HOLLYWOOD

premier – only to discover the grand opening of a new hot dog stand. And an evening with marionettes and Elsa Lanchester (*The Bride of Frankenstein*) at my fabulous Uncle Harry's famous Turnabout Theater, its walls covered with autographs of his fans. Everyone from Clifford Odets to Lana Turner to Alfred Hitchcock.[5] An entire Welsh village has been created on a sound stage for Bette Davis's *The Corn is Green*. A bevy of dancers jitterbug amid flashing neon signs on a stage where *Hollywood Canteen* is being shot. And David and I spend a wild couple hours blasting Junkers and Messerschmidts out of the skies over Burbank from the turret of a mockup of a B-29. Betty Grable, the "girl with the million dollar legs," isn't around for us to ogle, but there are enough aspiring starlets in hot pink shorts zipping about Warner's on messenger bikes, or roller skating out to serve us burgers and malts at a Sunset Boulevard drive-in, to more than satisfy an eleven-year-old whose hormones are starting to percolate.

The summer has been an inspiration. For the next two years, I soak up movies. Anything and everything, from cheesy reruns and B westerns at the Rialto (before it crumbles into decay), starring Lash LaRue, Johnny Mack Brown and Roy Rogers, to Buster Crabbe as Flash Gordon, in *Perils From Planet Mongo*, to *Girls in Chains*, to *I Walked With a Zombie*. I swallow my bubble-gum when George Zucco, as yet another creepy scientist, goofing around with ancient Egyptian gases, goes to his deserved reward in *The Mad Ghoul*, and am glued to my seat as Gary Cooper captures a hundred plus cringing Krauts in *Sergeant York*. I zip along beside *Captain Marvel*, in his wrinkly cotton tights, as he roars through the clouds in a weekly serial. And who cares if we can see the wires holding him up?

During one week in the summer of 1945, I take in a movie every day. Like most kids, I often don't know what the film I plunk down my fifteen cents for is about. I just want to be entertained. With

---

[5] California mainstays since their first arrival in 1929, Uncle Harry and his partners in The Yale Puppeteers achieved their greatest success from 1941 through 1956, when their unique little playhouse on La Cienega Boulevard sold almost every ticket, every night, for 4,535 performances. For more about their fabulous careers see Chapter 33, "Turnabout." (And my book, *Rare Birds*.)

no rating system we see everything. Of course, there's no raunchy dialogue to assault tender young ears (let alone any leave-nothing-to-the-imagination sex, or bloody chainsaws ripping terrified teens in two).

And I'm sufficiently smitten with movie magic to write Pop, explaining that I can buy a sound projector for "only" $248.00, which I'll be able to afford "when I am about five hundred years old." The guilt trip doesn't work and I settle for a $24.98 Keystone model, earned by peddling White Cloverene brand salve door to door. A few extra sales and I have enough to buy a four-minute reel of the Joe Lewis – Max Schmelling heavyweight title match, plus a *Felix the Cat* cartoon.

Whenever a movie Pop has written shows up at the Bardavon, I rush to tell friends. *Northern Pursuit*, starring Errol Flynn as a Mountie outfoxing a pack of Nazis who land in Canada, opens in Poughkeepsie. Admission is an $18.87 war bond. Mom earns little more than that in a week, so Pop generously provides bonds for each of us.

By the autumn of 1945 movies have me hooked, though mainly as diversion. From what? Oh, from wondering when I'll reconnect with a father who is three thousand miles away. From wishing that he and Mom would get back together (even though Pop has married again). From the continuing struggle Mom has to support David and me. And maybe from an unconscious feeling that life will probably always be lived as close to the edge as it was back in Brooklyn, when, at six, I sold *Superman* comics for a nickel each on a street corner in order to help buy groceries. (Oh, for a time machine, to whisk me back to retrieve those comics! Not to mention the posters in the Rialto.)

But somehow, we struggle through. Mom, who raises David and me mostly alone, has an attitude kind of like Wilkins Micawber in *David Copperfield*. "Something will turn up," she'll say, when we're scraping by on pennies a week. And somehow, something always does. If the landlord has to wait for the rent, or if the lights are turned off every few months, Mom always finds a couple of dimes to get us through one more day. Until my later years my attitude is much the same. Influenced perhaps by her creative side as well as by Pop's, I drift through life little concerned with storing nuts in the big oak tree against a frosty winter. Brother David, on the other hand, somehow gets it into his psyche to opt for steadiness and security as he grows up.

Like many children, my early goals are short term and seen in fuzzy focus. I operate by the seat of my emotional pants and try to make sense of the confusions swirling in my head. Kids simply survive the best way they know how. But mothers as fine as David's and mine play a big role in helping us learn how to cope with life.

FADE IN

INT. OUR APARTMENT. POUGHKEEPSIE. 1945 — EVENING

Danny swallows hard, hoping his request will be granted.

> DANNY
> Mom, can I go see *Frankenstein*?

> MOM
> How much does it cost?

> DANNY
> It's a special Halloween show… fifty cents.

A long pause, then –

> MOM
> Well, I guess we can manage that.

> DANNY
> It starts at midnight.

> MOM
> That's pretty late, Danny. I don't think so, it's --

MONTAGE

DANNY
Gosh, Mom, it's Halloween! There's no school tomorrow. And I'm thirteen!"

She pauses for a moment, smiles, then goes to look for her purse.

FADE OUT

Halloween, 1945. It's midnight. I'm thrilled; the Bardavon is jam-packed with deliriously screeching teens, and even though this is decades pre-*The Rocky Horror Picture Show*, Wolf Men and Mummies and Draculas proliferate in the audience.

The show scares the pants off me. And I love it.

As I leave the theater, my entire body's atingle. Although I know it's all been make believe, as I navigate home through the longest, darkest three blocks on Earth, I expect that at any moment the Creature will lurch from a doorway and carry me off to Castle Frankenstein, where evil Igor, rubbing his hands in fiendish glee, will slobber with delight as Victor dismembers me bit by bit and stuffs my parts into immense jars of formaldehyde.

Poughkeepsie, June 1946.

Time to leave for California. Our second trip, this time for good. Mom will close our apartment, sell the furniture and follow in two months. Until she negotiates new digs, David and I will bunk with

Pop. Though no longer a contract writer at Warner's, he still ekes out a living scripting movies.

The Great Rialto Adventure (as I then thought of it) is history. Eddie and I promise to write one other. We never do. In Chicago, David and I transfer from the New York Central to the *Chief*, heading west. With part of the fifteen dollars Pop provides each of us for the trip, I rent a radio (*The Shadow* and *I Love a Mystery* are mandatory listening). In Albuquerque, I get off the train to buy a Mexican sombrero. As I'm about to climb back on, a large black passenger looks down at me and says, with a deep, rumbling smile in his voice. "That's a mighty big hat you got there, son." Back in the car, our porter, also smiling, stops me in the aisle

"You know who that was?"

I shake my head.

"Count Basie," he says, with some pride.[6]

Having swept past Navajo hogans – where wretched-looking children seem to stare enviously at David and me, air-conditioned passengers – we return to "chatting up" (as my English wife Jeanne would say) two cute sisters in the next compartment. Then, as Arizona falls behind and we're crossing the muddy Colorado River, I find myself anticipating time with Pop, evenings at Uncle Harry's Turnabout Theater, and encounters with more movie stars.

---

[6] Pianist and bandleader William "Count" Basie (1904-1984) was a leading figure in the swing era of jazz. Along with Duke Ellington, he was an outstanding representative of the big band style.

Montage

"Hollywood," says the voice in my head, "here I come!"

George McManus, the first professional cartoonist to encourage me.

TWO

cartoonery

Beverly Hills, California. August 1946.

With the $35.00 Pop gives me for my fourteenth birthday burning a hole in my pocket, I race to a local art supply store, where I've spotted a huge, professional drawing table. I have to have it.

A drawing table, because in spite of my passion for movies I didn't start out to become a filmmaker. From the age of twelve, I wanted to be a cartoonist. And a drawing table I must have because days earlier I had discovered, under "artists" in the Beverly Hills phone book, that George McManus, legendary cartoonist and creator of *Bringing up Father* (Jiggs and Maggie), has an office in the building next to the art store. And how can I knock on the Great Man's door and claim to be a cartoonist myself, without a drawing table?

Tongue-tied but fearless, I've knocked. And have been ushered in by a haggard-looking fellow with owlish glasses. "Uh, Mr. McManus?" I utter. "Nope, I'm Zeke," says owl glasses. Beyond, a short, pudgy man who seems glued to his chair and whose stub of a cigar never leaves his mouth looks up. McManus himself, Jiggs incarnate. When I approach his desk and manage to blurt out that I aspire to a cartooning career, McManus mumbles gruffly, "Let's see what'cha got, kid."

I have nothing. Except a few sketches made in Poughkeepsie that even I am convinced are pathetic excuses for cartoons. I don't tell McManus that, but I promise to bring some back "in a couple days." Thus the urgency to acquire the drawing table.

"Are you sure you don't want it delivered?" asks the bemused clerk in the art supply store.

"No, I can manage."

Pop, with whom David and I are now living, is at a script conference; otherwise I'd have asked him to transport it in his trusty 1940 Hudson.

The clerk shakes his head and clucks his tongue as he holds open the wide glass doors while I manfully heft the immense, long-dreamed-of possession out onto the sidewalk.

Edging across Beverly Drive with the table literally on my back and paying far too little attention to traffic, my mind drifts back to my first stab at drawing:

"Look at this," I shout, at age six, racing into the kitchen with my crayon rendering of a Spanish Loyalist bomber blasting a Nazi ship. Mom turns from the stove, where yet another pot of macaroni and cheese is cooking. Her "That's very good, Danny," spreads a grin across my face. "I'll send them to Pop," she adds. Pop is in Spain, fighting in the Civil War. And on paper I'm in the trenches with him, hugging the dirt as a gut-wrenching explosion follows the sickening whine of an artillery shell.

The blast of a car horn jolts me back to Beverly Drive. I edge the drawing table off my back and quickly drag it to the opposite sidewalk. With an inch-and-a-half thick, three-by-four-foot board and cast iron legs, the thing weighs a hundred pounds. But I press on. Have to get it back to Pop's. Have to start drawing. Have to show McManus what I can do.

No problem, I keep telling myself, I'm already miles ahead of where I'd begun, at age eleven, when I'd decided I wanted to be a cartoonist. And the work I'll show McManus will be a huge leap forward. Copying Porky Pig and Little Lulu have satisfied the drawing itch, but seeing original characters come alive under my pencil always sets the creative juices flowing.

CARTOONERY

Now I'm inching along a side street with the drawing table (less chance of attracting bewildered stares from curious onlookers). Grunt, grunt; drag, pull, push, carry. My shoulders ache. Sweat runs down my neck. But I'm on a mission, after all. Only fifteen agonizing blocks before I'll reach the corner of Crescent Drive and Olympic Boulevard, where Pop has rented a home from director Edward Dmytryk.[1]

An hour and a half of this teenage masochism and I arrive. In by way of the rear patio, then bump, bump, bump, down the steps into the Dmytryk "rumpus room," which holds a ping-pong table, tennis rackets decorating one wall, a set of barbells in a corner (Dmytryk works out) and twin beds where David and I sleep.

Pop, back from his conference, has heard the commotion and come down, along with wife Helen Clare, to investigate. I explain that I need to get busy creating new cartoons right away and since the Hudson wasn't available I've carried the drawing table home. Pop, testing the weight, strains to heft one side of it from the floor.

[1] Edward Dmytryk (1908-1999) became, along with my father, a member of the Hollywood Ten. He served six months in jail for contempt of Congress, later renounced his brief membership in the Communist Party, supplied names of his former comrades to the Un-American Committee, and went on to direct such films as *The Caine Mutiny, Raintree County, Walk on the Wild Side*, and *The Carpetbaggers*.

REELING THROUGH HOLLYWOOD

"You're nuts," he says.

"But dedicated," replies Helen Clare.

Three days later I again knock on McManus' door, this time clutching a manila folder containing half a dozen gag cartoons that I've poured my soul into.

"Come in," shouts a voice. I enter and announce that I have some cartoons.

"Lemme take a look," growls the roly-poly little man, his cigar bobbing up and down. As he scans my sketches my heart does a nifty imitation of a bongo drum. Do I note an appreciative raised eyebrow? Is that a cautious smile?

"Damn good," says McManus. "Hey Zeke, come here and take a look." Zeke, hunkered over his own drawing table, inking in the boss's blue-pencil originals of Jiggs and Maggie, gets up, looks at my work and nods approvingly.[2]

"Ya got talent, kid," adds McManus. "I'm gonna send these to King Features."

King Features! The premier cartoon syndicate in the country. That McManus has enough confidence in my scrawls to have them take a look, raises goose bumps.

All through September and October, in my freshman year at Beverly Hills High, I nibble my nails waiting to hear what King Features will say. Doing only fair in Art, flunking Spanish, and barely squeaking by in everything else, I present my first report card to Pop. He gasps. Then leads me into his den, closes the door and launches into a long, stern and (to me) boring lecture. I won't be able to go to college, he warns, unless my grades meet a certain standard. When I reply that I don't need college in order to be a cartoonist, his brows furrow into deep canyons of concern.

---

[2] Zeke Zekley, with McManus since the mid-1930s and nominally his assistant, was actually a collaborator, both of them sharing chores on the strip. In a total coincidence, I met Zeke again many years later, and directed a pair of medical films for him.

CARTOONERY

"College will help you learn to think," he insists.

"I already know how to think."

"You may decide on some profession that requires a college degree."

"If I do, I'll go to college then."

Stalemate.

Days later, I'm summoned to McManus' office. He produces a big envelope with the King Features letterhead, pulls out and hands me back my cartoons, then shows me the letter the syndicate has included. It thanks him for submitting and comments that while the gags "brought us some chuckles," and while "the boy's work shows a certain promise," a couple of years in art school probably wouldn't hurt.

I never do manage "a couple of years," but soon after Mom arrives in California, and she and David and I locate to Santa Monica, a local newspaper item announces that a well-known gag cartoonist, Jefferson Machamer, is about to open a cartooning school. I call Pop.

"You're still in junior high school, for Christ's sake!"

"I know, but he's got night classes too!"

Machamer, a flamboyant curmudgeon whose cartoons, often for *Colliers*, feature long-legged, busty and usually not too bright young women, quickly lays aside any qualms he may have about taking on a pimply-faced fourteen-year-old and pockets the two hundred dollars Pop forks over.

Although it takes several nights for me and the one other teen that Machamer has enrolled to stifle the giggles when our first model strips, I feel a growing satisfaction. I have entered the world of art! On through junior high and high school, most evenings find me at an easel, decked out in corduroys and a frayed sweatshirt daubed with oil paint, or scribbling away at a gag cartoon, or developing a comic strip that never finds a life beyond the drawing board. I'm at it until Mom calls upstairs to me to "Turn off the lights and get to bed, Danny, you've got school tomorrow."

I sleep the sleep of the righteous, certain that I'll eventually become a working cartoonist. And that the torturous hour and a half dragging my now India ink-splattered drawing table through the streets of Beverly Hills was eminently worthwhile.

Sketch for me by the author, in his book,
Laugh and Draw With Jefferson Machamer

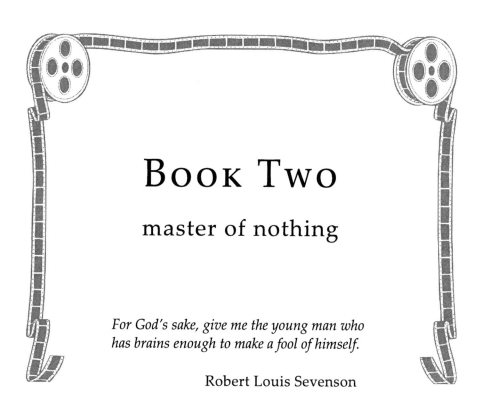

Book Two

master of nothing

For God's sake, give me the young man who has brains enough to make a fool of himself.

Robert Louis Sevenson

"I—I guess this means I don't get the chemistry award, huh, Mrs. Jones?"

THREE

signs by smith

Even before graduating high school, I'd become a published cartoonist. If you call winning a five-dollar prize in a small town advertising throwaway's cartoon contest getting published, that is. By 1950, several of my crude sketches had also appeared in Santa Monica High's student newspaper. But when my class put on the tasseled mortarboards and the long gray gowns and marched down the aisle to "Pomp and Circumstance," those of us who'd decided to pass on college faced parents whose glowering looks said, all too plainly, "How the hell are you going to get a job?"

OK, I'll show 'em!

Santa Monica, June 1950.

I've discovered an ad for a sign painter's helper, one with a driver's license. I realize, as I board the big, blue downtown bus, that I'll be biting the bullet; designing letters seems eons away from my fantasy of churning out hundred-dollar-a-shot gag cartoons for the major magazines. But what the hell, Signs by Smith will at least be a huge leg up from my ho-hum chicken and egg delivery route of the previous fall. Less sweaty than the weekend spent hauling rocks for a neighbor's retaining wall during spring vacation, it should also prove far safer than last summer's perilous pin-boy job, when I set two alleys simultaneously at the Broadway Bowl. Automatic pin setting is years in the future, so agile adolescents, working mainly for tips, hire on to scoop up the pins, toss them into a rack then push down on it, setting the pins in place again. Ducking fast is obligatory. (Has your noggin never felt the remorseless crunch of a jet-propelled bowling pin?)

As I get off the bus, a delicious image is starting to congeal. In a flowing smock and black beret, I stand next to an easel, creating a mélange of calligraphic designs with swift, broad strokes. Elegant letters flow from my brush in a profusion of color. Inevitably, I'll be called on to add eye-catching cartoons to the run-of-the-mill placards hawking blue-plate lunches. The staple of any sign shop. My future twinkles like a brilliant star in a Disney sky. Signs by Smith will be a springboard to New York, where my newly acquired skills will support me as I storm the bastions of *Collier's* and the *Saturday Evening Post*. Recognizing my immense talent, both magazines – *Esquire* and *The New Yorker* too, why not? – will fall over one another in a frenzy of bidding for my services. I'll be drowning in money.

Day one.

"I'm paying seventy-five cents an hour," says Smith. "OK?"

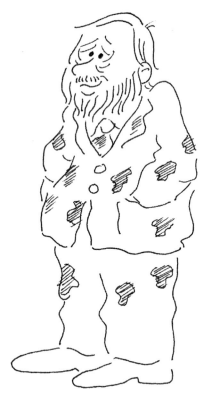

"Fine, wonderful," I reply, terrified to ask for more. At least it will be a cut above the fifty-cents Pop has warned me is the rock bottom hourly wage for any job.

"Terrific. First thing today we gotta put up a big sign. Here's the address." He hands over a greasy, crumpled slip of paper then meanders off, picking flecks of paint from his full red beard. I stare after him, fascinated.

Smith is a rumpled sofa of a man, a bemused hodgepodge. His baggy pants and paint-splattered corduroy jacket convince me that here is a real artist, a great talent whose nimble brain can't be bothered with narrow-minded concern

Signs by Smith

for appearance. Interviewing me for the job days earlier, he had disarmed me with a wry smile and a fuzzy, relaxed manner; which, I soon discover, comes from spending a lot of time with his good buddy Jack Daniels.

Still, I find myself in awe of him, paint-splattered jacket and all.

Smith's wiry assistant, Walt, has stepped right out of Dickens. Hunched, Bob Crachet-like, over an inclined table running the length of the sign painting room, he indicates a shelf to park my sack lunch. Then he gestures toward a jumble of wooden letters in a cardboard box. The letters, he tells me, spell out "Nick's Sea Cloud," the same name as on the slip of paper.

"How do I get to Nick's?" I ask, with an eager but goofy grin. Before Walt can reply, Smith ambles back in slurping coffee and instructs me to follow.

"You have a driver's license, right?"

"Oh, sure, I got it when I was sixteen." I do *not* tell him that it took me three tries to pass the driving test, nor that on the first attempt a frail old gentleman was forced into a nifty Fred Astaire imitation in order to dodge Pop's 1940 Hudson as I lurched from the curb.

In the alley behind the shop I meet Smith's dinosaur, a clunking 1928 Model T Ford truck. A weathered "Signs by Smith" can still be made out along the panels. Smith hands me the keys and starts back inside. Then, remembering, he hands me a second piece of paper, a diagram showing where the wooden letters are to be placed.

Fortunately, having owned a 1926 hand-crank model, bought for fifty dollars – a bargain even in 1949 – I am no stranger to the Model T. My trusty Ford's glory days had come to a clanking end, however, when I drove it down a flight of steps during a high school pep-rally. This deft maneuver ruptured the steering mechanism, so I had to turn the wheel left to drive right and right when I wanted to go left.

OK, yesterday's news. New York waits to throw itself at my feet. But first, pull on the messy coveralls Smith has supplied, then into the truck and off to Nick's Sea Cloud. Do I know what I'm doing? Of course not. But somehow, though it's a far cry from the Cartoonist's Hall of Fame, I see it as an exciting start.

Nick's is a bar, located in a small stucco building painted chocolate brown. I've been given a hammer and a ladder, but no instructions except to "Put the sign on the building like the diagram shows." Nick lets me use the phone. I call Smith.

"It's me. How do I get the letters onto the building? Nails?"

"No, no. Didn't Walt tell you? You gotta put the letters on a strip of wood, a two-by-two maybe, then use screws or something. Don't you have anything to put the letters onto? No? OK then, come on back and check with Walt."

Walt supplies the two-by-two, which I cut to length. The letters are too thick to nail, so I glue them to the board, then try to look busy sweeping floors until the glue dries. Smith has vanished again.

Signs by Smith

At Nick's once more, I nail the wooden strip to the building. Have you ever seen holes in stucco you could toss a basketball through? The lettering hangs out from the wall and tilts forward at a bizarre angle. The first stiff breeze and it will be history. Nick scrounges up a few screws. With enormous effort I force these through the two-by-two and into the wall. Amazingly, it holds. My ignorance of drills and toggle bolts is, at that point, complete. Nick comes out to examine.

"Hey, pretty damn good, kid. 'Course, ya gotta patch that stucco.

"Oh, sure, sure."

"What color ya gonna paint the sign?"

"Paint the sign?

"Probably should' a done that before you put it up, huh? Silver would be nice."

Whoops!

OK, back to the shop for stucco patch and a can of paint. Three minutes to gobble my sandwich. Back to Nick's, up the ladder and slather the silver paint across each letter. N-I-C-K'-S S-E-A C-L-O-U-D. Done! Nick will certainly approve.

"Kinda messy, ain't it?

I flash back four years: ninth grade art class. My garish oil painting, a blue ship on a sickly-green sea below a dirty-orange sky, was, mused my sensitive teacher, "either a new Van Gogh or a great mess." "A mess, a mess" chanted my 'buddies,' Richard and John. Wrong! I got an "A" for the mess. Ha, ha on them!

But this silver paint fiasco deserves an F-minus.

So back to Signs by Smith. Return to Nick's with a can of brown paint. It doesn't match, so a little dribble of silver, a splash of red (the truck holds extra cans) and it almost matches. But not good enough for Nick. Once more to the shop I go, stir up a gallon of paint approximating the color of Nick's Sea Cloud and spend the rest of the day repainting the entire side of the building.

My coveralls splattered with chocolate paint, I park the dinosaur and skulk in to face Smith and a humiliating end to an unpromising career. Smith scratches his beard. "Forget it," he says, "you'll learn. See you tomorrow, eight-thirty." Then he shuffles out the door and weaves through traffic toward his favorite bar.

Mystified, I try to figure why Smith is giving me a second chance. Probably the Jack Daniels. Well, no matter, I'll show him. I'll prove that I'm up to the challenge.

Day two.

When my distracted boss drifts in around noon, he remembers another uncompleted contract. At a nearby gas station he's installed a huge billboard. "You can't miss the sign," he says. "Owl Gas." My task? To advance on the station in the dinosaur. (*Don Quixote* springs to mind.) And once there, to varnish the sign as protection against the elements. A simple task, a child could do it. Smith produces my assault weapons – a gallon of spar varnish and a wide brush – and commands me to take the field.

About now, my stomach is grumbling. So a ten minute stop for a burger, then on to Owl Gas.

Smith has told me that the brakes on the T need tightening, so I've become used to pumping them whenever I stop. But I'm not prepared for them to fail completely.

They fail completely. Crunch! Clankety, clank, clank, clank! The spiffy new Chrysler I careen into rear-ends the Buick ahead of it. I leap out of the truck. "Are you OK, lady," I ask the trembling matron in the Chrysler. "Oh, I don't know," she moans, while rubbing her neck and rolling her eyes. A couple in the Buick, who remind me of the stoic farmer and his wife in Grant Wood's painting, *American Gothic*, are already out of their car surveying the damage and eying me like I'm Bella Lugosi on speed.

"The brakes gave out," I mumble apologetically.

Signs by Smith

The front bumper from the T lies on the ground, twisted like an abstract sculpture by Henry Moore. I smell something and look up. Smoke pours from vents in the hood. I jerk it open. Inside, flames dance along the engine block like the sequence in *Fantasia* (1940). The Prince of Darkness toys with his imps. The music from *Night on Bald Mountain* swells. My adrenalin boils. If the flames reach the gas tank, the matron, the *American Gothic* couple and me too will be so many body parts. Victor Frankenstein will arrive to collect us and begin a new project.

While the other drivers stand around discussing the ineptitude of teenage drivers, I bound across the street to a small frame house. I take the steps like Plastic Man, jerk open the door and race in. A chunky gent in a greasy undershirt is sprawled in a chair, snoring. "Fire, my truck's on fire!" I yell, as I rush into the kitchen. I grab a huge pot of what looks like day-old spaghetti, dump it into the sink, fill the pot with water, dash back to the T and cascade it over the engine. Hisssss . . . an enormous steam cloud rises and the flames die. Less than two minutes have elapsed since the brakes failed.

By now, sirens permeate the air. Flashing red lights race toward the scene. A hook and ladder pulls up, then a burly cop on a Harley. Fire and accident reports take half an hour. I'm coming unglued. And when the cop – who has the charm of Nazi Gestapo chief Heinrich Himmler – spits out, "It is strictly forbidden to drive without a bumper," I become a basket case. With strands of wire from among the litter inside the truck,

"Fire, my truck's on fire," I yell . . .

33

I reattach the bumper. Apparently satisfied, Heinrich Himmler drives off. Then I climb into the dinosaur and with one hand on the emergency brake, creep back to Signs by Smith at ten miles an hour. The Owl job is on hold.

To my absolute horror, I find myself still employed! Smith even chuckles. He confesses that he should have had the brakes fixed. So he and Walt push the T down the back alley to a corner garage to do just that. Though I've almost recovered my equilibrium, this unnerves me again. No fatherly dressing down? No words of wisdom about the sign business? No way. Not on Smith's agenda.

But Signs by Smith is wearing thin. Maybe I'll become an actor instead. Hey, Pop did that for a few years in his twenties. It's probably in the genes. Wasn't I runner-up for the Glenn Ford acting award at Samohi?[1] Didn't Pop arrange for us to rent the home of Lee Strasberg when we first moved to California?[2] The Actor's Studio will be honored to have me. Why not give it a shot when I get to New York?

Day three.

Back on the road, scouting for the Owl Gas sign. Easy to spot: a huge billboard with a big, wise-looking owl. It poses majestically, twenty feet above a gas-pump island in the middle of the brand new service station. Everything sparkles: the pumps, the red concrete surface where cars pull in, two clean-shaven attendants in starched whites who rush to greet customers. (The days before everything became DIY, folks.) Their guarded assessment of the dinosaur softens when I announce that I've been delegated to varnish the sign.

OK, here we go again. Smith's six-foot ladder won't do the job. How to reach the sign? I phone the shop.

---

[1] Samohi: short for Santa Monica High School.

[2] Strasberg, a friend from Pop's acting days in New York during the 1920s, co-founded the Group Theater in 1931 and later established the Actors Studio, where he became famous for "The Method," drawn from the teachings of Stanislavsky. He mentored future stars like Marlon Brando and Robert DeNiro and later appeared in films such as *Godfather II* (1974) and *Going in Style* (1979).

Signs by Smith

"Extension ladder's broke," says Walt. "Improvise."

Even on tiptoes I can barely reach the bottom of the sign. I wrack my brain. The station has a fifteen-foot-long pole with a rough-bristled scrub brush at one end, used to clean the sign. Brilliant idea: if I attach the brush to the handle I'll be able to reach the sign. I find a roll of string in the truck, tie the varnishing brush to the handle, dip it into the bucket and slowly raise it. The first time, the brush falls off before reaching the sign. The second time, it slides back down the handle after reaching the sign then falls off. The third time, it pulls loose from the pole, sticks to the sign – and stays there.

I have a gathering conviction this isn't art.

Still, I'm determined to complete the assignment. I turn the pole around, dip the scrub brush into the varnish and attack again, first knocking loose the stuck varnishing brush. By the time I finish, gas pumps, island and the brand new red concrete surrounding are awash in great sticky blobs. The wise old owl has become a multicolored dribble, curiously not unlike the nouveau Van Gogh my

ninth grade art teacher had praised. With the bewildered attendants looking on, I pile everything into the dinosaur and promise to return shortly with cleaning material.

I know it's a lie. I'll never come back. With luck, a twister will swoop down from the northeast and carry me off to Oz. If not, then Owl Gas will have to corner me atop one of their oil storage tanks, like Jimmy Cagney in *White Heat* (1949). They'll never take me alive!

By the time I get back to the shop, Owl Gas has called to express their vast displeasure. I receive a gentle reprimand and an admonition to use a drop cloth in future. For the rest, my shaggy employer says "I'll take care'a it, kid."

Damn Smith! Why doesn't he get mad and throw a brush? How come he doesn't dunk my head into a bucket of Nick's Sea Cloud Brown? Why doesn't he fire me on the spot? He's too damn *nice!* Is it the booze? He's never seemed obviously drunk, but the stuff clearly has just enough effect to maintain him in a state of permanent indifference.

I've become disgusted with myself. Unfit to serve. If Smith won't sack me I'll have to take action. I can't face a fourth day of abject failure. I mumble something about having decided to go to New York to study art and tell him I won't be back. Clearly disappointed, Smith nevertheless doesn't rip the nametag (which says "Bob") off my varnish-soaked coveralls and boot me out the front door. No, he wants me to stay! But a decision is a decision.

Smith looks at me like a pensive sheepdog. "I understand," he says gently. "You want to be an artist. I did too. Once." He pauses, a glazed look in his eyes. Then he shakes it off, trudges to his desk and makes out a check for three days pay: $18.00. "Let me know if you change your mind," he adds, "I think you've got a future in this business."

I promise to let him know. Then, pocketing the check, I slip out the back door, toss a last withering glance at the dinosaur and hurry off down the alley.

Signs by Smith

It takes more weeks of dangerous pin setting at the Broadway Bowl to earn enough for bus fare to the Big Apple. By late September I've traded in my curly locks for a crew cut, and am on the Greyhound, rolling out of L.A. toward San Bernardino. The sun is setting on the Mojave when I reach into the overhead rack and retrieve the portfolio of cartoons I've stowed there. Not bad, I decide, scanning each one carefully. New York will be impressed.

As the bus rumbles on through the night, across Arizona, New Mexico and then, with dawn, into the Texas panhandle, my thoughts drift to Pop. He's just arrived in Texarkana, a few hundred miles away, to begin a one-year prison sentence. Contempt of Congress was the charge, refusing to tell the Un-American Committee about his Communist Party membership. I feel sad for him, but also confident that he'll do his time with good grace. And I greatly admire his willingness to stand up for his convictions, even though, at eighteen, I have only the most general notion of what these are.

FOUR

nibbling on the big apple

to: Alvah Bessie, Prisoner #5853
Federal Correctional Institution
Texarkana, Texas

October 12, 1950

Dear Pop,

I saw the most horrible, most marvelous, most tremendous work of art that anyone has ever done, yesterday. I was walking through the Museum of Modern Art, looking at paintings. I turned a corner and what I saw made me almost break out crying. It was *Guernica*, by Pablo Picasso.

No one can possibly have any idea of what a masterpiece it is, until you see it for real. Not a thousand books on it, or descriptions could tell its story. I am convinced that the man who did it is not only the greatest living artist but also one of the great people in the history of the world. No art school could turn out a student to do this. No Leonardo de Vinci could produce a more marvelous thing.

It literally cries out to you to look at it. You can hear the screams and terrified cries of human beings and material objects. A man walked into the room and upon seeing *Guernica*, said, "What is this, a Virgil Partch exhibit?"

Love, Dan

So much for eighteen-year-old overkill. Picasso is one of my gods of the moment along with the great Virgil Partch, whose success I long to emulate.[1] So, first New York stop during the fall of 1950 is an audience with *Collier's* crusty, bald-headed cartoon editor, Gurney Williams. Feet on his desk, he leans back, studies my scribbles as if they were Rembrandt etchings, then allows, "They show promise, kid. Come back with more in maybe five years. Ever think about art school?"

Williams studies my scribbles as if they were Rembrandt etchings.

Hello! I've been to art school! Of course, I don't mention this. "For how long?" might be his next question. So I mumble grateful thanks and promise to return. Trudging along Madison Avenue with Williams' "Come back in five years" echoing in my noodle, I swallow hard and sign up for two classes at the Art Students League.

The League is a trip. Paint-box-toting students bustle along corridors, trailing cigarette smoke in their wake. Animated chatter bounces off the walls. Everyone seems "connected." In the cafeteria, shaggy-haired guys in paint-splattered jeans thrash out Camus or

---

[1] Virgil Franklin Partch (1916-1984), better known as Vip, began his career with Walt Disney then went into magazine cartooning. His six-fingered, loose-limbed characters, along with his uniquely warped sense of humor, made him one of America's outstanding comic artists.

Jackson Pollock over coffee, while adoring females hang on every abstract word. Gregarious and a "big wheel" in high school, here I feel like a fly on the lunchroom wall.

Still, life drawing is fun. More naked models to ogle, the first since my stint at Machamer's school three years earlier. At the League, Reginald Marsh, one of America's grand old men of painting, ambles in once a week to futz with the student's charcoals or pastels, most of which seem far superior to mine. I'll never be that good, I tell myself. But I don't cop to the notion that it takes work to get better at drawing. This isn't Santa Monica High, where my mediocre cartoons drew raves. Lacking genuine resolve, I last little more than a month

"When one is young," writes Otto Frederich, "one speeds nervously along in a kind of perpetual present."[2] And so it is with me at eighteen, wandering indifferent Manhattan streets, focused on nothing in particular after my cartoons aren't snapped up, and tracing in some weird way the aimless path my father trod between 1924 and 1935. Starting as a bit player on the New York stage, Pop then spent ten weeks haunting Paris cafes, returned to Depression America, married, survived on minestrone for two years, moved to Vermont, worked as a subsistence farmer, sired me and my brother David, discovered communism, and ended up becoming a serious writer.

Perhaps I need to "discover" communism too? I sign up for a class in Marxist philosophy at the Jefferson School for Social Science. But I barely comprehend most of the lectures so three sessions are all I attend. In a room across the hall I spy Dashiell Hammett, teaching creative writing.[3] (Looking back, I wish I'd taken his course instead.)

---

[2] From the preface to *The Grave of Alice B. Toklas* (1989). A penetrating writer, Otto Frederich's *City of Nets, a Portrait of Hollywood in the 1940s* (1986), is one of the more interesting books I've read on the film colony.

[3] Dashiell Hammett (1894-1961). His work made into films included *The Thin Man* (1934) and *The Maltese Falcon* (1941).

A flyer at the school announces actor tryouts. Maybe I'll give it a shot. Well, why not? I mean, wasn't I featured in the senior class play, opposite a *LIFE* magazine cover cutie? And doesn't Pop have all these "connections," folks he knew from his theater days? Like Clifford Odets, Elia Kazan, Frances Farmer and John Garfield.[4] And what about a famous dramatist he introduced David and me to on the beach at Malibu in 1947?

"Dan, Dave, I'd like you to meet Bert Brecht."

"Ach, zo . . . dis iss your zons, Alvah? Charmink, charmink," said Brecht.

I didn't know the name then, and wouldn't listen to *The Threepenny Opera* or see *Mother Courage* or *The Rise and Fall of the City of Mahagoney* for another dozen years. To me, at fifteen, Bertolt Brecht was simply a bandy-legged little man in swimming trunks, with sand between his toes.

Brecht, on the beach at Malibu. 1947

---

[4] I met John Garfield (1913-1952) backstage in Odets play *Golden Boy*, when I was five years old. If you're under sixty and haven't heard of this fine actor, rush right out to Blockbuster and rent *Body and Soul* (the 1947 version; there are several films with the same title).

Nibbling on the Big Apple

David and I dashed off to romp in the surf while Brecht and Pop sat on the deck, chain smoking and strategizing over Brecht's forthcoming appearance before the House Committee on Un-American Activities.[5]

New York again. Days later, heart pumping, I show up at the Jefferson School for the acting audition. The turnout is underwhelming. Me. Three sullen-faced thespians have me extemporize a scene set on a tenement stoop, playing opposite one of their number. Attempting to strike up a conversation, the only response I draw is an apathetic yawn. Clearly, I think at the time, I'm the toad who will never turn into a handsome prince. Even in make believe, I can't get a rise out of a girl.

"We'll let you know," says the tall, gaunt fellow heading the group. OK, I tell myself, so I won't become an actor. Broadway, eat your heart out.

I kick around New York for another month. In a scruffy overcoat, stubbly beard, smoking a pack of Camels a day and with a copy of the Communist Party's *Daily Worker* under one arm, I resemble a rock-ribbed Republican's caricature of a bomb-throwing anarchist. Of course, the image I see reflected in the window as the IRT rattles along beneath Lexington Avenue is romantic and Bohemian.

---

[5] On October 30, 1947, Brecht (1898-1956) was questioned before the Committee regarding the radical ideas expressed in his creative work and about his association with the American Communist Party. He smoked a cigar throughout his testimony and immediately after the hearings left for East Germany. The proceedings were recorded and in 1961 distributed by Folkways Records.

Every afternoon for a week I lose myself at matinees in shabby picture palaces along Forty-Second Street. Films not only kill time, they stuff my brain with more creative fodder. But for what, I have no idea. Does it register that my future might lie in the world of moving images? Nope, I'm clueless.

A week later, I check my wallet. Flat. The $150 I earned at the Broadway Bowl has shrunk to a lonely ten-spot. I start making calls. Pop's Spanish Civil War commander, Milt Wolff, gets me an interview with a lithography firm, headquartered in a dingy loft, where three middle-aged guys hunch over light boards, squinting myopically as they retouch negatives. If I join the lithographers union I can earn $125 a week – after a two-year apprenticeship.

The chance to grind pigments for an oil paint manufacturer seems hopeful, "except I haven't enough work to take you on right now," apologizes the affable, bearded gent who makes paint for a living so he can spend his free time creating art. "Leave your name, I'll let you know."

Failing to find a job, my wallet as empty as my mind and fighting tearful loneliness, I opt for the one safe place: home. Santa Monica. But I'm broke. So off to the swanky apartment of my Uncle Everett (Pop's brother) and Aunt Betty, on 96th off Park Avenue. Half a dozen guests, swirling pre dinner cocktails, eye this tattered curiosity of a nephew. My uncle takes in the frayed overcoat, the *Daily Worker* peeking out of a pocket. He glances at his friends, turns beet red and then says, "Dan, how nice to see you. Come on into the den."

As he closes the door I blurt out, "Uncle Everett, could you, uh, could you loan me fifty-five dollars for my bus fare home?" He smiles, produces his wallet and pulls out four twenties. "A little extra, so you won't starve on the way." Then, both of us breathing sighs of relief (for opposite reasons), my kindly uncle steers me past the dinner guests and out the front door.

After an all night meander around lower Manhattan, then four nights on the Greyhound and with just three hours sleep in five days, I arrive in L.A. Broke again. I call mom. She springs for cab fare home. That same night I hitch to San Bernardino to cheer on brother David as he fullbacks down the field for Santa Monica High. I stumble to bed at 2 a.m. and sleep for thirty hours straight.

Days later I take stock. I know I don't want to retouch negatives or grind pigments. The Art Students League has helped me affirm that I have a certain flair for drawing, even if the dedication to become a painter isn't there. And I've seen Picasso's *Guernica*.

Next year, I tell myself, I'd do it right, like Pop did in 1928. New York is for the birds. If I really want to study art, I'd go to Paris!

FIVE

befuddled

I don't go to Paris. Or to study art in Mexico at San Miguel's Instituto Allende (another daydream). I don't go anywhere. So what the hell *am* I going to do? I'll sacrifice anything to get into work I love. Which is what? Cartooning, probably. Or is it?

For me, in 1950, films are simply entertainment. That they might earn me a living hasn't occurred. My collisions with Hollywood have consisted of the 1944 visit to Warner's while Pop was a staff writer, and a screen test at Paramount to which my high school drama coach dragged me. My nerves were a dither until the execs let me know that "Your face tests too wide for movies." Clearly a lie. (My father's politics? Or was I just a lousy actor?)

I write Pop, still in the pokey, about my confusion. He replies:

25 November, 1950

Dear Dan,

If I were you I would not be too worried about what to do. You will find yourself in time; it takes most of us a lifetime, as I'm sure Mary [my mother] will tell you. The important thing is to keep what you already have – an open mind, sharpened sensibilities, watch, look, listen to everything you can, read, study, observe.

"Oh, that's a big help," I grumble as I read the letter. Ah well, he's got other things on his mind; like doing the five months remaining on his sentence.

Befuddled

By April 1951, he's free again. David and I are at LAX to meet him. As we become reacquainted, I continue stumbling through more false starts: counselor at a YMCA mountain camp, peddling my mediocre watercolors to family friends, and junior college classes. (I drop out half way into the semester, though I do take part in a nifty dramatization of "The Shooting of Dan McGrew" in the annual talent show.)

Then, in November, this ambling routine is interrupted with a romantic fantasy: the chance to ship out as a merchant seaman. One chilly morning, I hitch to the San Pedro docks, where, with Pop's labor connections, I join the Marine Cooks and Stewards. Rival unions, who hate the M C & S's radical politics, have dubbed us the "Marine Fruits and Niggers."[1] I sign on as a scullion: dishwasher, potato-peeler and all around kitchen hand.

Doesn't sound so romantic? Well, romantic enough. Two ten-day trips to Hawaii on the *Lurline*. Another on the *President Wilson*; Los Angeles, Honolulu, Yokohama, Kobe, Hong Kong, Manila, San Francisco, in forty days.

Rickshaws bump along dusty Hong Kong alleys. A shipmate and I are almost kidnapped in Manila. Like a woodblock print by Hokusai, Mt. Fuji's crest rises through a morning mist as the *Wilson* glides into Tokyo Bay. Hawaii is straight off a 1930s travel poster, with Kanakas strumming ukuleles at Waikiki. In a Honolulu novelty shop I have my photo snapped (for five dollars) with my arms around a sexy Filipina.

---

[1] The Marine Cooks and Stewards did attract a fair number of gays. Their work among well-to-do passengers aboard cruise ships seemed to be a safe cover. And as early as the 1940s and 1950s the union actively fought not only racism but anti-gay attitudes as well. Way before almost anyone else did.

"For fifteen dolla' we take other kind pit'cha," she breaths, as she scrunches her breasts against me. Temptation, however, gives way to medical graphics; images depicting ghastly, brain-munching diseases.

"Uh . . . I don't think so, gotta go meet the guys."

I'm a late bloomer. But frustration mounts, so by the time we reach Japan, where nearly every woman over forty is still wearing a kimono, those brain-munching images have flown the coup. Libido, along with Yoshiko in Kobe and Kimiko in Yokohama win out. At last! I mean nineteen-year-old virginity isn't exactly something to brag about to a pack of randy shipmates.

In the fall of 1952, the U.S. Coast Guard declares me a security risk. (Must be Pop's politics again; I haven't been involved in anything "subversive.")[2] Though I can no longer ship out, the Cooks and Stewards arranges for me to join the Longshoremen's Union.

With Longshoremen's Union head Harry Bridges (center, seated), at a Union banquet in Los Angeles

---

[2] The Coast Guard was in charge of issuing seamen's papers. A person "screened" off the waterfront as a security risk had no right to be confronted with any evidence or any witnesses. It was up to you to prove to the Coast Guard that you were not a security risk!

BEFUDDLED

I buy a grappling hook and spend odd days over the next several months unloading bananas and bales of cotton – and almost never get to write this book:

"Watch out!" yells a voice.

I spin around. A four-ton crate holding machinery, dropping precipitously into the cargo hold, is swinging toward me. In a flash I spot a man-sized depression in the bulkhead and duck inside – just as the crate smashes into it with a teeth-chattering clang.

"Quick thinkin'," shouts another voice, followed by a throaty laugh. "You was almost bug-butter, boy."

With women, I am bug-butter. Dumped after a brief fling, by a fellow counselor at a day camp I work at during the summer following my jaunt at sea, I'm open to the first nice person to come along. Rose Kuras, Brooklyn to the core, kind and generous, is the unlucky candidate. Unlucky because my reasons for getting married are as absent of conscious thought as anything I've done since tossing away that cache of posters at the Rialto in Poughkeepsie. I'm just one of Otto Frederich's young people speeding "nervously along in a kind of perpetual present." Pop says it best, when, years later, I ask him about his own choices: "I never planned a thing in my entire life," he replies. "It all just 'happened'." (Do I hear an echo?)

After getting Rose into bed, a guilty conscience wags a scolding finger and shouts that nice boys don't do that unless they're serious. Rose and I are married in January 1953. Wonderful! Shared values, regular sex, and the camaraderie of two lonely souls who enjoy being together. And though neither of us has given much thought to what the future might bring, somehow the marriage will last twenty-two years.[3]

---

[3] Our wedding party was held at my mother's tiny Santa Monica apartment. The kitchen and living room were dedicated to food, drink and conversation. One bedroom was taken over by poker players. In the other, one of Rose's former roommates, an aspiring singer who called herself simply "Odetta," belted out folk songs and spirituals to a small but captive audience. A few years later Odetta achieved worldwide fame as a concert and recording artist. (See also Chapter 33, "Turnabout.")

Reeling Through Hollywood

With my first wife, Rose Kuras

Putting my fantasies about Paris (or Mexico) on hold, we settle for San Francisco. Baghdad by the Bay. Pop has relocated there and I love the place. Scraping together $150, we buy a 1940 Chevy coupe to transport us north. And the $200 Rose produces from the lining of her suitcase, where she's pinned it for safekeeping, meets our immediate needs and pays the first month's rent for a modest two rooms.

Rose soon finds temp secretarial work. I find nothing. But one morning, a *Chronicle* item reports that the City of Paris department store (as close as I'll get to the City of Light for thirty years) is sponsoring a contest for "posters done in the style of Toulouse-Lautrec." I've always had a hankering to do posters. So, with Vesuvio's trendy bar and eatery as the setting (next door to the even more famous "hungry i," where Pop is announcing acts like Mort Sahl, Barbra Streisand and Woody Allen), I place a red-headed guitarist in my poster's foreground and Lautrec in the background, sketching.

BEFUDDLED

By now, Rose's temp job has ended. But she's seen an ad for sales clerks at the City of Paris, so off to the store. While she's busy applying for work, I suddenly remember the contest and... Well, a *Chronicle* piece appearing days later says it all.

> Last Friday the Bessies were down to their last five-dollar bill. Mrs. Bessie decided to apply for a job at the City of Paris. While she was at the sixth-floor employment offices, Don [sic] strolled into the exhibit rooms on the fifth floor where the posters were hanging. When he found his own, it was marked "$100 second prize; $100 first amateur prize.

Entering as an amateur made me eligible for the professional awards too. I'm floored. When we show up days later to claim the prizes, we are lionized. (For half an hour.) Joe Rosenthal, *Chronicle* staff photographer who shot the famous World War II photo of Marines raising the American Flag on Iwo Jima, snaps photos.

We've been in San Francisco less than two months. But with no job prospects for me, and having recouped Rose's $200, we scurry back to the safe familiarity (and more available jobs) of Los Angeles.

And over the next two years, work does come alone. But creative, fulfilling assignments they are not. Pouring jugs of mustard and mayonnaise into immense vats for Milani's 1890 French Dressing; deburring plastic frames for TV picture tubes on the Packard-Bell assembly line; operating a machine that coats athletic trophies with gold or silver paint.[4] And more work on the docks. Which, though irregular, pays better than mixing salad dressing, deburring, or coating bowling trophies. But still nothing I've tried since leaving high school seems to hold much promise.

So, with Rose this time, another stab at a New York art career (what, again?). In spite of a six-month effort the jaunt is notable only

---

[4] Tragically, a month after I quit the guy who ran the same machine was killed when it exploded.

51

REELING THROUGH HOLLYWOOD

for a stint in the printing department of the Hudson's Bay Company, a fur auction house. And for pleasant hours batting around ideas for a youth magazine with a captivating young woman, Lorraine Hansberry. [5] By the late summer of 1954 Rose and I are on the road back to California; in a 1941 Buick bought for $95.00 that literally collapses the instant we reach downtown Los Angeles.

Emulating Pop, I begin dabbling in left-wing politics. And spend no time searching for opportunities in the world of art. Visions of cartooning still dance in my head, but by July 1955 I need to support a growing family. For now we are three, with a happy and loving but also somehow "different" (we aren't yet sure why) daughter, Lisa. Jobs find me up to my elbows in diatomaceous earth and other noxious solvents while testing hydraulic valves for aircraft gas tanks, or soldering door frames onto cars for American Motors, or stocking shelves and trucking supplies up and down the coast for the Fuller Paint Company. One free weekend, I create a series of smutty posters for a guy who plans to make copies and sell them. He never does.

At least I have the good sense to wonder why I'm drawing this crap. Can't I find a way to do something more rewarding? I'd love to make a living as a cartoonist. But how? Should I hire on with Disney? Ha! I've had zero training in animation and Disney is way the hell over the mountains, in Burbank. MGM, however, is just twenty minutes away and they also do cartoons. Why not give it a try?

Had I not been flying by the seat of my pants those past seven years, maybe the call would have long since been made. Water over the dam. I phone MGM and ask for the animation department. Almost immediately, a friendly male voice comes on the line. "Schipek," it says.

What's a "schipek," I'm thinking. Woops, that's the guy's name. I tell him that I'm looking for a job.

---

[5] Then working as a waitress, Lorraine Hansberry was, she told me, "trying to write a play in my spare time." The play, of course, was *A Raisin in the Sun* (1959) and became the first drama by a black woman to be produced on Broadway. *"Raisin"* also won the New York Drama Critics' Circle Award as the best play of the year. Lorraine, a lovely and gifted human being, died of cancer in January 1965. She was only thirty-four.

Befuddled

At the kitchen table in Santa Monica,
creating designs

"Got a portfolio?"

"Portfolio? Oh, sure, sure."

"Bring it in Tuesday morning and let me take a look."

I have no portfolio. So for the next three nights I'm red-eyed and high on coffee until 2 a.m. Wising up by now, I have a lightweight portable drawing board instead of the monster I'd lugged through the streets of Beverly Hills at age fourteen. Balancing it on the edge of the kitchen table, I sweat out a dozen advertising designs and cartoon sketches. I also dust off a small stack of unsold watercolors. Come Tuesday, out on deliveries with the paint truck, I stop in at MGM's cartoon studio. Bill Schipek, he of the friendly phone voice, scans my work. Is that an approving nod he betrays?

"We may be taking on a few apprentices next year," he allows. "I'll let you know."

"I'll let you know." How many times have I heard that? My heart, racing until now, grinds to a halt. Well, almost. "Next year" might as well be when I reach sixty-five. Am I condemned to driving a paint truck for the rest of my life? The possibility Schipek holds out is so vague that, thrilled as I am to stroll the sacred corridors where Tom and Jerry hang out, right now I just want to go home and drown my sorrows in a peanut butter and jelly sandwich.

Three months later. I've forgotten about MGM. But my kite is flying a bit higher, because I've recently joined the Teamster's Union and a gnarly business agent has shown up to browbeat my boss into raising my salary from $55 to $85 a week. On a Friday I return home after a sweaty afternoon hefting boxes and fifty-gallon drums in the Fuller Paint stockroom, and sink into a welcoming bath. Rose comes in and sits on the edge of the tub. "MGM called," she says. "They want you to call back." It's 6 p.m. The cartoon department will be closed. I fret for two days. Monday morning, I phone from the callbox outside Fuller Paint and ask for Bill Schipek.

"How'd you like to start here as an animation apprentice," says Bill.
"Wonderful," I reply, "when?"
"Week from today."
"Fine, great... Uh... What's the starting wage?"
"Union minimum. $36.45 a week."

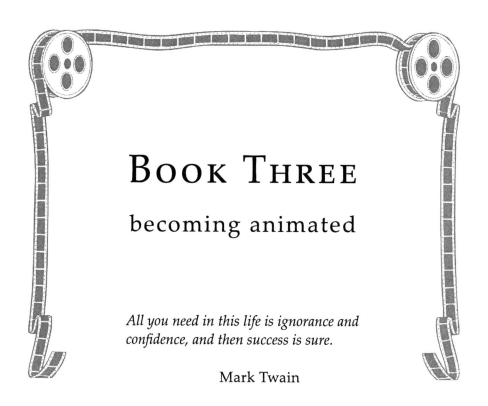

Book Three

becoming animated

All you need in this life is ignorance and confidence, and then success is sure.

Mark Twain

SIX

down the rabbit hole

MGM's Cartoon studio. January 1956.

Is that Jack Nicholson staggering down the hall? Sure is. But he's not tipsy. Not at all. He's staggering under an armload of film cans. And nobody knows he's Jack Nicholson. I mean, they know that's his name, of course, though most simply call him "Jack," because this is the eighteen-year-old Jack Nicholson, a thin, wisecracking kid from New Jersey who has graduated high school and arrived in tinseltown determined to become a big star (as he tells everyone within earshot). But right now, as I pass him in the corridor, he's the "can boy," schlepping film back and forth across the street from the animation department to the lab on MGM's main lot in Culver City.

Like Alice, I've tumbled down the rabbit hole. Finally! To a wonderland world I've never struggled for, yet have dreamed of since age twelve. I'm a professional cartoonist. Or will be, as soon as I cash my first paycheck.

Approaching the cream-colored art deco structure, I flash back to 1944. On that first California visit, Pop had pointed out the Screen Cartoonists Guild; and later, Warner Brother's cartoon department, where Chuck Jones held court over a wacky band of jesters.[1] Animation studio, dingy loft, it made no difference; wherever cartoonists carved out designs with 2-B pencils or splattered India ink over drawing boards was a magic castle I longed to enter and for which I hadn't known the secret password.

Now, I've crossed the drawbridge. (At $36.45 a week!)

Oh, what the hell, I decide, working with a pack of hugely talented and (as I'll soon discover) occasionally demented cartoonists will be worth it. Anyhow, I'm inside the castle. Well . . . maybe not such a castle; more a rabbit warren. Fitting. Disney has long since been dubbed "The Mouse Factory," and Warner's cartoonery, initially housed in a dilapidated wooden structure, is "Termite Terrace."

"First, a short tour," says Schipek, as he leads me and two other new trainees along second floor hallways, off of which busy animators labor in smallish, cramped rooms. Each animator, along with their personal assistant, sits hunched over a big desk with a built-in light board, engraving slightly different poses featuring MGM's assembly of cartoon stars. Each drawing is numbered then noted on an "exposure sheet," a kind of chart indicating the sequence in which the drawings are to be photographed.

"These are Moviolas," says Bill, as we peek into another room holding clattery editing machines. "They're for looking at pencil tests of each scene, so the animators can see if they need to make changes."

---

[1] Legendary director Chuck Jones (1912-2002) won three Oscars in a career spanning sixty years. Helping develop Bugs Bunny, Daffy Duck, Elmer Fudd and Porky Pig, he personally created Road Runner, Wile E. Coyote, and Pepe le Pew.

Down the Rabbit Hole

Then we poke our noses into the first floor ink and paint department, where two-dozen highly skilled women transfer the art to celluloid (cels). Each drawing is traced in ink then the cel turned over and painted with pre-designated colors. And there they are: the cat and mouse. Tom and Jerry. Characters who, along with Bugs and Porky, Woody Woodpecker, Mickey, Minnie, Pluto and Goofy, have danced in my head since I first began to draw.

Other rooms house layout and background artists. One large windowless vault holds a behemoth-like animation stand. Mounted on it is a 35mm camera that can, Schipek tells us, slide up or down at graduated speed in order to move in closer on the art. The bed below the camera on which the animation is placed can shift artwork left or right in increments to achieve panoramic movement. "Almost any move that can be accomplished in live action can be duplicated in animation," says Bill.

The tour complete, it's time to get to work. So back upstairs and into a 20 X 30 foot room (facing MGM's back lot New York tenement street), where half a dozen twenty-something-year-olds, also hunched over light boards, are penciling in the "in between" drawings created by the animators and their assistants. "After the animator completes a scene," explains Bill, "making, for example, twenty or thirty rough drawings in a sequence of fifty, his assistant cleans up the roughs, adds more drawings then passes the scene on to me."

Bill sits at the front of the room, the chief wrangler in the "Bull Pen," as this corral of scribblers is called.[2] An animator himself, he hands out the scenes, solves problems and answers questions as his charges grind an endless supply of pencils to their nubs and burn reams of three-hole-punched 11 X 13 inch paper, struggling to meet a quota of fifteen film feet (about ten seconds of 35mm animation) each week.

---

[2] There were virtually no female animators, assistants or inbetweeners in 1956; most women were consigned to ink and paint, though a few worked as background artists.

Bill Schipek

Schipek hands me a test scene. "Work with a blue pencil first," he says, "then use it as a guide to finish the drawing with the 2-B."

Crass exploitation, I decide, as I cross to my assigned desk to begin the task. My family will have to scrimp. (Without the $15 or $20 a week my dear Mom ekes out of her nursery school teacher's salary, you might be reading here about my forty breathtaking years working for a paint company.) Anyhow, here I am, among the chosen, stumbling through Bill's test scenes: a box tumbling in space, its perspective constantly changing. Balls of various sizes bouncing into the frame then out again. Geometric shapes morphing into other geometric shapes. What have I signed on for? This is child's play. Bring on Tom and Jerry! I whiz through the exercises before lunch break.

Little do I know. Nor am I willing to acknowledge the time and dedication needed to master a craft that seems so simple but is in fact infinitely complex.

"That's not quite it," says Bill, as he riffles the scenes I've raced to complete. "See how the box wobbles back and forth as it's coming toward us? See how the ball gets too small in this drawing, then too big in that one?"

Animation, I soon discover, means producing a series of individual sketches that work so smoothly in sequence that the eye retains (for a twenty-fourth of a second) the image of each previous drawing, creating the illusion of movement. There is no actual motion; the eye does it all. My drawings don't capture the flow. My box jitterbugs. But at least I now understand the process. Something I of course had no comprehension of when, at age five, Disney's animation gremlins scared me silly with Snow White's evil stepmother.

By the time I arrive at MGM, Bill Hanna and Joe Barbera are running the show.[3] Nor is this the madhouse of yesteryear. Tex Avery, whose wickedly warped humor rocked the corridors, has left.[4] Creator of Porky Pig and Daffy Duck at Warner's, Tex's MGM classics like *Red Hot Riding Hood* (1943), *Swing Shift Cinderella* (1945), and *Drag-a-Long Droopy* (1954) have given way to marginally more genteel chase-em-ups. While there's still enough mayhem on screen to whet the appetite of a preadolescent Ted Bundy, Tex's lecherous Wolf character is no longer around to conk himself over the head with a giant mallet, or have his eyes pop from their sockets and roll along the floor ogling the sexy "Red" as she struts past. Nor (gratefully) does a terrified "mammy" leap onto a chair at the sight of Jerry as dice, a razor and a poker deck fall from under her skirts. Sure, kegs of gunpowder still explode next to Droopy (a character Tex also created), but the fast-clearing smoke no longer reveals him in blackface, with thick lips and with "pickaninny" pigtails. Though Avery never worked on Tom and Jerry his influence permeates every film: Tom opens a door and

Tex Avery

---

[3] In their first cat and mouse cartoon *Puss Gets the Boot* (1940), the cat was called "Jasper." The idea for a continuing series was first squelched by MGM. "Too many cats and mice" (Mickey, Felix, etc) said producer Fred Quimby. But when a Texas exhibitor wrote to express her admiration for the short, and when it received an Oscar nomination, the series was greenlighted.

[4] After MGM, Avery worked mainly on TV commercials. During one of my long periods of unemployment I dropped in on Tex at a one-person studio he ran. Unable to offer me a job, he chatted for a few minutes then returned to attacking a big stack of drawings for the "Frito Bandito."

races into a brick wall. His face squashes like a pancake when Jerry assaults him with a flatiron. Droopy walks off a cliff into thin air, looks down then turns to us and in a voice sounding as if he has a mouth full of marbles, mutters, "Oh, my," before he plummets a thousand feet. Only to reappear in the next scene – without a scratch.

Even with my peaceful sensibilities, I pay scant attention to the violent slapstick MGM cartoons are famous for. I am, I tell myself, learning a skill, so a detached attitude becomes part of the game.

Less than a month into my ninety-day trial period Bill Schipek examines my recent scenes and decrees, "OK, you've got it." He has already turned me loose on secondary characters, or props and other "business," but now he lets me take on the stars. Even though I'm simply drawing lines between lines, creating new poses of Tom and Jerry or Droopy make me feel like a pro.

And I'm slowly gaining a new appreciation for the craft. Great animators, I decide, are actors too, able to communicate subtle or outrageous emotion with pencil and paper. The designs these artists charge with life are extensions of human personality. At the same time, they caricature the attributes of the animals they represent. Though animators may never achieve the fame of a Charlie Chaplin, Buster Keaton, or Mae West, I feel they more than deserve such recognition.[5]

But these are human beings, with all the personality quirks of artists. And some drive their assistants crazy. One helper confides that his animator "just scribbles. I can't figure out what the action is supposed to be." Another complains that his animator, hired on from Terrytoons, "draws all his Toms like the alley cats chasing Mighty Mouse, so I spend all my time changing them."

Indeed, though creative and stimulating, the work is also repetitious. In any factory-like operation tedium inevitably finds an

---

[5] Animators on staff while I was at MGM included Irv Spence, Ken Muse, Mike Lah, Carlo Vinci, Herman Cohen, Ken Southworth, Lew Wallace, Jack Carr, Jim Escalante, and Bill Schipek.

outlet. Griping is certainly one. And there are others: "You gotta hear this," whispers Art, a fellow inbetweener, as he motions me into the hall one afternoon. I follow, to a room where animator Herman Cohen is on the phone. Seems he's decided to sell his golf clubs. He's speaking to an elderly matron who has told him she's "seen your ad and I want to buy the clubs for my husband." And she's agreed to Herman's price. But now, she's reneging. They are haggling, and Herman, already sweating a bit, is eager not to queer the deal. Half the cartoon depart-

O.B. Barkley

ment stands around, apparently sympathizing, for Herman is in a dither.

What I quickly learn is that in another room (with the rest of the department gathered around) assistant animator O. B. Barkley is also on the phone – faking the high-pitched voice of the elderly matron! Then all of a sudden, the "matron" says she has an errand to run, but will call back. In his room, Herman frets.

Soon after, the matron's "black maid" (O.B., with a different voice) calls back to tell Herman that her mistress has decided his price is too high. Herman asks to speak with the matron. Back from her "errand," she comes on the line again, but can't seem to recall that she had wanted to buy golf clubs. Then the maid takes over. Her mistress is sure Herman is trying to cheat her. Back and forth they go. And Herman becomes more and more confused, while animators, assis-

Herman Cohen

tants, inbetweeners and even inkers and painters shuttle back and forth along the hall between Herman and O.B., delighting in the charade.

My fellow apprentices are a collection unto themselves. Fernando, from a wealthy Costa-Rican family, has a huge ego. We all poke fun, asking why he slaves away with the peons at starvation wages when he might be overseeing a banana plantation back home.

Ralph, a tall wannabe stud, tinkers with magazine photos, disrobing women in the ads with a Pink Pearl eraser. Then he gobbles up chunks of studio time etching in their sexuality with an H-B pencil.

Another apprentice, Jerry, arrives at his desk each morning and immediately nods off. Waking an hour later, he yawns, ambles down the hall for coffee, then returns and sits pouring over his daily racing form. Then off to phone his bookie. By afternoon he's playing catch-up. Somehow, he always meets his quota.

Louie, impeccable in bow tie and slicked down blond hair, is the perfect Aryan. A short Aryan, the size of Joseph Goebbels.[6] In spirit (though probably not in fact), Louie seems to me like a typical Nazi. His big problem with Hitler is that he didn't finish the job with the Jews. Fernando and his fellow Costa Rican, also named Fernando, are inferior types, Louie tells me in confidence. Never mind that they happen to be the best draftsmen in the Bull Pen. Later that year, when the federal minimum wage is raised to a dollar an hour, a scowling Louie descends to the ink and paint department. Minutes later we hear shouting. Then hurried footsteps. Then Louie scurries back into the room and collapses at his desk, breathing hard. We all look

---

[6] Joseph Goebbels (1897-1945) was Adolph Hitler's minister of propaganda.

Down the Rabbit Hole

at one another. No one says a word. Later, we find out that Louie had barged in to tell the "girls" that with the increase to a dollar an hour they were being grossly overpaid. We further learn that he narrowly escaped a lynching.

Louie is also incredibly gullible. Presented one day with a huge stack of drawings for a Droopy scene, he starts plowing through them. When Louie goes on coffee break I cull a drawing from his stack and quickly create a series of sketches to match a static drawing of Droopy's body. (Long scenes are often broken into parts. For example, a character's head or mouth might move on one level of drawings, while the body, which remains static, is on another.) I number each one and place these near the top of Louie's scene, then tell the other guys (except Bill Schipek) what I've done.

INT. MGM BULL PEN — DAY

Louie returns to his desk, sits and picks up a drawing. He stares at it for several moments. Then he pours over the exposure sheets.

ANGLE. THE ROOM

Inbetweeners are snickering.

LOUIE

Finally, he picks up the drawings and exposure sheets and crosses to Schipek.

> LOUIE
> Uh . . . I don't see this sequence anywhere on the sheets.

Bill riffles the drawings, stifling his own laughter at the sketches — a sequence in which Droopy's limp schlong slowly becomes erect.

REELING THROUGH HOLLYWOOD

SCHIPEK
I'm afraid someone's been pulling your leg, Louie.

A cartoon light bulb pops up over Louie's head. His face reddens. He turns and stomps back to his desk.

LOUIE
Very funny!

The Bull Pen cracks up.

Besides noting Jack Nicholson running film cans to the lab, I also pass in the halls three times – I count them – a knockout of a young woman. Carolyn Keeler. Tanned and blonde, I'm certain she's stepped off a 1940s Coca Cola tray. I don't have the nerve to do more than return her Pepsodent smile, though I do find excuses to duck into the ink and paint department (where she works) to drink in her All-American looks. And this very goofing off is no doubt the final motivation for Schipek to summon me to his desk one morning. "Dan," he says, "there's too much yakking going on in here and not enough work getting done, so . . ."

Yep, I'm the yakker. Too many arguments with Louie over his racism. Too much chatter with fellow apprentice George Cannata Jr. about his notion that "it's not the objects in a painting that are key to understanding the work, Dan, it's the space *between* the objects."[7] I am also bored. I've become skilled enough to scrape by, but have made little effort to improve. (Except for the dubious art of curling an index finger around a pushpin and hurling it like a dart, with some accuracy, at a photo of Richard Nixon.)

I have let myself be pulled in too many directions. Left wing politics, mainly. It will take years before I fully understand that

---

[7] Today, George Cannata Jr, "an accomplished painter and a well known animation designer and director, has won awards such as the New York Art Directors Gold Medal, a Cannes Film Festival Silver Lion, and an Academy Award nomination. He teaches at the Art Students League in New York" (where I lasted two months back in 1950).

DOWN THE RABBIT HOLE

becoming highly skilled in animation means hard work, and that with focus, mastering a craft can make it far more interesting, not less. Scattered thinking, in film as in most other aspects of life, frequently adds up to mediocrity.

Banished. Schipek consigns me to a tiny room at the end of a remote corridor, at a desk behind that of animator Jim Escalante. Jim's specialty is "effects": fire, water, explosions and earthquakes.[8] In his fifties, he still lives with his mother. "When she passes on," he tells me, "I'm going to join a holy order up in the Santa Monica Mountains. The brothers spend all their time in solitude and prayer. Doesn't that sound wonderful?"

"Wonderful," I reply, secretly rolling my eyes.

"I can't wait," adds Jim.

I need to be more generous. When Jim isn't painting word pictures about pools of bubbling sulfur that await my atheistic soul (how appropriate for an effects animator), or showing me photos of the Shroud of Turin – proving beyond doubt, he says, Jesus' crucifixion and resurrection – I manage to dip into his toolbox of special effects expertise and over the years become modestly adept at this specialty.

During coffee or lunch breaks I escape the monastery, wandering out onto the New York street set to exchange a few words with thirty-one-year-old Paul Newman with his broken nose (fashioned of putty), playing boxer Rocky Graziano in *Somebody Up There Likes Me*. Or catch a glimpse of Grace Kelly, fresh from her final take on her final film, *The Swan*, as she dashes for a limo that will whisk her to the airport, from where she'll fly off to marry the royal croupier of Monaco. Or I cross to MGM's main lot and lunch at the commissary, where Bing Crosby, looking terribly alone, sits at the counter munching a sandwich.

---

[8] Jim Escalante's key animation for the "Night on Bald Mountain" inferno sequence in Disney's *Fantasia* is a masterpiece.

REELING THROUGH HOLLYWOOD

Soon after my son Joe is born in August of 1956, the ax falls. MGM decides to fold the animation department. By October I'll be on the street. With budgets ranging from $45,000 to $65,000 per cartoon, with theaters showing fewer and fewer short subjects and with television creeping in, the work is no longer profitable. Besides, the studio has a backlog of three hundred shorts they can recycle forever.

So goodbye, kind Bill Schipek. Goodbye, wild and wonderful Bull Pen crew. To the unemployment line I prepare to go, along with ninety percent of the oddball collection called the cartoon department.[9] Inattentive as I've been to the craft, breathing life into characters with pencil and paper has been a kick. And I yearn to do more. During ten months at MGM, union-designated raises have brought my paycheck from $36.45 to $65 a week. I've become a middling craftsman, can draw a passable Tom and Jerry and will amuse children of friends by doing so for the next forty years.

Though it isn't clear how my little family will survive on a $30 weekly government stipend, Bill Hanna and Joe Barbera promise to refer us to other studios. Some of the crew eventually joins them at their new TV operation. One of the two Fernandos becomes a top background artist. Louie, who I run into at meetings of the Screen Cartoonists Guild now and then, remains a troglodyte. Carolyn, the drop-dead-gorgeous blonde I passed in the halls, I also finally connect with. And though my lecherous daydreams about her never inch beyond lecherous daydreams, we go on to work together and become close friends. We laugh a lot, argue politics, get plastered on mai tais in Honolulu and I crash on a futon on her lanai. Alone, that is, after she marries one of the cast of Hogan's Heroes and moves to the Islands. And it's at the Royal Hawaiian Hotel's bar that she bumps into an old acquaintance from MGM – Jack Nickolson. Fresh from a big splash in *One Flew Over the Cuckoo's Nest* (1975), his surprised reaction is much like mine when I first saw her walking

---

9 A few artists were kept on to complete work in progress. Between 1961 and 1986, when Turner Broadcasting acquired all rights, Tom and Jerry was revived as a series three different times, with varying success. Then, in 1989, Hanna-Barbera Productions began a new series, featuring the cat and mouse as children, which proved highly successful.

Down the Rabbit Hole

down the cartoon department corridor. "Oh yeah," says Jack, with a broad grin, "I remember, you were that blonde surfer gal!"[10]

Before I stroll down those hallowed halls and out the door for the last time, Bill Hanna provides a two-day respite from my back room penance with the evangelizing Jim Escalante. He leads me downstairs and into a storage room. There, a hodgepodge of scenes from past productions – drawings, backgrounds and inked and painted cels – are wedged into and falling off of floor to ceiling shelves. With orders to "toss anything that doesn't seem worth keeping," I put the drawings in each scene back in order, stack the backgrounds in neat piles and cull thousands of cels in varying stages of decay (and many not so decayed). I fill trashcan after trashcan with Tom and Jerrys and Droopys. And I dump Tex Avery's Wolf, his jaw dropping as The Girl strolls by.

Just like that pitiable scene in Poughkeepsie's Rialto, out go thousands and thousands of dollars in future collectables. Though I do roll up and store Avery's extremely long pan cel with the Wolf's sporty car, the one that drives endlessly across the screen in Red Hot Riding Hood. But I don't take any home. In 1956, animation cels are dime-a dozen-curiosities, good mainly to hand off to neighborhood kids and get a wow reaction from them. Today, some bring in over $10,000. Each!

I can still hear my mournful cries echoing across the decades.

---

10 She was indeed a "surfer gal," hanging out during the early 1950s with celebrated wave riders like Buzzy Trent and the Cole brothers, Peter and Corny. (All of who, like me, had attended Santa Monica High School.)

SEVEN

faking it

July 1958, late afternoon.

As my 1953 Plymouth station wagon burns rubber through hundred-plus degree Arizona heat on Route 66, a killer headache has overtaken me. One of dozens I suffer from my twenties into my forties, this is certainly the mother of them all. I'm numb. And oblivious to what I've gotten myself into as I head for New Mexico, where I've signed on as animation director for Bandelier Films.

"Animation director?" you cry, flabbergasted. "Weren't you a lowly apprentice? Weren't you just sacked by MGM?" Right on both counts. Sacked, and now an animation director. One great thing about being a creative person is our ability to blissfully ignore the inner gremlin wagging a stern finger to warn us of our middling talent while we go on to shoot for the moon.

Actually, it's been a year and a half since Tom and Jerry and I'm antsy to do more than carve lines between other people's lines. I want to create those lines and feel the magic, as absurd big-nosed characters flow from my pencil and parade across the animation paper. Never mind that my skills are still, shall we say, a bit "limited?" Never mind that the only animation I've completed has been a

FAKING IT

seven-second TV commercial in which a little Scotsman pops from a cash drawer and declares, "Hoots, mon, somebody saved!" (For which I received $65) and a twenty second spot, one of a trio warning against H-bomb testing. That aired once.[1]

The anti-nuclear commercials were produced in my spare time, during the six months I worked as an assistant animator at Quartet Films in West Hollywood. Art Babbitt, another cartoon legend, was one of the owners.[2] The fatherly Les Goldman was another; and a clutch of fine talents still lingered from the days when the innovative John Hubley ran the studio and called it Storyboard.[3] The budget for the anti-nuclear commercials totaled $650. Two great animators, Bill Littlejohn and Emery Hawkins, as well as ink and paint and camera services had donated their labor, and this had been my first independent project.

That's Hollywood. If, like me at twenty-six, you're no Orson Welles, or haven't mastered the skills guaranteeing success, you can always kick yourself upstairs and head straight for entrepreneurship. Sort of like Walt Disney.

Still in Arizona. Still with the headache. I've left 66 to detour past Sedona's red rock hills and am chugging through Oak Creek Canyon. I pull over, climb out of the Plymouth, retrieve a washcloth from my luggage, dip it into the cooling stream then lie back against a tree with the cloth over my throbbing head.

Lines from a TV commercial accentuate the throbbing; a commercial I had inbetweened at Ray Patin Productions soon after leaving MGM in the fall of 1956 (and before hiring on at Quartet). In

---

[1] Produced for the Los Angeles Sane Nuclear Policy Committee (SANE).

[2] Art Babbitt (1907-1992) Disney animator. Helped to develop Goofy, and was a key animator on *Snow White* (1937), *Fantasia* and *Pinocchio* (both 1940), among other films.

[3] John Hubley (1914-1977) began his career on *Snow White*, co-founded United Productions of America (UPA), creators of Mister Magoo and Gerald McBoing Boing, and was among several animation artists blacklisted. Along with his wife and collaborator, Faith, Hubley won short subject Academy Awards for, *Moonbird* (1959), *The Hole* (1962), and *Tijuana Brass Double Feature* (1966).

the spot, a frustrated Chinese toddler is trying to eat Jell-O with chopsticks, while an announcer, in stereotypical Pidgin English, explains the child's dilemma. Politically incorrect poison today, in 1957 Madison Avenue thought this cute. Other spots I worked on for Patin's "videoblurbarie" (*Daily Variety* lingo) included everything from Bardahl oil additive to Schlitz beer to Ken-L-Ration dog food.

For a time, although inbetweening was no challenge, simply being part of a creative team provided satisfaction. Ray Patin's animators were as inspired as those at MGM, with several "old timers" (in their 40s and 50s) having made the leap from Warner, Walter Lantz, or Disney to TV commercials. I spent a year there, working

FAKING IT

on scenes that, unlike MGM cartoons, were still mostly inked and painted and photographed in black and white.

Along with a stimulating environment and a raise to $75 a week, I got to preview the finished commercials we turned out. And studio manager Gus Jekel encouraged my desire to learn to animate by running pencil tests I'd created through camera and lab. Plus, the assistants spent extra time trying to help me improve my drawing.

One assistant, however, was anything but helpful. Ken Mundie, hugely talented but bubbling with angst, never stopped ragging me about one thing or another. Then, one day while my back was turned, he slammed an oily piston he'd removed from his MG sports car into my wastebasket. As my eardrums reverberated, I hit the ceiling, leaped to my feet and promptly challenged him to "step into the alley." Ken snickered then followed me outside. As workmates gathered to watch, Ken picked up a tiny chip of wood and placed it on his shoulder.

"Knock this off," he snarled.

Mistake! I busted him in the chops. He immediately covered his face with both hands, but I kept pummeling. Twenty seconds into the fray, insistent arms pulled me away and we were both sent off to cool down. Ken shook a fist and vowed to "get you after work!" But when I saw him that evening on the way to my car, his threatened assault had become a deep glower at me from across the street.

Ken never spoke to me again. Whenever I bumped into him over the years he would simply glare then stomp off.[4]

[4] Ken Mundie went on to direct Bill Cosby's first *Fat Albert* TV special (1969), an assignment I'd been led to believe I'd get. In retrospect, he was a far better choice than I would have been. Don't know if he realized I'd been up for the job, but if he did, his revenge must certainly have been sweet.

Back in Oak Creek Canyon. The headache has abated and I'm on the road again. An hour later I'm on 66 once more, whizzing past rickety compounds with gaudy painted letters advertising "Live Snakes! Gila Monsters!" Or trading posts that peddle blankets and "Genuine Navajo silver."

Genuine? Here I am, wondering how I'll fake it in Albuquerque, how I'll parlay my meager experience into running an animation department at Bandelier Films. And what the hell does "Bandelier" mean?[5] Is it a corruption of that broad belt slung across the chest, with pockets for carrying ammunition? Like Wallace Beery wore in *Viva Villa*?

I ruminate over my six months at Quartet Films.

Hey, I am an animator, I tell myself. Well, at least an assistant animator, pulling in ninety-five big ones a week. But when animator Art Babbitt handed me an inch-thick stack of drawings for, say, a Western Airlines commercial and said, "just nice, careful inbetweens," I had to look hard to find any, because in a sequence of

---

[5] The studio borrowed the name from Bandelier National Monument, near Los Alamos, New Mexico. Named for the 19th Century anthropologist Adolph Bandelier.

FAKING IT

three hundred drawings, Art had completed all but half a dozen. And they were so close together there was barely room enough from one drawing to the next to squeeze in an inbetween. This was no more creative than at MGM. Frustration mounted.

All over America, stress like this leads stifled egos to blow their coworkers away. In Hollywood, it only turned me into a chain smoker and pushed me into seeking a better opportunity.

I'm in New Mexico now, passing through Gallup and fretting about what lies ahead. But hey, didn't I hustle that anti-H bomb assignment? And produce the commercials myself? I should be able to pull this off. Just like I landed the gig with Bandelier in the first place.

Tooting my animation horn beyond credibility, I had walked into the Helen Edwards Agency on Wilshire Boulevard and signed up. A businesslike, middle-aged professional, Helen Edwards hustled jobs for folks seeking work in advertising. She had nothing at the moment, so I went home and forgot about it.

A month later, I was still at Quartet. Lines between lines. Borrrrring! Helen called. "I've got a job here, Dan," she said cheerfully, "Animation director for a film company in New Mexico. It starts at . . . "

"I'll take it!"

" . . .one twenty-five a week. And after you're there for ninety days, and. . ."

"When do they want me to start?"

" . . .they'll reimburse your moving expenses, up to two hundred fifty dollars. They want somebody ASAP."

"Sounds great."

"Uh . . . you are an animation director, aren't you?"

"Absolutely."

So goodbye Quartet Films. I tuned up the Plymouth, arranged to have movers transport everything from our modest one bedroom rental in Santa Monica to New Mexico, borrowed money for plane fare for Rose, Lisa and Joe, who would follow as soon as I found a place to hang our hats, and adios Santa Monica. So long to the Hollywood dream factory that had been less dreamy than I dreamed it would be.

And here I am, heading down 66. A twilight haze hangs over the Rio Grande Valley and the lights of Albuquerque twinkle in the distance.

Bob Stevens, owner of Bandelier Films, is a loud, glad-handing but pleasant Chamber of Commerce type. Along with Bandelier, he owns the adjacent Robert Stevens Advertising, a company he founded in 1948, two years after mustering out of the Army. Bob tours me through the studio. Three rooms; one for myself and another artist, a dark room with a jerry-rigged animation stand, and a long, narrow room set up for the dozen dollar-an-hour inkers and painters Bob confidently expects to hire, "now that we've got a big Hollywood animator on board," he bellows, as he claps an arm around my shoulder.

The room holds a twenty-five-foot-long inclined table. Constantly nickel and diming, Bob explains that he plans to run a conveyer belt above the table, with heat lamps over it, so a painter can apply a color to the rear of a cel then place it back on the belt. By the time the cel reaches the next painter, the first color will be dry. The second painter will snatch the cel, fill in a second color, then return it to the belt, and so on. I eye him quizzically. He guffaws, then admits that he's already scrapped the idea, having concluded that the time needed for each cel to move to the end of the belt would actually slow down production instead of speeding it up. Then he adds, "I was gonna hire Navajos to do the work. There's a lot'a skill in those people, ya know. Except, they're not reliable. Anytime some pow-wow or festival comes along they'd just take off."

Is this another Louie (my fellow MGM apprentice), I wonder? I think about calling Stevens on the slur, but it's day one and he's the boss, so I let it pass.

Next, I met Doyle, a tall, gaunt Texan and the ad agency's art director. He's been doubling as animator and figuring out how to make characters move by studying a Walter T. Foster instruction book, *How to Draw Animated Cartoons*. And he quickly lets me know how delighted he is I've been hired, since "I kind of only know about half way how to do this, Dan."

Bandelier's new Oxberry animation stand, acquired after I left.

I also discover that the "animation department" consists of two people: Doyle and me. So much for cracking the whip over a couple dozen animators, assistants, background artists and inkers and painters.

But if my fancy has flown, Bob's hasn't. He has plans. Big plans. And he's already putting them into operation. A flyer promising "a fully animated twenty-second TV commercial, from your storyboard, for $495," has been sent to a couple of thousand ad agencies. And this includes a round trip airfare to Albuquerque for an "interlock." (Viewing a work print of the animation, along with the sound track.) Though it will take me several days to grind out twenty seconds of animation and another week for it to be inked and painted, photographed and the film developed, Bob reasons that with the wages he's paying (he obviously doesn't cop to them being skimpy) he'll just about break even. "Anyway," he brags, "I'm building for the future."

In a way, Bob, with little background in the field and with only a novice animator (me) signed on, is doing the same kind of thing on a business level that I've been up to as a cartoonist: blundering ahead and taking a chance.

Unlike the modest burg of fifty thousand that Albuquerque had been in 1944 when brother David and I first came through on the Santa Fe Chief, cookie-cutter adobe style housing tracts now march across the East Mesa toward the Sandia Mountains. By 1958, nearly two hundred thousand call it home. After several nights in a cheap hotel, I locate a two bedroom house for rent then phone Rose to tell her the movers should be called and that she and the kids can come ahead.

Animating at Bandelier Films, 1958

Meanwhile, I've started work. At Bandelier, several of Stevens' local newspaper and radio accounts have stuck their big toes into television waters. Since, like Doyle, I "kind of only know half way how to do this," I take a deep breath, plunge in, and just do it. What Bob and Doyle don't know is that when they aren't looking I peek into my own trusty copy of Walter T. Foster's *How to Draw Animated Cartoons*. (A book I've had since age sixteen.)

For Robert Bronson Insurance I create a cat burglar character tiptoeing around inside a house, only to escape through a window just before the police show up. For the New Mexico State Fair I not only voice the announcer and create sound effects but also paint the cels. And Doyle teaches me to man the animation stand, so I soon become a low level jack of all animation trades.

Within three months, Bob's $495 blue plate special is paying off. Small regional accounts are sending in storyboards for bids.[6] I hire a shy young woman, Janet, who quickly learns to ink and paint. After Janet and I (aided by Doyle) work like beavers for three months to complete assignments on Bob's absurd budgets, he realizes he'd better hike his prices. So he sends out another flyer, raising his offer on twenty seconds of animation to $695. Still including the round trip airfare to Albuquerque.

---

[6] A storyboard is something like a comic strip, with panels describing the main action in a TV commercial, or live or animated film.

Reeling Through Hollywood

And the work continues coming in. A job arrives from Canada. I animate, help paint cels and run the animation stand, as a nutty Dalmatian skids across a kitchen floor slathered with Success Wax. In another spot, chipmunks sing the praises of Gambrinus Beer. Why chipmunks, I haven't a clue. But what the hell, didn't Tex Avery use a bear for his Hamm's Beer commercials, the "land of sky blue waters" and all that?

Though I'll often spend ten to twelve hour days fattening Bob Stevens' wallet, there are perks. He gives me the key to his mountain cabin near Jemez Springs for a family weekend. There are trips to Sandia Crest, looming east of the city, and to the adobe magnificence of Old Santa Fe. As we walk through town I expect Errol Flynn to appear along the dusty streets, leading a cavalry charge. Another visit, to Albuquerque's crummy zoo, with sad-looking animals pacing in tiny cages, isn't so grand. Nor are the windstorms that sweep across the mesa, drifting sand in under the doors of our modest home.

Six months along, more regional accounts roll in. Up to my ears in animation, I hire a young man with excellent drawing skills to spell Doyle on background art. Two more cel painters begin working with Janet, so ink and paint can keep up with me. Another young man is taken on to run errands and do odd jobs. Bob Steven's twelve-year-old son, Allan, sweeps floors, sets titles on the "hot press," and sometimes hands off cels to whoever is running the camera, so the work moves faster. Resumes from artists seeking employment arrive weekly, along with sample reels by filmmakers looking for assignments. One features a series of spots for Wilkins Coffee, popular in the Washington, D.C. and Baltimore areas. The spotmakers have created a clutch of odd-looking hand puppets advertising the brand. "Muppets," they call them. Bob loves them. I find them amusing, but tell him I much prefer my Uncle Harry's old-fashioned marionettes.[7]

---

[7] Kermit wasn't a frog in 1958; he was simply "Kermit the Thing." Miss Piggy was still a gleam in Jim Henson's eye.

FAKING IT

January 1959. I've become fairly puffed up. Have been doing a great job, I believe, of humbugging my way along as an animation director. Though mediocre, my work is so much better than what Bandelier had turned out before my arrival that even with a seasonal slowdown (common in the animation biz) I figure it's time to ask for a raise. I've also been agitating Janet and other employees to knock on Bob's door and demand more money. Squeamish about risking their jobs, however, they decided to wait to see what happens when good old Daniel blunders into his office. So I swallow hard and . . .

"Uh, Bob, I've been thinking . . . it's seven months now, we're doing more important work, you're up to over two grand for a minute of animation and I thought, well, maybe you could squeeze out another twenty-five dollars a week. You see, I -- "

"Gee, Dan, sorry. Wish I could, but as you know we're in a slow period. Never sure when it might pick up again and I'm squeezed to the wall. Maybe in six months." He smiles indulgently then asks, "Anything else?"

I sigh, and then vaguely mumble that if that's the case I'm not sure I'll be sticking around.

"Your choice," he replies, picking up the phone to make a call.

OK, if that's how he wants it!

That night I make a train reservation for the next day and ask Rose to call Bandelier in the morning to report that I'm down with the flu. And then I start packing. Late the next evening I'm in Los Angeles. And the day after, knocking on animation studio doors. No immediate jobs present themselves (the seasonal downturn) but everyone expects business to pick up soon. So a couple days later I'm back on the train to New Mexico, feeling semi-confident.

When I arrive, I discover that Bob, certain I'd been bluffing, and with Doyle in tow, had shown up at our front door. Rose had told them I was still sick in bed. Though they asked to see me, she wouldn't let them in.

Two days later, after "recovering from the flu," and having decided to stick it out for another month, I report to work. As I enter the studio Bob looks up from his desk, beckons me into his office – and immediately fires me. Then he grills me on where I've been. When I tell him I've been at home sick, he smirks and shakes his head. "I'll have a check for you by noon," he says.

One week later. Route 66 again. Rose, Lisa, Joe and I – along with Cookie, a half-pint half Collie we've adopted from the Albuquerque animal shelter – are in the Plymouth, heading west. Toward, I hope, a decent paying job, because after selling our furniture and paying a flock of bills, all we have left is a bit over $300.

But I'm confident I'll land something in L.A. And it's a crisp sunny morning as we roll up out of the Rio Grande Valley, cross the West Mesa and head for Gallup. Soon after, as New Mexico disappears behind us and we approach Flagstaff the sky rapidly turns black. Rain starts falling then quickly turn to snow. Then we are in the mountains west of Flagstaff, driving through a blizzard – with no chains for the Plymouth's well-worn tires. Ahead, the lights on the back of an enormous semi suddenly flare. I jam on the brakes. With no traction, we skid into a house trailer parked by the side of the road. Three-year-old Joe catapults over the front seat and into the dashboard. Blood gushes from his forehead. Rose quickly stanches the flow and he seems OK, just a small cut above one eye.

I jump out. The entire right front of our car has been crushed. Water leaks from the radiator. And an elderly guy is shuffling toward me, along with his wife, who has received a nasty gash in her leg when the trailer shifted as we careened into it. I fumble an explanation. We confer and decided that since the guy's car is OK we'll all pile into it and head back to Flagstaff to find a hospital. As we're getting into the car, a tow truck pulls up. Can he tow the Plymouth to Flagstaff? Sure. Twenty-five bucks. We are not the only orphans of the storm; the driver is flush with business. We're number five in line. It's six p.m. now, he'll have our car back to his garage by midnight.

FAKING IT

After one doctor attends to the woman's laceration and another cleans Joe's eye, puts a Band-Aid on it and promises that it's "nothing to worry about," we're into a motel for the night. By morning the snowstorm is no more. By noon, so is two-thirds of our remaining $300. The garage has straightened the Plymouth's front end and repaired the radiator well enough so that we can start hobbling back toward California.

My feelings are mixed. On the one hand, while I understand that bullshitting to get a job has been unwise I give myself credit for pulling it off. Then too, maybe getting canned served me right? With a family to support, my twenty-six-year-old impetuosity was hardly a brilliant move. Even though Rose (who doesn't want to live in New Mexico anyhow) takes it all in stride, my lack of foresight has led us down a road much bumpier than it needed to be.

By the time we stop for dinner in Kingman, Joe's eye is bright purple and big as an egg. A frown from the coffee shop waitress tells us she suspects we've beaten the poor kid. Since the Flagstaff medic had said that Joe's cut was nothing serious, we (unwisely) dismiss the waitress's suggestion to have him seen by a local doc. Then we limp as fast as we can across the Colorado River, through the Mojave, over the San Bernardino Mountains and to Mom's house in Santa Monica, arriving at midnight. Early the next morning we drive Joe to the doctor. It takes a weeklong regimen of antibiotics to keep him from losing the eye. But then, mercifully, he's back to normal.

Three weeks later, after making the rounds in L.A. looking for work and finding none, the phone rings. Bob Stevens is on the line. He has a TV spot for me to animate. Just the drawings, Bandelier will take care of ink and paint and camera. Not a word about firing me. No ill will, no recrimination. Simply a pleasant voice offering me four hundred bucks for a one minute commercial. Two weeks to create all the drawings, based on a storyboard he's about to put in the mail.

That comes to two hundred a week. I've got my raise!

On that February day in 1959 there is no way to imagine that I'll continue churning out animation for Bandelier for forty more years, with Bob flying me to Albuquerque now and then to meet with a client. Or that even before he retires, his son Allan will be running the studio and sending me work. And haggling with me about how much I'll charge. I'll always ask for more than he offers, and we'll inevitably settle for a figure somewhere in between. I also can't foresee that during the late 1990s, when I'm living (alone by then) in Santa Cruz, Allan will ship his own son Tim to California for a week so that I can offer him pointers in animation and give him a gentle but firm nudge into the field.

I provide as much advice as I can, but it does give me pause. Do I want to see young Tim chained to a hot light board for the rest of his creative life? Is this the career he really wants to pursue? I can't tell. He seems ambivalent. Well, I guess he'll figure it out. It's the kind of decision we all have to make

And it seems to have worked out. During an Albuquerque stopover not too long ago Allan confided that Tim "lives and breathes for animation," and that "even though I'd never tell him so, he's probably one of the best animators in this part of the country." I'm delighted to hear it. Like me, Tim may never become rich or famous. But as long as he's not grinding down 2-B pencils simply to please his dad, maybe he's experiencing some of the same satisfaction that I eventually did as I began to master the craft, and slowly became a real animator.

EIGHT

tent show

"Bears," intones the spindly, consumptive-looking ad agency account executive; "I want bears. Fat bears. Skinny bears. Tall and short bears. Odd looking bears. Bears with hats on. Bears without hats. Bears doing stuff. All kinds of bears. Design me a big page of bears. I've got a hundred dollars budgeted." Then he turns from the curtains he's been clutching – with his face buried in them – asks me to phone as soon as I've corralled his bears, and vanishes out onto La Cienaga Boulevard.

July 1961. Los Angeles. My first production company, Circus Films, has been open a year. But even as partners Thom Smitham and Dick Ravell and I stifle our laughter until the exec (who reminds me of Ichabod Crane from *The Legend of Sleepy Hollow*) is out of earshot, we all know that the doors on our tiny two-room empire are about to close for good.

We had started the company with a burst of energy and a shoestring budget: Dick Revell's $1000 investment. We started it because TV commercials were booming, because I had (I thought) solid client connections and because we were sure we'd make pots of money (some of which would pay for special schooling for my daughter Lisa.[1])Also because, after the House Committee on Un-American Activities hauled me before them in October 1959, I wasn't sure anyone would hire me anyhow.[2]

After the HUAC hearings, an occasional freelance job came along. I knocked out two spots for Bandelier, then a segment for a Mr. Magoo TV series. I drove one studio head into a screaming fit when I charged him seventy-five dollars on a job for which he'd assumed I'd bill forty. And through Hal, a friend at National Screen Service, a company producing movie trailers but which also had TV ambitions, I animated a Puss n' Boots cat food commercial.

Deep down, I had nourished hopes that my uncle Leo Burnett, whose agency advertised everything from Marlboro cigarettes to the Jolly Green Giant, would throw some business to Circus Films. And maybe one of his clients would take a look at a cartoon series idea I'd create.

Sky-high ambitions and a thimble of thoughtfulness. Yet sometimes this kind of chutzpa pays off.

With its hint of boisterous fun, Circus Films was, we all thought, a terrific name for an animation studio. Revell's $1000 let me create a letterhead, business cards and a direct mail flyer. I spent hopeful days addressing then stuffing and stamping envelopes and sending them to a thousand small ad agencies. The biggies (except for Leo

---

[1] Soon after returning from Albuquerque, doctors confirmed what Rose and I had begun to suspect, that Lisa's sometimes-odd behavior and quirky mannerisms were the result of organic but undiagnosable brain damage. She was mentally retarded.

[2] The hearings, a circus in themselves, were held to investigate "Communist activity in the western section of Los Angeles." I sparred with the Committee and declined, on Fifth Amendment grounds, to answer their questions. At the time, I'd been back at Quartet Films for three weeks. When the news broke two days later, I was told that I need not come in the following Monday.

Burnett) we planned to tackle after we'd batted a few home runs in the bush leagues. I had also put together a short 16mm sample reel of the few TV commercials I had copies of. Then we sat back, anticipating a deluge of assignments.

The deluge had been a slowly dripping faucet. Half a dozen agencies requested our sample reel. We'd made six copies, so I sent them all out. Two eventually came back – after numerous polite letters and expensive phone calls, intercepted by secretaries who usually feigned ignorance about ever having received a reel.[3] A single storyboard arrived for a bid. We didn't get the job.

Six months slipped by. Nothing. My letters to Pop, who had his fingers crossed for me to sell TV projects and hire him, ranged

---

[3] Today, a dollar or two will duplicate a sample reel on VHS. In 1960, those half-dozen five-minute 16mm sample reels cost us $250.

from the absurd to the pathetic; boasts about starting on my "life's work," an animated feature about Paul Bunyan, to pleas for cash to help with Lisa's eighty-dollar-a-month schooling. He sent a ten or a twenty whenever he could. And Rose made a few bucks selling her wonderfully warm *New Yorker*-like sketches to a library journal. A ten second commercial for Bandelier Films also helped.

July 1960. The Democrats were in town to nominate John F. Kennedy. I haunted the convention, picking up campaign buttons, the beginning of what would grow into an impressive and valuable collection. (Maybe I'd learned something from the Great Rialto Fiasco?) Most days, I came into the office and made a few phone calls, maybe lunched with a friend, made more calls then spent the afternoon developing new ideas for a TV series, knocking out bad poetry on my Smith-Corona, or drumming my fingers on the desk.

Then, in the spring of 1961, my contacts began to pay off. National Screen Service hired Circus Films to produce a twenty-second spot for Richfield Boron gasoline. Soon after, my friend Hal (having left National Screen, and now on his own) contracted animation segments for a series of three spots for local TV station KNXT. The budget was $2500. We received $500 up front, so I plunged in to turn out the drawings. With everything camera ready, we received another $500. We'd been paid less than half the money when Hal previewed the finished work. Great. He loved the spots. And KNXT approved. Double great.

Two weeks later, Hal called to say he'd run out of cash. The TV station, shooting the live portion of the spots (under his direction), had been charging a staggering fee for special video equipment.

He'd never figured this into the budget. He was broke. Dum, de, dum, dum . . . ! The theme from *Dragnet* ran through my head.

Smitham and Ravell were livid. Hal owed us $1500. "We'll take him to court," said Thom. But that would be expensive and we had less than zilch in the bank. So, over my objections, they hired a repo man to snatch Hal's brand new Olds and his wife Elaine's brand new Chevy. (In spite of his poverty plea, Hal clearly had money to burn.) Madness, I thought. Ultimately, I got them to return the cars. Hal and Elaine were dear friends, so what could I do? But Circus Films never saw an additional penny. Back to drumming my fingers on the desk.

Over the past couple weeks I had also completed a nifty storyboard for a TV series. After several attempts I set up a meeting with the L.A. branch of my uncle Leo's ad agency. On the appointed morning, a friend took off work for an hour to pose as my secretary. And I arranged for others to call during the meeting, so it would seem as if the Circus Films pot was bubbling. Or at least simmering. (Typical Hollywood hokum.) Smitham and Ravell were also on hand. Two agency people appeared and listened politely as I pitched the concept, *The Magic Egg*, in which a gawky, stork-like bird laid a gigantic egg, out of which hatched a short, fumbling wizard. The adoring bird, deciding the wizard was her son, followed him everywhere. To the wizard, the bird was a smothering nuisance, so he kept trying to shake her. The Leo Burnett folks smiled in all the right places, but ultimately didn't feel "this is exactly what Kellogg, or any of our other clients are looking for at the moment."

OK, then why not make a half hour pilot on our own? We'd show the world what we could do. So we put an ad in the *L.A. Times*, seeking investment. A fundraiser called, certain that for a hundred-fifty bucks (against a ten percent commission) he could find the money. He made an honest effort (we thought), but didn't turn up a dime.

The phone rang again.

"Hello, I saw your ad. Intriguing. I represent some folks back east who are eager to get into TV."

"Wonderful," I replied. "When can we get together?"

"Here's the thing," said the jocular voice at the other end, "I'm just flying back to Cleveland to meet with my contacts. I'll get to LAX about 5 p.m., could you come out there?"

No problem. At five, I was at the airport. The fellow was a friendly, down home Iowa type. We had dinner. He ordered lavishly: a thick Porterhouse with all the trimmings. And two glasses of Cabernet Sauvignon. As he dined, I nibbled. He chuckled over my presentation of *The Magic Egg*, took my storyboard and budget figures and tucked them into his briefcase, and was "sure this is exactly what my eastern contacts are looking for."

Dinner complete, he patted his stomach and sat back with a satisfied grin. Then he excused himself to go to the john. "Won't be a minute," he smiled.

The minute turned to ten. Then thirty. By forty-five minutes I got the idea. I'd been had. And left stuck with a fifteen-dollar tab. And he'd run off with my storyboard! Pissed as I was, as I trekked to the parking garage I had to give the bastard credit. Clever ploy. He was probably nicking free meals all over the country with this scam.

Tent Show

July 1961. The office on La Cienega. Circus Films' first year is limping to a close. I sit at my desk, doodling and wondering where to go from here. The phone rings. I am almost too depressed to answer, but what the hell ...

"Circus Films."

"Dan, hi. Sid Hecht here."

Sid, a pleasant, balding hustler, is the client at National Screen Service for whom we had turned out the Richfield gasoline spot a few months earlier.

"How'd you like to come to work for National Screen," he asks, "We need an animation director."

Well, why not? What else is on my plate?

Oh, the bears? I draw them, of course. A hundred bucks is a hundred bucks. When the Ichabod Crane agency guy drops by to collect them a few days later they aren't quite right. So I draw another dozen bears. For another fifty dollars. He leaves Circus Films, content. Neither the Ichabodish ad man nor the bears are ever heard from again.

NINE

hustlers

Two weeks later I am still at my same desk. But in another studio. In a dark hallway now, at National Screen Service. Circus Films is no more. And I'm in the hall because National Screen's loud, bearlike head honcho, Bud Brody, in the midst of remodeling the studio, has nowhere else to put me. But I'm feeling mellow because even though Circus Films has wrapped its tent and tiptoed into the night, we've put aside just enough out of the dribble we did earn to return Dick Ravell's $1000 investment. Not quite the disaster I thought it would be when friend Hal stiffed us on those commercials.

Brody and his second in command, Sid Hecht, are gung-ho to set the TV commercial world on fire. There'll be work for years, they promise. Plus which, the remodel is transforming a shabby warehouse-like structure into a modern and pleasant workspace

National Screen has been churning out previews of coming attractions trailers since forever (1920). Along the same hall where I camp, a staff of writers, squeezed into windowless offices, bang out snazzy copy to promote a huge number of Hollywood movies. In addition to trailers, National Screen produces publicity stills, lobby cards, half sheets, one sheets, three sheets, six sheets, twenty-four sheets and other advertising paraphernalia of various sizes. They also create an occasional main title.

This is Bandelier revisited: I'm the animation department. Within two months, and even with some thumb twiddling while Sid and Bud hustle work, I direct and animate a Skippy Peanut Butter commercial (peanut butter goes great on bananas; don't forget to peel 'em), along with a series of promos soliciting business. Then I create a title concept for a film Otto Preminger is about to produce. Or direct. And never does. But along with a National Screen writer, I get to hobnob with the legendary Viennese for ten minutes in his office at Fox. He's just as curt and dismissive of my storyboard as if he's still Oberst Von Scherbach, the Nazi officer he portrayed in *Stalag 17* (1953).

"Dis iss an interestink idea, I vill let you know, boys. But chust now I am very buzy, zo . . . " He lets us know nothing, of course.

And the arresting title graphic I've created (and which we actually film) for the now classic Kirk Douglas film *Lonely are the Brave* (1962)[1] doesn't make the cut either.

Nor is our pitch for a tender Judy Garland and Burt Lancaster film, *A Child is Waiting* (1963) successful. For the movie, which concerns mentally challenged kids, Rose creates a drawing of Lisa that seems to epitomize the feelings of these children. National Screen agrees, so we present the sketch to producer Stanley Kramer – who decides that the image is too stark for the publicity campaign he has in mind.

Otto Preminger

Though having ideas shot down is a bummer, there are occasional ups. Like the animated lettering I create for the trailer announcing the re-release of Elvis Presley's *Jailhouse Rock* (originally distributed in 1957). And the work is steady. Sid Hecht likes me. Bud Brody

---

[1] *Lonely are the Brave* was based on Edward Abbey's novel *The Brave Cowboy* (1956). Abbey also wrote *The Monkey Wrench Gang* (1975). Ten years later I found myself working for *Lonely are the Brave's* producer, Eddie Lewis. (See Chapters 16 and 19, about *Executive Action*.)

likes me. A $250 paycheck, the promise of big things in the future, and a steady dribble of animation keep me optimistic.

Finally, with remodeling in high gear, I'm liberated from the hallway and installed in a building across from the main offices. There, I work mainly on a series of animated intermission trailers, the kind we still see off and on, urging us to rush to the lobby and load up on overpriced pop-corn and soft drinks.

I've never understood how it's possible for theaters to pop a nickel's worth of corn kernels, scoop it into a bag, toss a little salt and butter on top and sucker patrons into forking over three to five bucks (or more).[2]

Early in 1962 Sid Hecht flies me to New York to consult with the U.S. Army Signal Corps film unit at Astoria, Long Island, for which National Screen has contracted to produce the animated portion of a film on tuberculosis.[3]

While there, a Brody sycophant, a brother-in-law as I recall (I should have suspected skullduggery back on the plantation), hands me the card of a friend who runs a fashion house in the garment district and urges me to "get a little something for the missus. On the expense account." Torn, and feeling guilty, I finally buy Rose a stylish seventy-dollar orange dress with a white collar.

By the time I return to L.A., massive new leather couches grace Bud Brody's office. Expensive but tasteless art adorns the walls. He has also ordered himself a new Cadillac. Sid's office is less flamboy-ant, and he only gets a Buick. And a short, middle-aged Filipino in

---

[2] Sixty percent of exhibitors profit comes from the food concession. Amazingly, when I left Santa Cruz, California in 1999, the Capitola Theater, a rerun house, was still charging no more than thirty cents for a generous bag of popcorn.

[3] During World War II this same unit employed such talents as Frank Capra, Darryl Zanuck, John Huston, and Theodor Geisel (Dr. Seuss) to turn out morale building and propaganda films.

white jacket and bow tie is bustling about, polishing the huge new inch thick glass doors leading to the executive offices, vacuuming the plush red carpets that run the length of the main hall, and keeping Sid and Bud and both their secretaries supplied with coffee. The "houseboy" is right out of *The Green Hornet*.[4]

An aura of tension also pervades the studio. I suspect that my career at NSS is slipping away. I write my father about it:

April 19, 1962.

Pop,

Situation here at National Screen is BaaadddDD!
1. Bosses spent too much money remodeling studio, promoting business, etc.
2. New York office unhappy.
3. Not enough work coming in.
4. Bosses have apparently been fired.
5. New boss coming in (an s.o.b; he worked here before).
6. Many people will probably be fired because of lack of work, including yours truly. Who knows?

More later, love, Dan

Two weeks after I complete animation for the TV trailers, the studio is awash in east coast higher ups and accountants. Bud and Sid wear worried frowns. Rumors of "irregularities" are spreading. Next day, Sid hands me a pink slip: two weeks' notice. New York is taking no chances on how far the malignancy has spread, so everyone hired by Hecht or Brody during the past year is being suspended. Sid doesn't supply details, but does clue me in that he and Brody will be leaving National Screen to set up their own TV commercial business. Whisperings have it that Brody and his brother-

---

[4] *The Green Hornet* began on radio in 1936, and played until 1952. The first *Green Hornet* comic was published in 1940. Two films were made during the 1940s, and the first TV series (with Bruce Lee as the Hornet's "faithful valet," Kato) was produced in the 1966-67 season. A made for TV movie appeared in 1990, with Gordon Jones as Brit Reid (the Hornet), and Keye Luke as Kato.

in-law have been receiving kickbacks from every contractor they've hired to remodel the studio. Tens of thousands of dollars, we hear. I panic. Will they find out about that seventy-dollar orange dress?

Coincident with this shady business, the Un-American Committee arrives in town on their own shady business. A picket line has been organized to greet them. I take off for an afternoon to demonstrate my opposition. The picket line stretches completely around the Los Angeles Federal Building. A thousand people. Press and police photographers are snapping pictures of everyone.

When I stroll into National Screen the next morning the receptionist motions me over and whispers, "Better take a look on the bulletin board by the camera room." Curious, I wander down the hall. On the board, someone has pinned a newspaper photo of the anti-HUAC picket line, a tiny section of eight people (out of the thousand who were present). And there I am, smack in the middle.

A red circle has been drawn around my image, with big, fat red arrows pointing directly at it.

I hear snickering. I turn to discover a low-level employee, a man I've never liked. "Gotcha," he chortles, then disappears.

I soon discover that he's tacked copies of the *L.A. Times* photo on two other bulletin boards. Each copy has me circled, along with the arrows. My two-week notice turns into the next day. By which time, warns the new high-muckety-muck, I have to vacate.

My job is history.

Hecht and Bud Brody don't get off so easy. Though I animate a couple spots for them after they set up their new operation, within six months Brody is carted off to the pokey for a two-year stretch. Sid, having perhaps covered his tracks more carefully, avoids the same fate. Gradually, we lose touch, and a few years later I learn that he has died of a rapidly spreading cancer. Crooked or not, to me, Sid was a kind, helpful and generous fellow.

Me? I'm "at liberty" again. But every time I look at Rose in that new orange dress I feel a twinge of conscience.

TEN

hey culligan man!

Once in a great while our lives cross paths with a person who is kind, honest, talented and a warm and friendly human being all rolled into one. Yiddish speakers have the perfect word for such a treasure: Mensch. Dallas Williams was a mensch. The world would be a far better place if we had more mensches.

Fall 1962. Bounced from National Screen Service, I'm at home in Santa Monica, fretting over where our next rent payment will come from, when the phone rings. I pick up.

"Hello, this is Dal Williams," says a genial voice, "I got your number from the Screen Cartoonists Guild and I understand you do animation."

With this call begins a creative association that will last twenty years and a friendship that will last thirty. Dallas is looking for a capable someone to take over where Lee Mishkin, original designer of the Culligan soft water commercials, left off after their debut year. Starting in 1961, the animated TV spots for Culligan, featuring an ever patient announcer (voiced by Dallas) and a coy but ditzy housewife (voiced by his former wife Jean) go on to become a hugely popular series, and the housewife's "Hey Culligan Man!" cry becomes an icon of American advertising. Indeed, Dal Williams is, along with the great Stan Freberg, one of the very first to integrate comedy into commercials.[1]

---

[1] Freberg's fifty plus years in show business include everything from cartoon voices to syndicated radio and TV commercials, to spoofs of popular shows and songs, to his masterpiece album, "Stan Freberg Presents the United States of America." (1961)

Dallas Williams

A straight shooter, Dallas immediately lets me know his budget. Less than Mishkin wants, he implies, thus the call; for I'm acquiring a small reputation as an animator who works fast yet turns in a professional job. And because of this speed and reliability, on most assignments – few as they've been since leaving National Screen and although I'm able to quote a lower fee – I usually earn above Guild scale. (Though I don't tell this to clients.)

Dal Williams is the perfect image of the man in the gray flannel suit: impeccably combed hair, horn-rimmed specs and a handsomely chiseled face. But unlike most agency guys he's low key, thoughtful, considerate and never one to pressure another creative soul. His humor is ubiquitous. He drives an older model Rolls Royce with a personalized license plate that proclaims, "Flaunt."

Working with Dal is a joy. We meet for lunch, perhaps at the

Nickodel near Paramount, or across the street at Lucy's Casa el Adobe, where Orson Welles, probably weighing over three hundred pounds, holds court with a clutch of youthful admirers. Over a club sandwich or Lucy's enchilada combo,[2] Dal and I develop story ideas for the next "Hey Culligan Man" series. He'll toss out a concept, I'll toss some back, and then he'll dream up a couple more. By the time the check arrives (he always insists on paying), we have roughed out the basics for the three to five spots I'll direct and animate for him. Then Dal goes back to his office and types up the copy; dialogue mostly. I stop by, pick up the scripts – or he mails them to me, or sometimes just phones me the lines (the fax hasn't come in yet; or at least neither of us owns one), and then I execute the storyboards.

We repeat the process every year for the next twenty. Close to a hundred commercials. And since almost every spot features the same two characters – the little announcer standing on a rectangular box with the Culligan logo on the front, with the housewife standing next to him – all we have to do is come up with different lines. Invariably, each spot reaches a point where the guy asks the gal to "just call your Culligan man." And she does!

Pencil drawing for a Culligan storyboard

[2] More than forty years later, Lucy's Casa El Adobe is still in business. Try their salad; the dressing is wonderful

Hey Culligan Man!

A typical situation:

He's on the box with the logo; she's beside him.

HE: "To get soft water, just call your Culligan man."

SHE SCREECHES: "Hey Culligan Man!"

As the words appear above her in large block letters he falls flat, terrified; then he looks up and says —

HE: "But Culligan means soft water."

SHE: "Oh." Then, gently, "Hey Culligan Man."

Soft, flowing letters spell out her words; flowers appear, birds tweet. He sits up.

HE: "Now, isn't that better?"

She nods in agreement.

Sometimes we use props instead of just the little guy standing on the box. In another spot, he and the housewife are next to a big washing machine, atop of which sit boxes of bleach, detergent and water softener.

HE: "Why go to all that expense and bother? All you need is soft water . . . and a Culligan Water Conditioner gives you an unlimited supply. Why'n'cha' call your Culligan Man?"

As she screeches "Hey Culligan Man!" his reaction sends him head first into the washer. She watches him spin around and around for a moment, then turns to camera and says, "I'm gonna give Culligan a whirl."

OK, Abbott and Costello it isn't. But the gags bring a chuckle. Often, we idle away an hour tossing darts in Dal's office before knocking out ideas. Or yak about politics. He being a liberal, me a lefty, our discussions are amicably thoughtful.

Once I've created the storyboards Dal ships them to Culligan's ad agency for approval. During our twenty-year collaboration, minor changes are suggested only two or three times. Culligan respects Dal's work and Dal respects mine. So the frustration I often feel working with some clients invariably dissipates when the phone rings and I pick up to Dallas's cheery voice. I also look forward to his calls because long dry spells and layoffs – along with being in hock to my friendly Santa Monica Consumers' Federal Credit Union – are finally broken when he does.

Following storyboard approval, Dal and Jean record the sound tracks. Then I have them "read" by a film editor – who translates the sound from 16mm magnetic film to exposure sheets, so I know exactly where to open and close the character's mouths. After I complete the animation (three weeks, on average) the drawings are inked and painted on cels (transparent sheets of 9 X 12 inch celluloid, like at MGM).

And this is where Carolyn, the stunning young woman Jack Nickolson remembered (also from MGM) as "that blonde surfer gal" comes in again. I bump into her at a Screen Cartoonists Guild meeting while I'm in the midst of my first Culligan assignment. With a reason now to talk, I muster the courage. Sure, she'd love to handle ink and paint. And so she does, with expert skill, each year for the next twelve, until she splits for Hawaii. (As I write, she's long since turned in her ink and paints and is marketing Carolyn K's Hawaiian style Olde English Toffee out of her home on Oahu.)

When Carolyn returns the completed cels, I'm off to animation camera. And get chewed out for getting cigarette ash in the scenes. The film is then sent on to Consolidated Film Industries. Dal picks up the developed film (called "dailies"), has an editor add sound effects, mix those together with the dialogue in another recording session then sends everything back to the lab for an answer print. Which, after that's approved, also makes copies to be sent to TV stations all over America.

Whew! My family can scrape by for another few months; and we can manage the modest sum (not modest for us) charged by the special school Lisa now attends, an hour's drive from Santa Monica. And son Joe can have the new bike he's been hoping for.

Beyond merely eking out an existence, that first Culligan money is also enough, Rose and I figure, for ten percent down on a home of our own. So we scour the San Fernando Valley, checking out model homes mushrooming across the landscape from Van Nuys to Tarzana to Woodland Hills. Most new developments are beyond our means, so we settle for already lived in. And locate a cozy three-bedroom two-bath number with a generous yard at 7313 Zelzah Avenue in Reseda: $21,500 bucks.

Stills from Culligan TV commercials

When Pop first drove David and me through there in 1944, the Valley was studded with chicken ranches and walnut groves. By 1963 freeway-to-freeway tract homes disgorging office-bound dads, and moms shuttling Bennys or Suzys to Little League or ballet lessons, saturate the Valley. We've become firmly ensconced in the Great American Middle Class. Thank you again, Dal.

After a long bout with cancer, Dallas Williams, astonishingly cheerful to his final day, died on June 2, 1991. Apparently, as his widow Gaye told me, "a clipboard and pencil were too high tech for the funeral parlor." Dal's body was stuck into a walk-in cooler and forgotten. For four months. Someone else (Gaye never learned who) had been cremated in his place. As Gaye said, about the urn on her sideboard, "I had no idea who I was talking to all those months." One of their mutual friends said she wasn't surprised at the delay in straightening everything out, because "Dallas was the biggest procrastinator I've ever known."

Dal would have appreciated the irony.

When the correct ashes were finally scattered, off a boat on Puget Sound, there was a single cloud in the sky, with a rainbow over it. "Dallas couldn't have designed it better himself," said Gaye. "Or maybe he did."

ELEVEN

ups and downs

Up is Down, animated in 1968, signals the point at which I begin using my growing skill for something beyond selling soap and soft water. It's the point at which my pencil begins to do more than scribble funny characters. It's also the period during which the cycle of employment and layoff gives way to more steady work.

Not that this six-minute epic for Goldsholl and Associates, a highly regarded film and design studio near Chicago, rescues the family from financial oblivion. The fee is $1000. But simply being recommended for the job by Les Goldman, my former employer at Quartet films and a man I deeply respect, then having the film win fourteen international awards, is a big fat feather in my psychological cap.[1]

In *Up is Down*, a young boy walks on his hands "so he can see things close up, explore the earth, intimately." This gives him a keener perspective than most folks. But the boy's attitude disturbs people. He's got to be straightened out. So he's subjected to "therapeutic treatment": spun centrifugally, given simultaneous hot baths and cold showers, brain washed, and bombarded with red and blue radiation. Finally, the boy stands up on his feet – and sees the world for what it really is, discovering that mealy-mouthed leaders who talk about cooperation really mean competition. That what they call depth is superficiality. That beauty is ugliness, and that peace is war. He goes into a spin and lands back on his hands. "If you

---

[1] Among its awards *Up is Down* won a CINE Golden Eagle, a Golden Dove at the Atlanta Film Festival, a Chris Statuette at the Columbus Film Festival, and First Prize at the Baltimore Film Festival.

want me to stand on my feet," he says, "you'll have to make some big changes first."

Dedicated to Martin Luther King Jr., *Up is Down* sends a strong, supportive message to those who are vilified because they look at the world in a fresh and original way, unbound by the "shoulds" of tradition. It is also among my first work, since the anti-nuclear commercials a decade earlier, that has something important to say. After *Up is Down*, more personal satisfaction begins creeping in, because much of my creative life becomes involved in more than simply entertaining. And while I don't knock work that entertains, to me, as to many creative folks, using your art to say something that may help make the world a little better place can be enormously rewarding.

But before *Up is Down*, life is still a roller coaster ride.

Spring 1963. Along with seventy percent of animation workers, I'm out of a job. And have exhausted unemployment benefits. Rose has found work in a nursery school, but this doesn't pay the mortgage. With almost no assignments until the Culligan spots bail us out in the fall, I borrow from Pop. Mom helps too, and for several days I earn three bucks an hour addressing labels for the Longshoremen's union. The year slips by. By March of 1964, Rose is eight months pregnant with our third child.

And then I'm arrested.

Long story short: at a party in the Hollywood hills, police bust in and haul away a teen they've spotted guzzling beer in the street. Soon, more police arrive. Friends and I decide they had no right to enter, so we barricade the door. Mistake! (Don't mess with the cops. Cooperate. Then go find a good lawyer.)

Soon after, they break in again, cuff three of us, drag us to waiting squad cars, and we spend hours in the lockup. Weeks later we're on trial, in what our attorneys decide is a big civil liberties case but which turns out to be a Keystone Cops one-reeler. The officers who had arrested the teen – a sixty-second drama – lie outrageously about being "threatened and harassed" for fifteen minutes on their initial entry.[2]

Maybe the eight women on the jury find us innocent (all the men find us guilty) because of Rose's entry into the courtroom with Timothy Hugh Bessie (born April 7) in her arms. I'll never know. The judge has us apologize for "interfering with officers in pursuit of their duty" then dismisses the charges.

July 1964. After another six jobless months, Ed Graham Productions hires me to help animate one of the Saturday morning kids' shows popping up like warts on a frog. This one features the King of the Beasts.

Not *The Lion King*, he won't appear for another thirty years. This is his less growly cousin, *Linus the Lionhearted*, produced for CBS. The characters, based on those appearing on Post cereal boxes, feature voices by Carl Reiner, Ruth

---

[2] We later learned that a pair of uptight young female partygoers saw blacks and whites dancing together, freaked out, and decided to phone in a report on underage drinking.

Buzzi and Stiller and Meara. Sheldon Leonard, a B-movie gangster, assays Linus. Sugar Bear, Rory Raccoon and an assortment of other cuties back up the king, whose throne is a barber chair.

Shows cost $90,000 each, and my $300 a week is decent money for 1964. But since Graham is short on space I put in my eight hours at home, in the garage, where I've set up my animation desk. This leaves me free to chauffeur Lisa to school and back, or pop up to Topanga Canyon to pick up Joe, who (on scholarship) is attending a summer day camp.

The Linus crew is a talented and gregarious bunch: layout designers such as Corny Cole,[3] and directors like Clyde (Jerry) Geronomi, a roly-poly, good-natured old-time Disney hand.[4] Nearly everyone has a terrific sense of humor; even our boss, Ed Graham. Soon after he shows up with a new car, we find a memo on the bulletin board:

No Mustang for me, but I do pay off $1500 in accumulated bills, including $150 owed to Pop, who has recently lost his job as publicity man for the San Francisco International Film Festival.

After the usual Christmas layoff, softened financially by the annual Culligan spots, my job with Ed Graham comes to an end.[5] The following spring I sign on with Grantray-Lawrence Animation, turning Marvel Comics' stable of superheroes loose on TV.

---

[3] In addition to being among the early surfing crowd in Santa Monica, Corny Cole worked as a production designer on features such as *Shinbone Alley* (1971) and *Raggedy Ann and Andy* (1977). He went on to teach at California Institute of the Arts.

[4] Jerry Geronomi (1901-1989) worked as a supervising director on Disney's *Sleeping Beauty* (1959), and as co-director on films such as *Cinderella* (1950), *Alice in Wonderland* (1951), *Peter Pan* (1953) and *Lady and the Tramp* (1955).

[5] *Linus the Lionhearted* lasted five seasons, until the Federal Communications Commission yanked the series, confirming what everyone knew: that despite the high class talent and spiffy writing, Linus and his pals were basically a half-hour commercial for Post cereals.

This is 1965, remember, twenty years after World War II. And Captain America is still rounding up Nazis. Except for the Sub-Mariner, a deep-sea oddball with wings on his feet, most of these muscle-bound fantastics start out as runts in "real life." Captain America, an emaciated G.I., morphs to super size when injected with an experimental serum. The Mighty Thor is a skinny doctor, but when he taps his cane he turns into the Norse god. Iron Man, a millionaire inventor with a hunk of shrapnel embedded in his chest, creates a bulky metal suit to keep himself alive, provide invulnerability, and add the power of flight. The Incredible Hulk is the by-product of another whacko experiment, with scientist Bruce Banner transformed by gamma rays into a half-naked green creature with humongous strength and a gnarly disposition.[6]

Perhaps more appalling than the fact that kids (adults too) devour this Pablum, is that I often earn more than $600 a week churning it out. Though my base salary is $250, we're on a quota system and are paid generously for extra footage. Easy to beat the quota, since drawings are xeroxed straight from the comic books, and the animation largely consists of making eyes, mouths or limbs move.

[6] The Hulk, of course, went on to even greater glory when it became a major live action motion picture in 2003, directed by Ang Lee.

REELING THROUGH HOLLYWOOD

While I often resent the time spent on these doodles, I put up with it. We have to pay for Lisa's special schooling, and our 1959 Volvo is constantly falling apart. And I keep telling myself that I'm "perfecting my craft." Also, my fellow animators are a kick. Tall, bald Ralph Somerville has a curious attitude toward his own eventual death; he's looking forward to the "great adventure."[7] The pixyish Ruben Timmons keeps me doubled over with bawdy jokes. And whenever I bitch about the job, the gruff Fred Grable brings me up short with, "You hired on as an animator, kid. If you don't like it, ship out."

A year later, after I've been laid off then rehired, another Marvel character leaps aboard the Grantray-Lawrence express: Spiderman. Nope, nothing to do with Tobey Maguire; nor is Willem Dafoe's Green Goblin cavorting across the screen. That's live action, circa 2002. Maguire isn't even born in 1967 when I find myself carving out Spidey in this first animated TV series.

In a building across from Universal that once housed a seedy motel where studio execs whiled away saucy hours with ambitious starlets or horny secretaries, a half dozen animators are on staff. Myself among them.

George Cannata, father of the apprentice I did battle with over abstract art at MGM, is there; smoking, like me, two packs a day. (I got up to three before finally quitting at age thirty-five.) Another, soft-spoken Don Sloat, drives two hours each way to work from his home near San Diego; where, in his spare time, he raises orchids and tends koi.[8] And by now, we're off the quota system. The number crunchers have wised up. My paychecks are an unchanging $300 a week.

---

[7] Ralph Sommerville died in February of 2000. I hope he's on that great adventure he so looked forward to.

[8] I recently learned (isn't the internet grand?) that Don, an Army medic on Bataan during World War II, survived a Japanese prison camp in the Philippines, and has memorialized on canvas the horror of one hundred thirty-nine of his fellows, who, on December 14, 1944, were shot, bayoneted, and burned alive by their captors. While I worked with Don at Grantray-Lawrence, he never mentioned his World War II experience.

Ups and Downs

Still, the work isn't difficult. Previously completed "stock" scenes have Spidey gliding from one rooftop to another, or squirting the goop he uses to swing from or trap the villains with. Close-ups of our hero have also been created, with a series of drawings describing his mouth movements, while his head and shoulders remain static. So, while we also create new animation, whenever Spidey talks or bursts into action all we need to do is grab one of these scenes from a shelf, take it to our desk and recopy the numbers onto our exposure sheets. (The graph-like charts detailing how many twenty-fourths of a second each drawing appears and which serve as a guide to photographing the scenes. In 35mm film, twenty-four frames equal one second of screen time.)

The titles of each show are straight from the comic books and geared to a nine-year-old imagination: "Where Crawls the Lizard" (featuring The Lizard), "The Menace of Mysterio," and "Electro the Human Lightning Bolt." Spiderman's recurring nemesis, the Green Goblin, is there too, in "The Witching Hour."

While Spidey bounces off buildings, I bounce with ideas, eager to do more than plod along as the journeyman animator I've become. I want to make my own films. Or at least move into directing. Hard to do, since the Saturday morning circuit is tied up by former Disney men or directors from other studios. Most are secure in their positions and are relied on (rightly so) to bring in shows on time and with professional skill. So, frustrated, I use up buckets of nervous energy running around on weekends looking for political campaign buttons. And become involved in left wing politics.

And fret about the family.

REELING THROUGH HOLLYWOOD

In the three years since Tim's birth, and (at least partially) because we lack the special parenting skills needed to cope with an exceptional child, Lisa's problems have become more severe. Unable to articulate her feelings and tormented by our attention to her younger brother, she takes it out on him, physically. At almost twelve, Lisa is strong for her age. So we worry that she might injure Tim. Or worse. Teasing from neighborhood kids increases her frustration. Facilities with staff skilled enough to help children such as Lisa are few and far between during the 1960s, and beyond our means. So, frustrated ourselves, agonizing over what course to take, and advised by professionals (and since we see no other option), we sign our precious daughter over to the care of the State of California. In January of 1968, Lisa is admitted to Pacific State Hospital in Pomona.

This devastates Rose. Me too, but I manage a brave face. It's "for the good of the family," I tell myself. In a way, life at home parallels my life in film. I'm doing the best I know how to figure things out as I stumble along. But I often don't get it right. And the guilt over the decision to commit Lisa will haunt me for much of the next forty years.

With seasonal layoffs in the industry and with freelance assignments sporadic, I constantly nose about for steady employment. For years, a close friend, Gary Horowitz, has been working as a film editor. By 1966, he's in the TV commercial business, in partnership with the soft-spoken, bearded cinematographer Kent Wakeford and the gaunt, creative, John Orloff. Together, they've established Wakeford-Orloff Inc. (Later, just W/O.) Gary is the third partner. John and Kent, both already well known in commercials, attract agency work. But from a business standpoint, Gary (sans Horowitz on the letterhead) runs the show.[9]

---

[9] Kent Wakeford also freelanced as a cinematographer on more than twenty features, including Martin Scorsese's *Mean Streets* (1973) and *Alice Doesn't Live Here Anymore* (1974). After Wakeford-Orloff eventually folded, John Orloff stayed in commercials, forming another company. With Gary Horowitz no longer at the helm, it never matched W/O's success. John died in 2000.

Ups and Downs

If they're doing TV spots, I reason, why not animated spots? This makes sense to Gary, so during the spring of 1968 he takes me on as W/O's animation director. At $500 a week. For the first two months I have little to do but shoot pool in the back room. Though I do spend time reading books that might translate into features, because Gary is hot to make movies. Quality movies too, which excites me. And the three weeks I take off to complete *Up is Down* adds to my feeling that good things are about to pop.

But commercials are Gary's bread and butter (mine too), so I shift the Culligan job to W/O that year. The tidy budget of more than $8000 helps Gary's partners feel like he's actually building an animation department. Wakeford-Orloff can add these to their reel of TV spots to show clients. Soon after, a twenty-second animated tag for a McDonalds commercial comes in. After I redo it twice, the agency is satisfied with the speed at which the Golden Arches appear. There are other small animation bits to whack out too; then I go back to whacking billiard balls in the back room. But gnawing at my insides is the notion that although I'm skilled, even very good sometimes, my animation is unlikely to match the high standard in the live action commercials turned out by John Orloff, Kent Wakeford, or W/O's other commercial directors.

"Not to worry," says Mr. Horowitz. "Be patient. Big plans are afoot. But right now, we've got to keep cranking out the commercials."

TWELVE

it's plastic, it's fantastic

*I'm a Barbie girl, in a Barbie world
Life in plastic, it's fantastic
you can brush my hair, undress me everywhere . . .*

From *Barbie Girl*, by Aqua

Man in Toys-R-Us to Saleswoman:
"Does Barbie come with Ken?"
Saleswoman: "No, Barbie comes with G.I. Joe.
She fakes it with Ken."

Herb Caen, *San Francisco Chronicle*

Every successful enterprise whether a project, family, organization or business, needs a central driving force. Could be an idea, a winning concept, a solid plan, or a dynamic individual. At Mattel Inc, it was Ruth Handler, creator of the impossibly well-endowed Barbie. At Wakeford-Orloff, Gary Horowitz is that individual.

How to describe Gary? Not tall, usually smiling, easy going, friendly and direct. When preoccupied he runs both hands through his rapidly thinning hair. During the years we work together he sports a moustache. And since a childhood bout with rheumatic fever, he has maintained a solid, wiry body through diet and exercise.

Gary is the kind of guy of whom it can truly be said, "he could sell ice boxes to Eskimos." He's such a charming hustler that whenever he isn't positive about something, he nevertheless convinces you he is. A skillful manager and soother of bent egos, he's an ideal front man for a company dealing with TV commercial clients like Pepsi, General Motors, TWA, Braniff, Bank of America, Coke,

IT'S PLASTIC, IT'S FANTASTIC

Texaco and Standard Oil. The perfect CEO to deflect the ire of a client frustrated by delays or mistakes and somehow convince them, when a job goes over budget, that it's *their* fault and they need to come up with extra money.

February 1969. While waiting for Gary's promised big plans to materialize, I find myself helping W/O palm off more products on a gullible public. Two jobs stand out.

Item: I help seduce millions of pre-pubescent girls into manipulating mom and dad into forking over hard earned bucks for the latest permutation of Mattel's stock in trade, Barbie. In this case, I'm assigned to produce (but not direct) a thirty-second "Barbie and Ken in love" spot. As it happens, Mattel's ad agency, Carson/Roberts, has muffed their deadline. So the job, normally four to six weeks work, has to be shepherded through animation, ink and paint and camera and be ready to screen in ten days. Ten days? My stomach turns somersaults. No time for anything but bullshit. I'll leave that to the art director, since my first meeting with him, in which he blames Mattel for the short deadline, convinces me that, like Gary, he's a master of the art.

Twittering birds are to be featured, flying around Barbie and Ken. Disney run amuck. But no Thumper or Bambi, just birds. Birds are adorable. Birds sound happy. Birds sell "being in love." The whole spot will be backed by an insipid chorus chirping out, "Barbie and Ken, they've got a special world; Barbie and Ken . . ." (You get the idea.) Indulgent moms will storm toy counters all over America.

I phone an animator, Bob. He drives in from Malibu. Thirty miles. W/O is located in a Spanish style courtyard next to Mu Ling, a Chinese restaurant on Sunset Boulevard.[1] Bob has a reputation for working even faster than me. He will knock out the designs too. That evening! I explain what is needed then phone the client

---

[1] The charming ventriloquist, Edgar Bergan, who owned the building, wandered through the courtyard now and then. Upstairs in his office, in a big trunk, were his dummies, Charlie McCarthy, Mortimer Snerd and Effie Klinker. Larger than life.

to assure them we'll have the sketches the following day. At ten that night I drive to Malibu to pick up Bob's sketches. Back in the office by eight the next morning, I paste them onto a big presentation board and then rush to Carson/Roberts on Melrose to drop it off by nine. At eleven a.m. I'm back at the agency again for the big meeting.

The Mattel folks are already there. Three of them. One, younger, is primed, ready to see that we do right by Barbie. The other two, older, bored, are eager to get through this in time to dive into their lunchtime Martinis. The art director goes into his spiel.

"First," he lied, "we worked on this concept."

He unfolds a presentation board with eight or nine birds and points to a group of five. Although these are the same birds animator Bob has drawn, this is not my presentation board. Between nine and eleven he has peeled all the birds off the one I'd prepared and pasted them on two different boards.

"But we didn't feel they'd quite sell Barbie and Ken's budding romance," he continues. Then, pointing to a group of three, he says, "And these felt a bit too cutesy, so we worked on these." Now he indicates the last group, while at the same time sizing up the reactions of the three execs. The younger guy is expectant, eager for

It's Plastic, It's Fantastic

the punch line. His companions yawn. (Knowing how agency folks work, I suspect they are wise to his dog and pony show.)

"But they were just a tiny bit too subtle," the AD goes on, smiling, "so we finally came up with these!" Now he unfolds a second board, with three more of Bob's outrageously Disneyesque bluebirds pasted to it. "We're convinced they add just the right pinch of sex appeal," he concludes.

Mattel is sold. The AD has turned a frantic twelve hours into what sounds like a two-week slog. And the animation is done just as quickly, with Bob the animator injecting himself with coffee into the eye-reddening hours, and me shuttling to Malibu to grab his scenes and race them through ink and paint, camera and editing.

Barbie, of course, is thrilled. Girls are gaga over Barbie and Ken in love.[2] And Barbie goes on and on, reaching new plateaus of commercial stardom. By 2006 girls can get Barbie along with her clones, Tori or Simone, and can sing along with the dolls Karaoke style, just like on *American Idol*. Batteries not included.

But take heart, fellow citizens; not too long ago, the Barbie Liberation Organization, taking advantage of similarities in the voice hardware of Teen Talk Barbie and the Talking Duke G.I. Joe action figure, absconded with several hundred of each and performed a change operation, then replaced them on store shelves. Even today, somewhere in deepest Nebraska a small boy may rip open a Christmas gift and find his G.I. Joe blurting out an adenoidal,

---

[2] According to Mattel's press release of February 12, 2004, the romance is over for Barbie and Ken. But they will "remain friends." The company says that the couple, who need "quality time apart," met on the set of a TV commercial in 1961 and have been inseparable ever since. (As of 2006, reports indicate they may be getting together again.)

REELING THROUGH HOLLYWOOD

"Let's go shopping." His pig-tailed sister, happily squeezing her Teen Talk Barbie, might hear her growl, "Vengeance is mine."

We move on to item #2, John Orloff's Great Gallo Wine Fiasco. And if you don't know about the Gallos, check out an interview with Gina Gallo in *Wine X Magazine*, in which she talks about growing up in a "typical Italian family," with herself one of seven kids, "kinda like Jan Brady . . .but without Alice and the wood-paneled station wagon." Or read *Blood and Wine* by Ellen Hawkes (Simon and Schuster, 1993) described as a "revealing look at the California wine business . . .an epic account of violence and passion, deceit and ambition, it takes readers behind the scenes to watch Ernest and Julio Gallo build the winery that today dominates the industry, amassing a fortune for themselves and then using their money and power against their younger brother."[3]

No wonder I believe the story Gary relates; that when he traveled to Gallo's headquarters city, Modesto, California, he was driven along a street where all the company execs live. A cul-de-sac. Ernest's home is at the head of the street. The first vice-president's home sits next to Ernest's, on the right. The second VP's is across the street to Ernest's left, and so on down the block. "And if you're promoted in the company," says his host to Gary, "or demoted . . . you move!"

Gary has received a call from Young and Rubicam. They want him to personally supervise a thirty-second spot for their client, Gallo. Gary's hot for the account, this will be W/O's foot in the Y & R door. He accepts. Even though partner John Orloff tells him the concept Y & R has in mind can't be done. "So what," replies Gary. "Even if we fall flat on our face, they'll love us for trying."

One guess who is called on to make the impossible, possible? Right. Yours truly.

---

[3] Tom Allen, on *WineSquire.com*, said he thought that Ernest was trying to corner the market on these books. "I loaned my copy to a Gallo salesman years ago," he said, "and never saw it again."

It's Plastic, It's Fantastic

The commercial is supposed to work like this: artwork of a young man pouring Champagne into a glass will draw itself onto the screen. As this happens, the camera moves in. Animated wine pours. Then, as the camera pulls back again, the animated bubbles are to transition to live bubbles, effervescing faster and faster. Continuing to move back, we'll see the couple come to life, toast one another, look deeply into each other's eyes then kiss.

Not difficult to execute in a world gone digital. Immensely complicated in 1970, even using optical tricks. After the artwork draws itself on (easy to do) and the camera moves in (easy to do), the bubbles have to gradually transition from art to live action. Drives me crazy trying to figure out how to do it, because the bubbles have to match exactly and this is all supposed to happen as the camera pulls back. The job could be attempted using a process called rotoscope, in which the completed live footage is projected down onto the bed of an animation camera stand. Then the animator (me in this case) will trace each live element in each frame onto separate pieces of paper: bubbles, glass, swirling Champagne, the man pouring, the toast, the kiss. Problem is, since all this is supposed to occur with the camera in motion, the sheer number of drawings we need will be double prodigious. And the process will take months. Plus which, the likelihood of creating a smooth and matching transition will be virtually nonexistent.

To solve the endless labor and reams of animation paper this would normally require, John Orloff has (he thinks) a brilliant shortcut: I am to have a series of big color prints ("C" prints) made from the live action footage of the couple. In effect, a "live" series of animated photos so that each animated bubble will match a corresponding live action bubble, and as the animation dissolves away and the camera pulls slowly back it will seem as if the whole picture "comes to life." Except that it doesn't work. John makes a test, which I take to a nearby photo service. But the photo service can't achieve the required accuracy with the "C" prints. They tend to shrink. Or expand. So the gradual transition John has in his head simply isn't possible.

"Oh," says John, when I convey this news. And he walks off, mumbling under his breath.

Thousands are spent on "C" prints, tests, my salary, meetings and more tests. Finally, Gary (as usual) comes to the rescue, convincing Gallo's agency that they actually called for a different kind of transition in the first place! "We did?" reply the puzzled execs. "OK, go for it." Naturally, they end up paying for everything. Amazingly, Gallo is delighted with the final result.[4]

> There's a lesson here; if you want to play in the big boys' sandbox and you only half understand what you're doing, you have to know how to cover your ass.

What I didn't discover until years later is that Gary was wracked with guilt about doing a Gallo commercial. Caesar Chavez's United Farm Workers, a group he supported and to which he'd given free office space and a phone at W/O, was conducting a strike in the vineyards of California's great central valley against Gallo and other growers. When he talked his dilemma over with the UFW's staff person, she told him he'd be crazy not to accept the work. "Give the profits to the union," she suggested. "That way, Gallo is supporting the strike!" Problem solved. But W/O didn't make a dime on the job.

My two years with Gary involve more than suffering agency fools or playing matchmaker to Barbie and Ken. Six months after hiring on, I find myself animation director for not only W/O, but

---

[4] Gallo's ad agency, Young and Rubicam, also spent tens of thousands of their advertising budget flying to London to have the famous John Barry create elaborate music that might as easily have been created by three musicians in a Hollywood garage.

It's Plastic, It's Fantastic

for two more companies as well. Gary's "big plans" are happening. Wakeford-Orloff has become part of a conglomerate. And, announces Mr. Mogul, "We're going to produce features."

Movies? We're going to make movies? I can relate to that. Actually, I've already been involved in one . . .

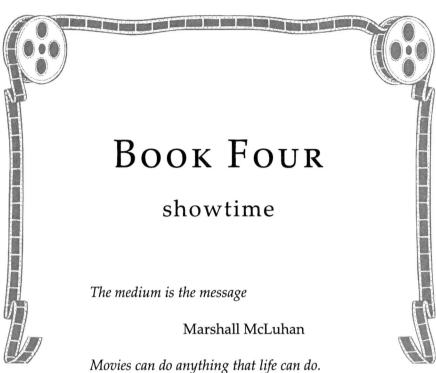

Book Four

showtime

The medium is the message

        Marshall McLuhan

Movies can do anything that life can do. They can move you, they can teach you, they can make you meditate and they can make you dream. They're a simulacrum. This is their great power.

        Donal Richie

We are drowning our youngsters in violence, cynicism and sadism . . . The grandchildren of the kids who used to weep because the Little Match Girl froze to death now feel cheated if she isn't slugged, raped and thrown into a Bessemer converter.

        Jenkin Lloyn Jones

THIRTEEN

flashback: salt of the earth

Summer 1953. The film *Salt of the Earth* is grabbing two days of pickup shots in Topanga Canyon north of L.A. Director (and Hollywood Ten member) Herbert Biberman,[1] who has been in jail at Texarkana with my pop, is strutting around in riding breeches and knee-length boots. No monocle, but he does have a megaphone. And a beret. He reminds me of a tall, Jewish, Eric von Stroheim.[2]

Turning up as an extra, I suddenly find myself appointed as assistant to the assistant director! "Dan," says the AD, an arm around my shoulder, "round up a bunch of those extras and have them stand by. We're going to need them later, up on the hill."

Salt of the Earth dramatizes an actual fifteen-month-long strike by miners in Silver City, New Mexico. In the film, Latino and Anglo miners over-

---

[1] Herbert Biberman (1900-1971). Among his five directing credits were *Meet Nero Wolf* (1936) and *The Master Race* (1944). He's also the subject of the 2000 film, *One of the Hollywood Ten*, starring Jeff Goldblum and Greta Scacchi.

[2] Eric von Stroheim (1885-1957). The Vienna-born director of primarily silent classics (*Greed*, 1924; *The Merry Widow*, 1925), also acted in more than seventy-five films, and is perhaps best remembered as Gloria Swanson's faithful chauffeur in *Sunset Boulevard* (1950).

come differences in order to do battle with an absentee owner. In a major sub-plot, miners' wives, struggling for equality with their men folk, take over the picket line when a court injunction prevents miners from striking.

The screenplay is by Michael Wilson. He'll receive a posthumous Oscar for *The Bridge on the River Kwai* (1957).[3] But in 1953 he's on the film industry's blacklist, as are director Biberman and producer Paul Jarrico.[4] During principal photography the *Hollywood Reporter* snips about "H'wood Reds . . . shooting a feature-length anti-American racial issue propaganda movie at Silver City, N.M." Screen Actors Guild president Walter Pidgeon alerts the FBI, State Department, House Un-American Activities Committee and the CIA. On the floor of Congress, Santa Monica representative Donald Jackson calls the film "a new weapon for Russia." Fabricating scenes that were never in the script or even dreamed of by the filmmakers, Jackson claims that *Salt of the Earth* has been "deliberately designed to inflame racial hatreds and to depict the United States as the enemy of all colored peoples." Movie and aircraft mogul Howard Hughes writes to Jackson, outlining steps that will prevent the movie from being completed or exhibited.[5]

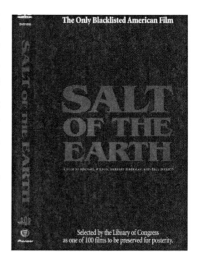

---

[3] Michael Wilson (1914-1978) also wrote *Friendly Persuasion* (1956), *Lawrence of Arabia* (1962), and the original *Planet of the Apes* (1968).

[4] Almost forty years after the film's completion, on October 27, 1997, the American Federation of Television and Radio Artists (AFTRA), the Directors Guild of America (DGA), the Screen Actors Guild (SAG), and the Writer's Guild of America, west (WGAw) honored Paul Jarrico at a "Hollywood remembers the blacklist" event. Tragically, in the small hours of the following morning Jarrico was killed in an auto accident while driving home.

[5] Neither Jackson nor Hughes had read the script. A detailed history of the effort to prevent the film's production, completion, and exhibition can be found in *Salt of the Earth, The Story of a Film*, by Herbert Biberman (Beacon Press, 1965).

Flashback: Salt of the Earth

On location in New Mexico, a mob stops the filming, knocks over the camera and punches out members of the cast and crew. The distinguished Mexican actress and star of the picture, Rosaura Revueltas, is hustled off by INS agents, grilled about her politics during a long ride to El Paso, held for ten days, labeled a "dangerous woman" by government attorneys and pressured into leaving the country before her scenes are complete. The final shooting takes place under near siege conditions, with the New Mexico Highway Patrol guarding the roads. When the crew leaves, a union hall is burned to the ground, along with the home of one of the local cast. Back in Hollywood, seven labs refuse to process the footage. The film has to be edited and the music scored and mixed in secret.

And in 1956, after a three year struggle to get *Salt of the Earth* shown on a handful of screens in the U.S., the film wins the Académe du Cinéma de Paris award for the best film made anywhere in the world exhibited in France during the preceding year. Vive la France!

So why the hullabaloo? Simple: the U.S. is in the grip of rabid anti-communist hysteria, and folks who are pariahs in Hollywood because of their political views are making *Salt of the Earth*. With the filmmakers run out of New Mexico, with their star exiled and with a key sequence that ends the story still needing completion, the producers decide to film the missing scenes in Topanga.

Topanga Canyon, a rustic, oak-studded enclave north of Los Angeles, is (even in 2006) sprinkled with non-conformists, conforming to their own funky lifestyle. In 1953, it's a venue for hootenannies. But also in 1953, millions are petrified of the crimson paintbrush being wielded by Senator Joe McCarthy and his disgraceful band of witch hunters. So only word of mouth leads thirty or forty unintimidated souls up the winding canyon road to listen to Pete Seeger, Cisco Houston, or Woody Guthrie thrill us with everything from "Hard Travelin'," to "Good Night Irene." Such is the paranoia of the times that we feel like a bunch of Christians secretly meeting in ancient Rome, expecting the Centurions to break in at any moment and drag us to the lions.[6]

Back to the movie. First, the phone rings. A friend is on the line to tell me that a film, about which I know nothing, is being shot on the following weekend. Extras are needed. Sounds like fun. So I call a dozen other friends and ask them to join the party. Then, on Saturday, wife Rose and I pile into our intrepid 1940 Chevrolet and chug along Pacific Coast Highway and up into the cheap hills to the staging area, Will Geer's bohemian family compound in Topanga.[7]

The sequence being filmed is the climax, in which the bad guy sheriff (played by Geer) and his deputies show up to evict the Quinteros, the family at the center of the story. Rosaura Revueltas is

---

[6] The paranoia was perhaps justified. The Senate Internal Securities (McCarren) Act, passed in 1950 over President Harry Truman's veto, not only called for registering communists and so-called "communist organizations," but also provided for setting up concentration camps to incarcerate anyone considered a danger to the nation.

[7] Blacklisted himself, Will Geer (1902-1978) went on to star as Grandpa in *The Waltons,* and appeared in more than a hundred features or TV shows, including a film I co-produced (see Chapters 16 and 19 "Executive Action.")

Flashback: Salt of the Earth

Esperanza Quintero, but since she's been booted out of the country a stand-in doubles for her in several over-the-shoulder shots.

Except for Geer, Revueltas and two or three other pros, the cast consists of real miners, their wives and friends. Juan Cachón, newly elected president of Local 890 of the Mine, Mill and Smelter Worker's Union, plays Esperanza's husband, Ramón. He has only a couple pickup shots, but sticks around for the full two days, smiling broadly at everyone. Clearly, he loves being a part of movie making as much as I do.

Film shoots have an infectious energy. Everything is supposed to run efficiently and on time. Sometimes it does, more often, not. There's a reason for this, as I quickly discover. Much has to do with so-called "producers" who don't know their ass from their elbow in terms of the logistics involved in making a film and controlling a budget. Even on this shoot, although the filmmakers have a plan they are clearly improvising.

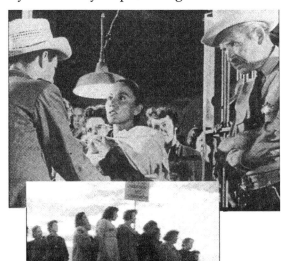

Scenes from *Salt of the Earth*

For the next two days I shuttle back and forth between a shady spot under one of Will Geer's big Canyon Black Oaks where the extras are parked (Topanga is a frying pan during the summer), and the assistant director, to await orders. "Tell them we'll need them in fifteen minutes," says the AD. I start off. He checks his shot list. "No, wait, Biberman is shooting a different scene. Tell them an hour."

Two hours later we gather thirty women for a sequence at a location duplicating a road near the entry to the zinc mine. The extras, my wife Rose among them, are to match a scene shot in Silver City in which a group of mostly Mexican-American women stop a sheriff's car trying to run them down. Our group, mostly Anglos, is to pull the deputies from the car and run them off. With a hand-held camera and slam bang inter-cutting that emphasizes the few Latinas in the crowd, when the film is complete it's hard to tell that one part of the sequence was filmed in New Mexico, another in Topanga.

For me, this is heady stuff. I've been jumping from one job to another for three years, and since constant motion is part of any film shoot my assignment feels more like play than work.

During the second day's filming the sheriff and his men arrive to evict the Quinteros.

I round up the extras again and fifty of us trudge up a long hillside in the broiling afternoon sun. Then I'm wearing a miner's helmet and riding in a truck with a group of other guys. In the completed film the shot is five seconds, part of a montage in which angry miners and their supporters trek in from all over the country-side to support the Quinteros. They move along a dusty road, past a Chrysler convertible, from inside of which two company bosses eye the gathering crowd. Except that an actor playing one of the execs has been injured in a car accident and isn't on the set.

Biberman looks around at the crew. Then at me. "Here, Dan," he calls, "put on this jacket." (I'm wearing Levis and a blue denim shirt.)

"But I don't have a white shirt . . . or a tie . . ."

FLASHBACK: SALT OF THE EARTH

"Never mind," says Biberman.

"And here's the hat," adds the AD.

Then I'm in the Chrysler, in sports jacket and a Stetson. The other actor, David Sarvis, plays the zinc company's slick east coast rep. A gentle, kind man, he nurses a Chesterfield and does his best to look sinister. As we gaze at the crowd moving toward the Quintero home, Biberman directs me in a couple of hand gestures. Then a nod of the head and my celluloid moment is history. And the shots make it into the final cut. For years after, whenever I watch the film with friends and the sequence runs by, I'd call out "That's me, that's the back of my head!"

As the miners and their wives and kids frustrate the eviction by carrying furniture being removed from the Quintero house back inside, the camera sweeps across two hundred people come to stare down "sheriff" Will Geer and his deputies. He stops in his tracks and sizes up their steely determination. A long, dramatic moment, then Geer tosses his cigarette, motions to his deputies and they are into their cars and peeling off in a cloud of dust. A huge cheer from the crowd, congratulations all around, and then one by one the miners and their supporters drift off, having achieved one small victory.[8]

Voice over, Esperanza says, "Then I knew we had won something they could never take away – something I could leave to our children – and they, the salt of the earth, would inherit it."

Brief as the experience of working on *Salt of the Earth* has been, it brings home to me the sense of family that is created on almost any shoot. People who may previously have been strangers suddenly became bosom buddies.

Visiting the Warner Brothers lot with Pop in 1944, I had only been a spectator (and an ogler of messenger girls in short pants).

[8] Movies often just create a world we'd like to see but that doesn't exist. Although *Salt of the Earth* closely parallels actual events, the New Mexico strike was eventually lost and the miners had no choice but to return to work.

131

Reeling Through Hollywood

Here, I became involved, a tiny part of something larger. And I loved it. Though I didn't know it in 1953, this family feeling would be recreated again and again during the next forty years, with folks coming together for a day or three or five, or a month or more. We'd meet on the first morning like old friends, scarf donuts, schmooze, bicker and complain, laugh and play practical jokes, do good work (and sometimes lousy work). Then, as the film wrapped, there'd be tight hugs all around, knowing we might not work together again for months or years. Or ever.

Hanging around during the Topanga shoot are two gangly preteen girls, Will Geer's daughters, Kate and Ellen. Thrilled to be working on an actual film, high on coffee and movies, I barely notice them. I'm a month shy of my twenty-first birthday that Topanga summer and do little thinking beyond the moment. And even if I'd been able to, how could I guess, in 1953, that more than thirty years in the future I'd be directing Ellen Geer in a film of my own?

As the flashback ends we drift back to 1969. To Hollywood. To Wakeford-Orloff and to my friend Gary Horowitz's promise that we're going to produce features. OK, I'm ready; let's go for it!

FOURTEEN

mogul fever

Mogul mania is rampant in any business. Movie-making is no exception, and once having scrambled up Everest it seems as if the only thing left for a successful producer to achieve is to own the damn mountain.

Even those of us who claim we don't give a fig about mogulhood often find ourselves driven by a weird sense of competitiveness that finds us comparing our progress to that of an actress friend who has "made it," a screenwriter we know who "has a deal," or a producer who is "excited about my project." Instead of applauding their success and rolling up our sleeves to do better, we find ourselves in a psychological rut. We're in a sturdy, reliable, 1987 Jeep Cherokee, spinning wheels in a ditch along some muddy road, while lusting after a racy new Jaguar that will zip us down Sunset to our gated Beverly Hills mansion

But hard as we try, our ambition often outstrips the results. Or, as the poet so neatly puts it, "The best laid schemes o' mice an' men gang aft a-gley."

Gary Horowitz's "big plans" never get off the drawing board. Though Wakeford-Orloff (W/O) becomes part of a publicly held company that raises millions for investment, the cash set aside to promote features soon dribbles away.

133

Hollywood is all about image, so $100,000 that might have funded a high quality, but modest budget attention-grabber, goes instead to equip an elaborate office complex inside a new Sunset Boulevard high-rise. Over the next two years another $350,000 evaporates. Filmsense, our theatrical division, founded by my former Quartet Films boss, the gently thoughtful, immensely talented but hopelessly un-entrepreneurial Les Goldman, produces zero features. But all through those two years we're constantly "on the verge of a deal." Once a week, Gary, Les and I, along with Les's nervously energetic assistant, Ron Lyon, meet at the International House of Pancakes (IHOP these days) to update one another on a raft of projects. Ron invariably becomes outraged when the same waitress, week after week, forgets that he wants his English muffin "fork broke." (Don't ask; I order blueberry pancakes.) Gary's friend Peter Fonda, hot off *Easy Rider* (1969), says he can get Universal to back (with himself directing) Kurt Vonnegut's oddly poignant novel, *Mother Night* (1966), the rights to which we've acquired. But Les nixes Fonda. Then Richard Benjamin (*Goodbye Columbus*, 1969) will direct. Then Fred Zinneman (*High Noon*, 1952). Then John Boorman (*Deliverance*, 1972) But Boorman wants total control and Les also vetoes that. Then Columbia makes cooing noises, and hints about Filmsense developing a script based on *The Passover Plot* (1965), a fascinating but controversial book about Christ's crucifixion.

Les Goldman

For a $7500 fee we hire my pop to adapt *The Hostages* (1966), a novel in which rightwing fanatics kidnap a busload of kids attending the United Nations International School and threaten to kill them unless the admission of red China to the UN is rescinded. Which the UN can't do, because the admission of China has defused an international crisis likely to precipitate World War III. At the same time, Pop is bombarding me with letters demanding to know why we aren't presenting his scripts to the studios.

With Les Goldman, I develop an updated version of *Alice in Wonderland*. We pitch it to Barbra Streisand. No dice. Then to Goldie Hawn. No dice again. Then to Diana Ross. Snake eyes.

Gary and I want to take on Dalton Trumbo's great and terribly moving anti-war novel, *Johnny Got His Gun* (1939), and Trumbo is willing (if he can direct). But with its provocative message, there are no takers.

Dalton Trumbo, who did most of his writing in a bathtub

Composer John Barry is also part of the team and will work on any feature we manage to launch. James Coburn becomes interested (if we come up with a successful script) in the true story of a Canadian surgeon who died in China while doctoring with Mao's army.

We try TV specials too, and pitch the comic strip *Pogo* to General Foods as a series of five specials. They don't bite. (More on *Pogo* coming up.)

REELING THROUGH HOLLYWOOD

And the projects keep birthing. And quickly dying. Nobody on board has strong enough contacts, nor are the projects wildly commercial (though we think they are). Barry Epstein, founder of W/O's parent company, will only use capital for development, never to fund a movie. By the end of 1970 he stops shoveling cash down the Filmsense drain. So one by one our tender grapes wither on the vine.

Perhaps we're ahead of our time (that's always a consolation when an agent sends your script back marked, "opened by mistake"). However several projects that we're the first to try to produce eventually do get made. By others.[1]

While the feature effort is a failure, I manage during these two years, with the help of a small creative team, to shepherd three short films through W/O's corporate and educational affiliate, Communications Group/West.[2]

And before leaving I'm privileged to add a smidgen of effort to one final project: *Pogo*. Not the TV specials we've pitched to General Foods that they don't pop for, but *Pogo* nonetheless. The great Walt Kelly, cartoonist, political satirist and creator of the lovably outspoken possum and his Okefenokee pals has developed *We Have Met The Enemy And He Is Us*, a razor-edged fable dealing with the environment. Kelly, a liberal Democrat who refuses to compromise his principals, has willingly let *Pogo* vanish from the pages of newspapers that demand he knuckle under by turning out less strident political comment.

---

[1] Dalton Trumbo's *Johnny Got His Gun* came out in 1971; Trumbo directed. *The Passover Plot* was eventually made (in 1976) and directed by Michael Campus, with whom I had worked on a TV project at Media. The Canadian doctor story, *Bethune: The Making of a Hero* was filmed in Canada in 1990 and starred Donald Sutherland. *Mother Night* was also finally produced in 1996, with Nick Nolte starring.

[2] The highly talented Sid Galanty, who had served as media director for Hubert Humphrey's 1968 presidential campaign, headed CG/W. For CG/W I directed *On Your Marks*, a film on punctuation marks from a book by Richard Armour, produced a short film on toilet training retarded children and turned out a corporate slide presentation for IBM - to be screened once only, at a conference in Mexico City.

Mogul Fever

Along with Les and Ron Lyon, I first meet Walt, for dinner, at the Hollywood Roosevelt Hotel. Rotund, engaging and with a cigar stuck in his mouth, he's clearly not in great health, but is determined to turn his concept into both a book and a film. He shows us a storyboard he's created. Sid Galanty's CG/W agrees to produce.

I work for two weeks with Kelly, getting his sketches ready to film. His tale finds the Okefenokee more and more polluted by industrial waste, with Pogo, Albert and Porkypine down in the dumps (literally) and trying to make sense about why this is happening. Walt himself narrates. He lays the major blame squarely at the door of corporations that care more about profit than human betterment. At the same time, he doesn't neglect the role individuals can play in finding solutions.

As originally planned, we're simply going to shoot Walt's storyboard. But as the days slip by he keeps adding more and more drawings. So many, that the film becomes almost fully animated. Although I've left the company by the time the job is complete, working with Walt has been a delight. He knows exactly what he wants but responds with reasoned consideration to the few minor suggestions Les or Dan Bessie or Sid Galanty have to offer. (Though he doesn't change a thing.)[3]

Walt Kelly

---

[3] When Walt turned *We Have Met The Enemy And He Is Us* into a book in 1972, caricatures of J. Edgar Hoover, Attorney General John Mitchell and Vice President Spiro T. Agnew decorated the cover. Walt died the following year. His widow Selby Daley completed the film, which CG/W distributed. Selby also continued the *Pogo* strip for another two years, and Walt's daring title became the rallying cry for a generation of conservationists.

W/O keeps busy with commercials. Gary brings the fine artist Bob Kurtz aboard and his company, Kurtz and Friends, becomes the animation department, pulling in business left and right. Sid Galanty continues distributing educational films, producing TV spots for Gary Hart's 1984 California presidential primary bid, Harold Washington's 1982-83 winning mayoralty race in Chicago and Tom Hayden's California campaigns for the U.S. Senate, state senate, mayor of L.A. and finally (successfully) the state Assembly. In the late 1970s, Sid begins to stash away a tidy fortune in fees, producing and directing Jane Fonda's wildly successful workout tapes. As I write this, he's scribbling away at his memoirs. He's written at least thirteen hundred pages so far. To date, he's reached 1966.

Ron Lyon hooks up with Jack Haley Jr. to produce a series of TV documentaries. He also makes a pot of money.

John Barry, who has previously scored films such as *Goldfinger* (1964) and *Born Free* (1966), goes on to compose music for umpteen more, including the 1976 version of *King Kong* and in 1990 Kevin Costner's *Dances With Wolves*.

Les Goldman grinds his teeth trying to launch more projects that never materialize. Secure as producer (with Chuck Jones) of not only the Oscar-winning short *The Dot and the Line* (1965) and the feature *The Phantom Tollbooth* (1970), as well as a flock of Tom and Jerrys for TV, Les is nevertheless short changed on credit for convincing Jones to produce the 1966 animated version of Dr. Suess's *How The Grinch Stole Christmas*. A founder of ASIFA, the international animation society, Les becomes a roving "ambassador of animation," moves to Santa Cruz and directs a film festival there for two years. Far too young and with a good deal more to accomplish, Les dies of a sudden heart attack at the age of sixty-nine. He is greatly missed.

With half a million dollars of W/O's money down the drain, would-be mogul Barry Epstein decides that media is not his cup of tea. He moves to Kentucky and returns to his first love, breeding racehorses.

Mogul Fever

Me? I'm suddenly on the dole again, painfully aware that the eighty dollar unemployment check will never maintain the ranch style home (with a fat mortgage and a swimming pool), plus a new 1970 Plymouth Duster in the drive that two years of steady work have made possible.

"We gave it a good shot," I tell Gary. "But what if, instead of pissing away a half million bucks on 'development,' we had made a movie?" He shrugs.

Water over the dam, huh? OK, I tell myself, that's how it is. And what is daydreaming about what might have been gonna get me? Echo answers: Nada!

So what now?

Thinking, thinking . . . Taking stock, I pump myself up a little with the knowledge that in addition to the shorts for CG/W, and inspired by those, and by my work on *Up is Down*, I've also produced (in my spare time) a pair of educational films. *Meet Lisa*, using Rose's artwork depicting our daughter, is a touching plea for understanding children who are different. *Learning to Observe*, which I hustle $4000 from an educational film company to produce, teaches pre-science concepts to learning-disabled kids. So, with two short animated films under my belt I begin to wonder, can I direct live action? Could I indeed get a feature off the ground? There's still *The Hostages*. W/O's option on the book has run out. Time to start my own company? Again? Hmmm . . . Dangerous move, since I'm essentially broke. Oh, what the hell, I decide. What's life about if you don't take chances?

FIFTEEN

look ma, I'm makin' movies!

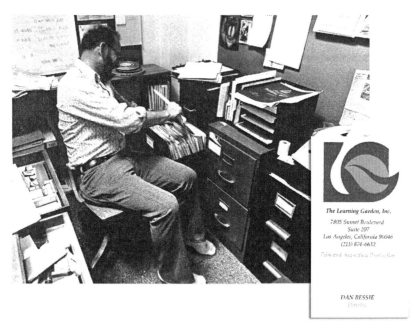

I'm at my desk, filing papers. (And sporting a beard.) When you're chief cook and bottle washer you get to sit around in stocking feet. No more nine to five. More like eight a.m. to eleven p.m. No more hustling TV spots like at my first flop, Circus Films. But hustling just the same, because entrepreneurship is the name of the being in business for yourself game.

A year and a half of steady income has temporarily bailed my family's sinking boat. Now I can once again set sail on the stormy seas of outrageous debt. In a dingy. So, off to see Belva Roberts, trust-

LOOK MA, I'M MAKIN' MOVIES!

ing holder of purse strings at the Santa Monica Consumers Federal Credit Union.

"Belva, how's about six thousand bucks so I can start a film company."

"What are you going to call it?"

"Learning Garden. I'm getting into educational films."

No sooner said, than bucks in the pocket. Belva knows I'm good for the loan, because through thick and thin I've managed to cut her a check every month of every year she's carried me on her books. Some of the $6000 rents a big airy space atop Westwood's Bank of America building. Another chunk pays for designing and printing a fancy brochure, since I've decided to distribute films as well as create them. Along with *Meet Lisa*, I pick up three more titles. Fifty dollars goes for a huge, double-winged animation desk that the Disney studio has retired and which dates from *Snow White*. (Worth a fortune today. Should have hung on to it. %$#@*&$$@!!)[1]

Right off the bat I have work. Another short film, to be sure, but this time I'll be in charge. *Buyer Beware* is a seven-minute live action epic (plus graphics) on wise food shopping, aimed at low-income folks. Charlotte Holtzkamper, big, stocky, consultant-type person funds the show through the California Bureau of Homemaking Education. With ten percent squeezed from the $3500 budget, I assign the script to Pop. Charlotte makes but minor changes. The Bureau wants a Spanish language version too, so I phone a talent agency. "I need someone who speaks both Spanish and English perfectly," I say, "with no accent in either language" (the client's requirement). The next day, three candidates show up at Learning Garden. Number one's English is heavily accented. Number two bats her eyes like shutters in a wind and makes it plain that if she lands this $125 gig, a hot time in the sack is on the agenda. (Gad!) I drum my fingers on the desk.

---

[1] *How's School*, Enrique, by Stan Frager, and *I Wanna be Ready* and *Learning to Learn*, by Lucia Capacchione, an artist who later became a self-help author, and forever a good buddy.

Linda Dangcil

Then Linda Dangcil flounces in. Perfectly bilingual. Perfectly charming. Perfect choice. By now, Linda's career has included roles as an Indian in the original (1954) Broadway company of *Peter Pan* (with Mary Martin), Sister Ana, who faints at the sight of Sally Field zipping around as *The Flying Nun* (1967-70), and as a singer and dancer in the film version of *West Side Story* (1961). Smart, perky (and happily married), as we fairly rapidly get to know one another, Linda laughingly brushes off my lust whenever it bubbles up, and our friendship continues for decades.

Until now, my vast live action experience had been limited to "directing" an empty hospital hallway to background the animation in a medical film. So I hire another novice to captain *Buyer Beware*. For $150. The budget allows for a two-person crew. A pair of Hungarians fit the bill. One operates camera and lights. His partner does everything else. Most of the show is set in a supermarket and they light the place in half an hour. Like the inside of Dracula's coffin. Talent is from the Ed Wood school of acting. (Go rent *Plan Nine From Outer Space*.) I dish out fifteen bucks each to the "actors," who are delighted.

I figure a half-day's shoot. Wrong. Takes a day and a half. Part of the learning curve. After we wrap the first day, the director tells me he has a dentist appointment the next morning. Hey, thanks! After a restless night, eight a.m. finds me, a mass of jelly. I'm inside a mom and pop corner grocery, directing another non-actor, the gracious wife of a friend. I stumble through the shots and the gracious wife is also pleased with her pitiful stipend.

Look Ma, I'm Makin' Movies!

The finished film looks grainy and awkward. Crap. There, I said it. But it does the job, and the Bureau of Homemaking Education is all smiles. Now Charlotte has a new thought: why not parlay this into an entire series. Cool! Well-heeled educational companies are shelling out decent money for product. Maybe one of these will spring for the $72,000 I figure it will cost to produce five more consumer titles. We start work on a proposal.

Suddenly busier than the legendary one-armed paperhanger, I begin scouting for helpers. Movie hopefuls are forever wandering through film company doors. That's where the work is, after all. It's the golden stairway to paradise, they hope, whether as actor, writer, producer, director, or flunky.

Franklin Koenigsberg is no flunky. This slight, soft-spoken and amiable twenty-year-old is hoping to avoid the draft – and a possible return ticket from Vietnam in a body bag. Only way to do that (without splitting for Canada) is with a letter from me saying I'll give him a job helping to make educational films. With my letter, Franklin receives conscientious objector status. He does odd jobs, answers the phone and fills requests trickling in for one of the four films we're distributing.

Fully half the time, Franklin is out there beating the bushes, trying hard to put together a film on the Zydeco great, Clifton Chenier. Also from within those bushes, he flushes out and drags into Learning Garden – usually while I'm on an important call

Franklin Koenigsberg

or hobnobbing with clients – an airy collection of lost souls. A busty young earth mother who reads auras, or a scraggly student who proclaims himself a "fruitatarian" and who plans to ultimately exist on nothing but air (!). Later, I spend a tiny sum sending Franklin to Arizona to photograph the copper mining ghost town of Jerome, thinking to create a film about the place. He returns with great photos and interviews with old timers. Like so many good ideas, the film is never completed, and I eventually donate Franklin's material to the Jerome Historical Society.[2]

Over the next several months, Learning Garden attracts more key players. I can pay them zip. Marianne Meyerhoff, tall, slim, red headed, determined to move up the ladder from production assistant, calls, comes in and makes me an offer I can't refuse. "Tell you what, Daniel," she says, "I'll give you a year's free work. At the end of that time you fund me in a film I want to make." I jump at the chance.

Marianne Meyerhoff

The phone rings again. An acquaintance wonders if "my friend Severo can come in and talk to you about a job." Of course he can. Talk is cheap, even though I have no job for him. Next day, Severo Perez arrives. He's smart, engaging, and with a bravado betraying an inner tension, Severo is a curly-headed eager beaver from San Antonio. Sensitive, bubbling with ideas, he's already turned out a couple short films and

---

[2] Franklin became a fine filmmaker. His short on Clifton Chenier was never completed, but he produced and directed *Conversations With Shaky Jake* (a jazz musician), as well as one of the earliest films explaining acupuncture. Tragically, Franklin developed bone cancer, and died in 1982. He was not yet thirty.

Look Ma, I'm Makin' Movies!

Mallory Pearce (L) with Severo Perez

is determined to make it in Hollywood. He too has an offer I can't refuse: "Just give me a desk and a phone," he says, "don't pay me anything. But within two months I'll bring in enough work to justify a salary." Deal. He hustles a couple assignments and these keep him going until we eventually land contracts that let me pay him an occasional pittance.

Several others cut their film teeth at Learning Garden. Eda Godel Hallinan has to screen one of our answer prints for a client while I'm off at another meeting. Unaware the film has to be wound from a core to a reel before screening, she fumbles the ball. Picking up the core without supporting the film's weight with her thumb, she watches in horror as endless yards of footage spool off onto the floor – while the client steams. Today, Eda's an Oscar and Emmy-winning producer. Just goes to show...

Meanwhile, from darkest Marin County Pop is inundating me with letters and postcards fretting over my efforts to cobble together a movie deal on *The Hostages*, the story we'd been unable to launch when I worked at Media. And I do try. With not too much urging, my accountant hustles $7500 so we can option the novel again, pay Pop $2500 for a rewrite and have enough left over for a bit of promotion.

After Pop completes revisions, a flock of scripts go out, one to Burt Lancaster. Weeks later, at a huge peace rally at the L.A. Sports Arena for which I've helped put together a slide presentation, I ask Lancaster (who is introducing the program) if he's received the script. He has. He likes it. But he's also afraid that a film showing right-wingers kidnapping a busload of UN kids "might give somebody the idea to do it." Even though he's chairperson of the Arts Division of the American Civil Liberties Union, Burt is clearly not ready to stick his neck out on such a project. Not yet, anyway. (Stay tuned.)

"Send out more scripts," cries Pop. "To John Huston, Paul Newman, Sidney Poitier, John Frankenheimer, Karen Black, Sidney Lumet, Mike Nichols and Roman Polanski." Several of these folks he knows, so I comply. On my own I send copies to Columbia, Universal, ABC-TV, half a dozen agents and a flock of other names, some even bankable. Most don't answer. Those who like it have no deal-making power. Others reply, "It's too political" or "It's not for me." Marty Ritt (*The Great White Hope*, 1970; *The Front*, 1976; *Norma Rae*, 1979) also doesn't feel it's his cup of tea but adds, "the only thing mitigating against selling this script is the terrible state that the industry is in."

My father Alvah Bessie (L) and director John Huston
at the San Francisco International Film Festival.
(Looks as if they're wrist wrestling.)

When I stop by the office of producer Bert Schneider (*Easy Rider*, 1969; *Five Easy Pieces*, 1970) I can't get past a secretary. So I return to my car, parked behind the building. Next to my Duster is a new 1971

Look Ma, I'm Makin' Movies!

Porsche. "Mr. Schneider" is stenciled on the parking barrier. I jot a quick note, slip it into the screenplay and push the script through a half open window onto the Porsche's front seat. Two weeks later *The Hostages* comes back in the mail with a note: "I liked the script but it's not for me. And it's a nice Porsche, isn't it? Regards, Bert Schneider."

"Not for me." The line heard so often by most who try to break into the industry with a screenplay. Still, if that's your dream you've got to keep banging on the gate, got to give it your all. (I seem to recall a story about a screenwriter who keeps tossing scripts over a producer's garden fence. But the producer's dog keeps burying them!)

The Hostages, however, is a topical script and after nearly two years has grown stale. Although there are two or three more attempts, by the following May I've basically laid the project to rest in Hollywood's Graveyard Of Good Ideas That Never Got Made But Still Ought To Be.

By June, Eddie Lewis, an important but low profile producer begins making noises about hiring me to work on *The Scalpel, The Sword*

REELING THROUGH HOLLYWOOD

the story of Canadian doctor Norman Bethune that Filmsense has been briefly excited about.

By October, I've hooked into Jane Fonda's Entertainment Industry for Peace and Justice committee. Naturally, Pop pushes me to lay his novel, *The Symbol*, on her. Plus *The Hostages*. At this point I barely know Jane (or her inamorato of the moment, Don Sutherland), so I decline.[3] Still, Pop and I and another Spanish Civil War vet have begun talking about a script we'll eventually write together, one we'll tailor specifically for Jane. After Pop comes back from Berlin (and Leipzig), that is, where he is off to attend a writer's conference.

So, with feature possibilities dead as a Dodo for now, it's time to concentrate on what I've begun to sense I might be able to do fairly well: produce small educational movies. When Charlotte Holtzkamper pitches *Buyer Beware* to the California Bureau of Homemaking Education as the pilot for a series, they swipe the idea and hire a company wired into their office to make the films. Fortunately, consumer education is "in" at the moment, so I recreate the idea with a little different twist, then zip over to the Hollywood office of Encyclopaedia Britannica Films and in one meeting sell them on five titles. Along with five filmstrips. But the big chiefs in EBF's Chicago wigwam need to approve, so for the moment, the consumer films are on hold.

Mid February 1972. There's that ever-ringing phone.

"Dan? Hi, this is Eddie Lewis. I've got a feature project I'd like to talk to you about."

"*The Scalpel, The Sword*," I ask, hopeful.

"Nope, something much more exciting."

---

[3] In November of 1971, I screened *The Hollywood Ten* for Jane and Don Sutherland. This short fund raising film, produced in 1950, explains the case of my father and his fellow blacklistees. Jane, though she felt it was "enormously moving," also found that "strange [because] I felt it was badly made to the point of being irritating." (All talking heads, and unimaginatively photographed.)

SIXTEEN

executive foreplay

February 1972. Learning Garden is still among the living. Educational distribution is going nowhere, but production chugs along nicely. With *Buyer Beware* in the can (grainy though it is), as well as a medical film, we're awaiting a go ahead on the Encyclopaedia Britannica consumer education titles.

Eddie Lewis

And Eddie Lewis has a project. But then, Eddie always has a project. Nineteen-Sixty's *Spartacus* was his, along with *Seven Days in May* (1964). Later, he'll captain such titles as *Missing* (1982), *The Thorn Birds* (1983) and *The River* (1984). He can also claim the forget-

REELING THROUGH HOLLYWOOD

table mish-mash, *The Blue Bird*, starring Jane Fonda, Cicely Tyson, Ava Gardner and Elizabeth Taylor, with the venerable George Cukor directing.[1] More often than not, Eddie's work has a socially conscious aspect. The project he wants to involve me in will be no exception.

Nine years earlier, President John Kennedy had been gunned down in Dallas. The Warren Report had done little but stir up conspiracy theories. Notable among those suggesting that our government could and did lie to cover up facts behind disquieting news, were writers Mark Lane and Donald Freed, authors of *Executive Action*, a lively and plausible fiction dealing with the event. Lane and Freed had sent the manuscript to Donald Sutherland, who in turn had taken it to Eddie Lewis.

Having known Eddie around the fringes of left wing politics, and even with his hype about me becoming involved in *The Scalpel, The Sword*, I'm flattered when he asks if I'll consider producing the film. To begin, he wants me to read a screenplay based on the book, a screenplay by Dalton Trumbo. Eddie sees *Executive Action* as a low budget docudrama, and has been negotiating with Claude somebody-or-other, a Canadian director with documentary experience. Sutherland is also Canadian, thus, I assume, the connection.

The picture will stir a hornet's nest, so Eddie guards the script like the plans for the D-Day landings at Normandy. He summons me to his swanky Bel Air home, ushers me into the library, plunks me down on a cushy sofa and hands me the screenplay. Then he asks if I'd like something to drink.

"Well, maybe a glass of white wine?"

Eddie's eyes pop as if he's just won the lottery. He turns and shouts down the hall to his wife. "*Millie* . . . Millie!" he cries, "He asked for white wine!" Then he turns back to me and blurts out, "That's what Claude [the director] asked for!"

---

[1] The International Movie Database called *The Blue Bird* (1984) an "oddball mess." This first US-USSR co-production found Taylor dressed "like a Mafia wife gone insane," and the whole project "so icky sweet [that it] makes Barney look like "Penthouse Forum" in comparison."

Executive Foreplay

Movie people grasp at shadows. If both the producer and director of a film appear to be in sync (the "white wine" connection in this case), it must be an omen. The film is going to make millions. Who can blame them? It's part of the dream.

Though I have other projects on tap, there is nevertheless a huge adrenalin rush to begin. Claude and his girlfriend (and sidekick) Josie are flying in from Canada. I'm to budget the show, scout locations and start hiring crew. Suddenly created a producer on the strength of one phone call and reading a script, I figure that I too need a "do everything" assistant. Someone (preferably female) whose personality melts butter and whose practical experience will make the gnarly logistics involved in organizing a shoot run as efficiently as a Toyota assembly line. I don't have far to look.

"The gal you want is Debbie Hooper," says the first person I call, an acquaintance at another company.

Debbie has served as production assistant on dozens of projects, and at twenty-three has a keener grasp on pulling together the elements of a film than anyone I've worked with until now. Nor does it hurt that she's impishly cute, and, coincidentally, was *Playboy's* Playmate of the Month for August 1969.

Claude and Josie arrive. Clearly swingers, they glom on to Debbie, eager for an "arrangement." Together or separately, I'm not sure. But Debbie isn't interested – which still doesn't cool their jets.

Meantime, we start going over the script. Claude is clearly a pro, knows how many pages he can shoot in a day, and the breakdown is accomplished in a morning. (Prior to budgeting, a screenplay is broken down into shooting days, with an attempt made to schedule filming of locations and actors in a sequence that avoids unnecessary expense.) Next comes the budget. "You've got $250,000," says Eddie. To me, this is a fortune; most educational films come in at no more than $30,000. (What do I know?)

Time mushes on. Claude and Josie return to Canada, as Debbie and I shift into pre-production mode. The film will require a variety of locations, from remote terrain where the movie assassins can practice, to a mansion where the wealthy men behind the plot confer, to a greensward able to pass for the tree-lined grassy knoll in Dallas, where (following the two killers theory) a hidden gunman gets off the death shot as JFK's motorcade slows down and heads toward an underpass.

We also need two crucial actors, doubles for Lee Harvey Oswald and for Dallas nightclub owner Jack Ruby, who killed Oswald. No one in the fat, multi-volume Academy Players Directory comes close. But gossip about the making of the film has been circulating and I've placed ads in two LA papers, seeking look-alikes. Letters pour in, most with photos. None bare the slightest resemblance to either man, though the respondents clearly believe they do. One Oswald wannabe is decked out as a survivalist, posed in front of a Nazi flag. Another has pasted his own face onto a magazine clipping of Oswald. Another offers a photo of himself buck-naked and holding a rifle. This is going to be a gnarly assignment. We don't bother interviewing any of the candidates.

Then, one morning, Debbie bounces in dragging a stubble-bearded, scraggly-haired friend (and ninth-grade sweetheart) she's tracked down.

"Who's this?"

"Lee Harvey Oswald!"

"Debbie, *please!*"

She smirks, grabs the fellow, Jim MacColl, by the hand and heads for the door. "Be right back," she promises. An hour later she returns with a clean-shaven and neatly trimmed Lee Harvey Oswald! Well, close enough. In *Executive Action*, Jim will portray a double for Oswald, hired by the conspirators to pop up around Dallas dropping false clues in order to set up the real Oswald as a patsy. (Recall coverage of Oswald's line to the press as he was led down a hall on that grim November day? "I didn't shoot anyone," he called out, "I'm just a patsy.")

Jim passes muster with Eddie Lewis and his stylish wife Millie, whom he consults on all decisions. Within days we also find Jack Ruby, a near dead ringer, in the person of Oscar Oncidi, a chubby-faced insurance salesman. Oscar's acting is another story. He would have trouble passing for a corpse.

More letters arrive. Some conspiracy buffs want to make sure we are on target with their pet theory. One note, from a painting contractor in Illinois, offers the tantalizing news that he "planned the assassination of President Kennedy and it was carried out exactly as I planned it." He also claims that he later had a "change of heart and informed the FBI . . . at least five or six times before the incident took place." He has declined to reveal this juicy information until now, because "a United States Marshall implied that I would be shot if I did so."

While Debbie and I zip around scouting locations in her MG convertible, which she lets me drive (until I grind the gears), Eddie sweats out the financing. Without a star – Don Sutherland isn't bankable on his name alone – and without a more important director than Claude, the project is too hot to handle. No studio will commit.

This scenario, familiar to anyone trying to get a movie bankrolled, has endless variations. As star likes a project but the director sees someone else in the role. A director is assigned, but financing falls through, or is unavailable until the director finishes another film. The star or director wants script changes, "to make it really great," but then the star is unhappy with the rewrite. And on and on until the project is eventually shelved. Or, like some pictures, actually gets made.

If my big screen dreams are going to disappear in a puff of Hollywood smoke, so be it. OK, I tell myself, Learning Garden will just keep plugging along with little movies for schools and libraries. Discouraging, sure. Especially after all the work Debbie and I have put in. But *Executive Action* seems dead in the water.

Debbie Hooper - Good friend and assistant on various projects

By now too, Debbie has fled. As has been clear from day one, Eddie's wife Millie is less than thrilled with her. Possibly, she can't imagine that a young, vivacious person has the skill to do the required organizing job. Maybe it's "all that boobs and butt" (Debbie's words). From Millie come not so subtle suggestions that I find someone else. Debbie, I reply, is the best, and working with her has shown me she'll do a great job. But finally, unwilling to deal with Millie's often nasty vibes, Debbie arrives one morning to say she's throwing in the towel. Though I've seen it coming I try hard to convince her to hang in. She won't budge. "Not worth it, Daniel," she says. With regrets, we hug and promised we'll work together again.

When Debbie had first arrived at our Woodland Hills home for a production meeting (and a swim), I was sure that Rose saw hanky-panky afoot. There wasn't. Regrettably, I told myself at the time, for getting it on with a *Playboy* centerfold had certainly been a fantasy. The entertainment world bubbles over with such mental meanderings: your movie featured at Cannes, that Mercedes in the drive, a star on Hollywood Boulevard's Walk of Fame. And, of course, gorgeous babes or handsome hunks ready to leap into the sack with you. In any walk of life, distractions are a dime a dozen. So it's easy for the sexuality associated with the allure of fame and fortune to run riot in a business like making movies. (As in politics.)

And for someone whose understanding of what makes for a loving and lasting relationship had, at that point, been as scattered as had mine, temptation was always as close as someone's beckoning finger. Or more likely, the distortions in my own head.

Debbie wasn't my first fantasy. Nor would she be my last.

SEVENTEEN

just desserts

For anyone hot to work in movies, it's easy to forget that even middling power can lead basically decent people to lust for more than a successful career. The human goodies available when you're in a position to hand out jobs, or exercise the phony attraction that being a person of influence brings can be staggering. I know. I was there.

Yes, there were occasional and always guilt-ridden infidelities. But my case was mild. For too many, sexual appetite runs rampant and innocent people are victimized. And the victimizers often feel no guilt. With regret and apologies for my peccadilloes, finger waggers and those wont to utter little tsking noises should be pleased to know that not every yellow brick road leads to the Emerald City.

Fall 1971. In spite of concern for the family (but with not enough for my marriage), I've separated from Rose for the second time. Not yet forty years old, with half my hair remaining and with a fire still simmering in the basement, it isn't difficult to find solace. But the avenging goddess of spurned wives is on duty, so a hoped-for jolly afternoon with a pottery maker of talent and verve is snuffed out when the flu bug lays me low. My ardor turns to chagrin when a hairy, many-legged creature peeking in at the window opposite her bed inhibits a roll in the hay with a painter who lives near Pasadena's Rose Bowl. Tarantulus interruptus. And as for the futile effort to get it on in a sleeping bag on a rockbound Arizona campground, in 20-degree weather, with a Swedish dwarf . . . Well, what can I say?

All of which leads to big time fantasy number two: Donna

Just Desserts

Michelle, *Playboy's* playmate of the year in 1964.[1] Though six years beyond her centerfold fame, if the cliché "drop dead gorgeous" applies to anyone on Earth, it still applies to Donna. And even beyond Earth, for Donna's is one of only two playmate photos selected to accompany astronauts John Young and Michael Collins when they blast off in Gemini X in 1966; the first women in space, seventeen years before Sally Ride.

Gary Horowitz first introduces us when I ask if he knows a photographer I can employ on a medical film then in production. And though I tell myself it will be like biting nails not to hire Donna off her looks alone, fortunately, her photographic skills are excellent.

When she isn't snapping photos we chat, I pester her for dates, and after much hemming and hawing on her part we start going out. One date is a visit to the L.A. County Museum of Art. Don't

Donna Michelle

[1] Donna Michelle. (Born December 8, 1945.) After appearing as *Playboy's* Miss December 1963 and then Playmate of the Year for 1964, she went on to rolls in films such as *Mickey One* and *Beach Blanket Bingo* (both 1965) and *One Spy Too Many* (1966).

ask what the exhibit was, I haven't a clue. For me, the company of a woman I see as a living goddess is seventh heaven enough. And so it apparently also is for a young stud in a Jaguar XKE, whose panic stop scorches tire tracks along Wilshire Boulevard when he spots Donna in the crosswalk. I'm positive he's going to leap from the Jag and abduct her. But then traffic backs up and horns blare, so lecherous ogling is as far as he gets.

Another time, I show up at Donna's apartment to find her attempting to mask depression with a cornucopia of pharmaceuticals. After an hour of her incomprehensible conversation I take off, frustrated.

Also about now, I have scored a month-long boat-sitting gig in the Marina at Playa Del Ray. (The owner has taken off for Europe.) And Donna has told me that although she'll be busy on a photo shoot in the Pacific Palisades (on Los Angeles's west side), we can get together afterwards. I'm to meet her at the shoot. So I time my appearance to coincide with the end of filming. About 5 p.m.

As she stows her photo equipment, we agree to go for dinner. I'm in my 1970 Plymouth Duster and suggest she might like to "drive down to the boat with me, I'll cook us a nice meal." It's December, the holiday season and the good fellowship often accompanying it abounds. Winter's chill permeates the harbor. Boats are festooned for Christmas. A candlelight dinner, a hot toddy, a warm and fuzzy man's arm around the waist. Who knows what might develop?

"Oh, I don't know," says Ms Playmate of the Year, "why don't we just go to a restaurant?" There goes my dream, I think, dashed against the shoals of libido.

"OK, sure, why not. I know a place."

"I'll follow you," says Donna.

Just Desserts

Sigh. OK, so I'm into the Duster and she into her silver-gray Porsche and I head down the coast highway toward Santa Monica, with Donna close behind. At which point the Porsche suddenly pulls ahead of me. What the hell is she doing?

Now we're in Santa Monica, driving along Lincoln Boulevard, and heading toward the Marina. I'm still wondering what's got into Donna. Maybe she's on something? Doesn't seem like it, and she's always been on top of her act while working, focused and professional. Annoyed, unaware of what she has in mind, I zoom up next to the Porsche, indicate in a slightly annoyed manner that she should follow me, then take the lead. Several blocks later I pull into the parking lot of a steak and lobster house on Lincoln. Donna doesn't say a word as we get out of our cars, enter the restaurant and are shown to a table. We each order a glass of Chablis then sit scanning the menus. Moments later I look up and ask, "What the hell were you doing back there?"

"Leading you to the boat," she replies with a smile. "Sounded like it could be kind of a fun evening. I thought something 'nice' might happen."

"Well OK then, let's *go*," I retort, starting to get up and mentally salivating over the fun and games about to take place in the boat's fo'c's'le.

Donna shakes her head. "Sorry, the mood's gone. Gotta strike while the iron is hot, you know."

I don't say it aloud but it's running through my head: "You certainly blew that one, laddie."[2]

---

[2] Donna eventually retreated to Mendocino County, California, became something of a hermit and struggled to keep her financial head above water. After I left L.A. we never met again. Sadly, she died too young, of a heart attack (age 58), on April 14, 2004. The world barely noticed.

Fantasies eventually have to end, and it's then that reality has a chance to take hold. If one is alert to the opportunity, that is. For me and for too many men I've known (plenty of women too), this understanding took longer than it needed. An unwillingness to ignore other female attractions had me wearing blinders that didn't let me work on my marriage, and made later relationships harder too. And because of it, my children probably went through more angst than they needed to. All part of how illusion distracts us from more important goals. It happens in life as much as it does in media.

Once again, those working in a field where illusion is a big part of what gets created have a harder time keeping focused. But better work comes of it, I guarantee. The best analogy I can think of is getting hooked on coffee. Some folks say, "I can't get started until I've had my morning cup." (Which often becomes three or five and on through the day.) I once felt the same. But just giving up the bean allowed me to think more clearly, not less.

So too with fantasies about playmates, a star on the Walk of Fame, or that new Mercedes in the drive. Letting go of illusions and zooming in on the possibilities is more likely to bring them closer. And don't forget, fantasies aren't the same as dreams. Ambition is good. Hope is good. Diligent work often leads to grand accomplishments. Keep that in mind as you tread the yellow brick road of life, to Hollywood or to any other land of your heart's desire.

As the great writer Langston Hughes advises,

> *Hold fast to dreams, for if dreams die*
> *Life is a broken-winged bird that cannot fly.*
> *Hold fast to dreams, for when dreams go*
> *Life is a barren field frozen with snow.*

EIGHTEEN

fumbling along in the land of enchantment[1]

New Mexico or Hollywood, take your pick. They both have their allure.

March 1972. By now, it looks like Eddie Lewis's JFK film is so much pie in the sky. So, on with the little movies that are Learning Garden's bread and butter. As the winter rains temporarily wash away L.A.'s smog and the trees are greening, I'm on the road to New Mexico in our 1964 Plymouth station wagon. New Mexico, because live footage for a medical film dealing with nerve deafness will be shot there. And because my former boss, Bob Stevens of Albuquerque's Bandelier Films, has agreed to find actors and locations and film the show for half what it would cost in L.A. With me is Jimmy Roden, a slight, and slightly frenetic director I've previously worked with.

We are also toting the big set of lights Bandelier has ordered for the shoot.

Zipping along at seventy and without even the courtesy of a spasmodic warning cough, the Plymouth goes into cardiac arrest. Deep in the Mojave. Fifteen miles east of Dinosaur City, Arizona (population, one gas station). What to do? While Jimmy snoozes, I

---

[1] For stay-at-homes, New Mexico's state slogan, emblazoned on every license plate, is "Land of Enchantment."

thumb back to Dinosaur City to make a call (no cell phones in 1972). Then I return to the Plymouth. Two hours later Triple-A arrives, hooks up and tows us seventy-five expensive miles to Flagstaff.

What the hell, I'm thinking, I'll make fifteen hundred or so profit on the film.

"Well now," drawls a shifty-eyed mechanic, sizing up this anxious Californian's potentially thick wallet, "be near a week t' fix this puppy. Give'r take. Gotta send t' Phoenix f'r the parts . . . 'bout seven hun'ert dollars, I reckon. Give'r take."

Seven big bills? That's nearly half of my profit. No damn way! So while Jimmy meanders off to score a cheeseburger, I hustle down the block to the local Nissan dealer. A telephoned OK from my friendly Bank of America VP in Los Angeles (the trusting sister of a high school buddy), and I'm in hock for a new, caramel-colored 1972 Datsun station wagon. Boxy yet serviceable. Jimmy and I transfer the film lights from the deceased Plymouth (now the not so proud property of Flagstaff Nissan) to the Datsun, pile in and take off east through the mesquite.

Albuquerque. A Friday. Bandelier has done nothing to prep for the shoot. No locations, no talent lined up. We have a cameraman (Bob's son Alan, just graduated from film school) and an assistant, and that's it. Production is to begin on Monday. (Fortunately, Alan has had the foresight to order film.) During the next twenty-four hours we set up a casting session by contacting a Baptist church – the client wants to feature an African-American family – and race to check out potential locations.

FUMBLING ALONG IN THE LAND OF ENCHANTMENT

In his spare time, Jimmy, with his "visiting firemen expect a playmate" Hollywood mindset (Bob Stevens laughingly offered his middle-aged wife), settles for hitting on a cocktail waitress at the Holiday Inn where we're staying.

By Monday morning everything has fallen into place. And to my amazement the shoot comes off without a hitch. Except that the housewife who has provided her location looks on, apoplectic, when we cater lunch. For our family of charming and talented African-Americans – mom, pop, grandma and three kids (along with the crew), devours huge buckets of The Colonel's greasiest Original Recipe around the Drexel Heritage table in her impeccably *House Beautiful* dining room. As we're wrapping she races around sweeping, scrubbing, oiling and polishing the table and stuffing linens into her washer before hubby returns to find the typical film shoot Armageddon.

Heading home on Route 66, I start mulling over who should direct the upcoming consumer education films. Jimmy perhaps? The Albuquerque jaunt has been a test, and in spite of his quirkiness he clearly knows what he's doing. As I mull, Jimmy jolts me back to the moment.

"You know," he smirks, "I scored with that waitress at the Holiday Inn. Except I was so stoned that I don't remember if I gave her a great time or not."

I don't believe a word. (Except that he was stoned.)

Jimmy puts his seat back and drifts off to Never-Never Land. Just as well, since I'm not in the mood for more of his befuddled cannabis adventures.[2]

By June I am feeling wonderfully upbeat. Encyclopaedia Britannia has signed for the consumer films, we've raced through production, all five titles are in editing and I'm looking forward to a hefty profit.

---

[2] A few years later, Jimmy, overflowing with angst, put a bullet through his head.

By September, the bubble has burst. Top execs at EBF, in a purple snit over the content of one film, have reneged on final payment. So now I'm in deep do-do. (What content, you ask? Stand by.) With a mind like that of a chipmunk treadmilling inside a cage, I sit in my Learning Garden office scribbling numbers on a big yellow pad. Trying to figure out how to pay off $38,000 owed to the lab, equipment houses and crew, who all keep my phone jingling. But since my bank balance is currently in tatters, the figuring only makes me feel more chipmunkish,

Where the hell am I going to find $38,000? A film shot in May for a school for exceptional children my dear daughter Lisa currently attends had been a labor of love, funded by $350 each out of pocket by the school's director and myself. Grant proposals submitted earlier in the year for an animated Native American folktale and for a series teaching sex education to retarded kids have gone nowhere.

And *A Crack in the Pavement*, a live-action short designed to interest city kids in nature, which I assigned Jimmy to direct, never worked. He botched the job and the client rejected the finished project. So while the consumer films were in production I spent six weeks redoing the entire eight minutes in animation. Leaving zero profit.

Still from *A Crack in the Pavement*

I've been holding out a thimble's worth of hope for producer interest in *The Symbol* (1966), Pop's novel drawn from the thinly disguised life of Marilyn Monroe.[3] Maybe selling that will bail the Learning

---

[3] Eventually produced in 1974 as *The Sex Symbol*, an ABC Movie of the Week, the film, which starred Connie Stevens and Shelly Winters, was widely panned. Pop, whose screenplay was badly mauled, complained bitterly about what he felt Hollywood had done to his novel.

FUMBLING ALONG IN THE LAND OF ENCHANTMENT

Garden boat? Never happens. Thus my puny bank balance. Thus $38,000 in the hole. How did I get into this pickle?

Well, since Jimmy has fallen flat in his last assignment, I turn to other directors for the EBF gig. Carol Ballard – pre *The Black Stallion* (1979) and *Never Cry Wolf* (1983) – is my first choice, but co-producer Charlotte Holtzkaper (she who acquired funding for my first consumer film, *Buyer Beware*), vetoes him.[4] So TV commercial director Buck Pennington gets the assignment. And produces fine work. Even though he turns Simon Wheeler, the actor playing a door-to-door salesman, into a bowl of Jell-O by shouting at him after every take. Which, I later learn, has been Buck's plan from the start; to make Simon come across as a sweaty-palmed, fast-talking sleaze, as he suckers a gullible young couple into plunking down hard earned working class bucks on a set of tinny pots and pans.

And it's this film, *Harry J. Woods is at the Door* that brings on Learning Garden's $38,000 debacle. When the five titles get to Britannica's Chicago office (I'd contracted the work through their Hollywood branch), the execs take one look and refuse to pay a nickel more; because *Harry J. Woods* exposes exactly the kind of high-pressure door-to-door selling tactics engaged in by their Encyclopedia salesmen! I mean, did they read the script? Or did I, in my impulsive delight over the witty approach taken by the writer, never consider the fact that Britannica's main business is selling Encyclopedias?

Charlotte Holtzkamper panics. With a quicksand of debt sucking me under, she's petrified she'll be stuck with the bills. A hand-delivered registered letter arrives, abrogating her role as co-producer and disclaiming further interest in or responsibility for the films. Since EBF's advance has been used as start up money for talent, location fees and film stock, and since the little I've taken out to keep the family afloat has long since evaporated, the wolf is huffing mightily at the door.

So there I sit, scribbling figures and wondering if I'll get a response to the two legalistic-sounding letters I've composed and

---

[4] Possibly a wise veto. Off the strength of his two most famous films, Ballard acquired a reputation for going wildly over budget.

sent to Encyclopaedia Britannica. And while a cartoon featuring a "for sale" sign next to the old walnut tree in front of our Woodland Hills home appears in my mind's eye – along with visions of cramming the family into a seedy dump in Venice (totally chichi now, but then one of the cheapest spots in L.A.).

Once more, the phone rings. I pick up.

"Dan Bessie?"

"That's me."

It's an attorney in EBF's Chicago office.

"Well, look, about the consumer education titles. We don't want to distribute them."

Oh, my God, I think, the quicksand is over my head. Before I can protest, the lawyer continues: "Tell you what; we'll cut you a check for the balance on the contract. As a loan. And the films are yours to do with as you want."

I'm flustered. I don't have the capital to take EBF to court. Or distribute the films myself. But maybe I can palm them off on someone. And since Charlotte has pulled out, I won't have to share the profits with anyone.

"Well," I equivocate, "I don't know . . . I'm not sure I can ever pay EBF back fully . . ."

After some haggling, we agree that I'll pay what I can out of whatever revenue the films generate. I'll simply owe the $38,000, refundable from any sale or distribution of the films, with no interest, until the loan is repaid – or not, depending on how well the titles do. But I'm not on the hook to pay the whole amount if the films never sell.

Saved. And a blessing too, because $4000 of EBF's balance owing is my take, and will keep Learning Garden (and the family) going for another few months.

Fumbling Along in the Land of Enchantment

The ups and downs continue. Soon, another medical extravaganza is on tap. Soon, I'll make deals with two distributors to take on the EBF films, the royalties from which actually will let me pay back most of the $38,000. Soon too, Gary Horowitz and I have enough extra cash to shell out $600 each to commission a screenplay from an idea pitched to us by Judith Parker, the young woman who had scripted the consumer films. We send her completed script to Eddie Lewis for his partner John Frankenheimer (*The Manchurian Candidate*, 1962; *The French Connection*, 1971). Frankenheimer sends it on to writer John Carlino (*The Great Santini*, 1979), who wants to do a major rewrite. Judith nixes the idea and the script gather's dust on her shelf.[5]

OK, I'm thinking, so I never will make a feature.

As 1972 winds down, *A Crack in the Pavement*, the short I redid in animation after Jimmy Roden's version flopped, is invited to the Fourth International Children's Film Festival. A local TV station features me talking up the festival along with Sheri Lewis, mom to hand puppet Lamb Chop. I am lively and gregarious during the segment, Sheri and I have a chummy time yakking it up, and when the cameras shut down she turns to the show's producers and says, "You know, this guy is good! You ought to give him his own show." The producers chuckle.[6]

Sheri Lewis and LambChop

---

[5] This script, however, landed Judith her first agent and she went on to a successful EMMY-winning career writing and producing episodes of *L.A. Law* (1986-94) and other shows.

[6] A week later Rose and I were invited to Sheri's stylish Beverly Hills home for a great party. A gracious and talented lady, Ms Lewis. The world is a little better for her time among us.

Reeling Through Hollywood

By the time I send out invites for Learning Garden's Second Annual New Year's Bash and Festival of Good Cheer, the wolf is no longer huffing at the door. And, surprise of surprises, the phone rings one more time. It's Eddie Lewis. "Dan," he says, "we've tied down the funding for the JFK movie."

No more foreplay. *Executive Action* is on again!

NINETEEN

executive action

Enough hanky-panky. Time to get it on. Make the movie.

In independent feature film trenches you'll slog through the endlessly sucking mud of production schedules, dodge the shrapnel of unimagined problems and get to squeeze nickels out of an already minuscule budget so the director can get in one last shot. You'll push the troops we call the crew, often working for poverty wages, into fourteen-hour days for the glory of being part of an important film.

If you're ready for all that, come along for the ride.

Little do I realize that my first experience producing a feature will drive me, if not to Southern Comfort, at least out of Hollywood – though it will take another five years to cut the cord.

February 1973. *Executive Action* is up and running. Eddie Lewis has a director. Though he lacks recent credits, David Miller's *Sudden Fear* (1952) and *Lonely are the Brave* (1962) are minor classics. Creative and gregarious, David sets up shop in my Westwood office. And I've found a new Cracker-Jack assistant, Carolyn (then called Caron) Beaver – who takes a lot of ribbing because of her last name. In no time she's into her casting books and plying David with headshots (close up photos of actors).

With a director, and with financing from a group of Chicago investors, Eddie now hooks a star: Burt Lancaster. Though Lewis, a name producer, has a winning track record (*The Blue Bird* notwithstanding), Lancaster, now in demand off the huge grosses for *Airport* (1970) hesitates. Could JFK, he wondered, have really been the victim of a conspiracy? Will critics shit on the film even before it opens? Eddie plies Burt with material backgrounding Kennedy's murder and questioning the Warren Report. From Burt, a long silence. Is that his answer? Then, as *Executive Action* is about to be shelved again, he phones Eddie from LAX just before flying off to do another picture. He'll do the movie. He'll play the role of Jim Farrington, a man thick into black operations who hires the assassins and supervises logistics. Moreover, he'll do it on Eddie's terms: SAG minimum of $750 a week, for two weeks. Plus 10% of the distributor's gross. Now, I have to shift into hustle mode.

Director David Miller (R), confers with editor Irving Lerner (L) and casting director Carolyn Beaver.

Eddie's office on the Fox lot is even smaller than mine. No place to run a major production out of. So I phone Gary Horowitz. Wakeford-Orloff (W/O) is still big in TV commercials and Gary has already produced a couple of low budget features. I put him together with Eddie and they work out a deal. *Executive Action* will be an "Edward Lewis Production," followed by "in association with Wakeford-Orloff" (in small letters). Since I've heard that Eddie has a reputation in the industry of a financial piranha, I find it remarkable that Gary is able to negotiate a four percent profit share for W/O. And a third of that (on top of a $7500 producer's fee) will be mine. Also, Gary and I nudge the budget to a more "realistic" $400,000.[1] Eddie furrows his brow but says he can live with it.

Eddie Lewis

Now, the pace quickens. Eddie wants to release the film by the tenth anniversary of JFK's assassination. With a star in hand, he trolls for a distributor. Carolyn Beaver casts the supporting players, while I hire crew and began to tackle the endless details accompanying any film shoot.

Eddie has also signed Robert Ryan, to play Foster, a man furious with JFK for championing Martin Luther King's civil rights struggle, and over his hints about withdrawing from Vietnam. I'm delegated to land Will Geer, who will play Ferguson, a crusty and initially reluctant conspirator whose millions are key to bankrolling the operation. When I phone to enroll him for the part, Will grumbles about Eddie's $2500 offer.

"Oh, he said that, did he?" says Eddie. "Remind him who hired him when he was on the blacklist and nobody else would touch him with a ten foot pole."

At Will's West Hollywood home, a gaudy antique neon boarding house sign hangs above the door. Flashing on and off, it warns, "We

Will Geer assaults me with a giant zucchini

---

[1] Today, that $400,000 would be around two million; still a pittance for most features.

do not take theatricals."[2] Pleasant and affable, Will, when I tell him about our tiny budget and why his participation is so important, quickly agrees to the role and does not need a reminder of Eddie's past help. Before leaving, I gracefully dodge Will's "come hither" handshake, which turns into rubbing my arm up and down, accompanied by a glint in his eye. Though Grandpa Walton is "ambidextrous," I'm not.

I spend the next month tracking down archival footage from CBS, NBC and ABC. All dealing with Kennedy speeches, press conferences and personal appearances designed to build his popularity and looking toward the 1964 reelection campaign.

Simultaneously, Gary and I put together a support team. Redheaded W/O production assistant Gerry Puhara scouts locations then handles wardrobe during the shoot. And finds time during pre-production to regale me with hysterical stories about the former Singer Midgets, some of who had been Munchkins in *The Wizard of Oz*.[3]

Myself, with production assistant and wardrobe person Gerry Puhara

[2] This kind of sign was common in many American cities during the period when stage actors were regarded as a pack of irresponsible deadbeats.

[3] While costuming the midgets for a commercial, one horny three-foot-eight Lothario kept coming on to her, promising, "Gerry, who else can suck on your titties, bang your box and kick you in the shins all at the same time?

EXECUTIVE ACTION

Severo Perez, my Learning Garden production manager, spends weeks scouting for an L.A. substitute for the grassy knoll, the embankment next to Dallas's Stemmons Freeway where JFK was killed. No luck. We search from Ventura to Orange County but never find the perfect spot. In frustration, director David Miller, on his third visit to a park we've picked for other shots, turns to a small hillock, miles from any freeway, and says in a loud, agitated voice, "OK. The grassy knoll!" With a prop sign, a wooden fence constructed in front of a stand of trees, and remembering the truth that only what the camera sees is real, audiences will have no clue that we didn't film the scene in Dallas.

Late into pre-production, screenwriter Dalton Trumbo is diagnosed with lung cancer. With researchers David Lifton and Penn Jones Jr. fussing about inaccuracies and inconsistencies, and with our insurance underwriter also demanding changes, the script is in rewrite until the first day of shooting. (What else is new in the movie game? Check out *Round up the Usual Suspects*, Aljean Harmetz's intriguing peek at the making of *Casablanca*.) With Dalton unable to work and with Eddie needing the security of another writer, I fly my father in for a conference.

"Here's the way I see it, baby," says Pop to Eddie, when Lewis asks what ideas he's come up with.

"Baby?"

Eddie eyes my father sideways. I hold my breath. Out of the loop for thirty years, Pop has time-warped back to 1943, to the writer's building at Warner's. Once past that, he writes fine bridging dialogue for several scenes, quickly and professionally. For a minuscule $750.

Pre-production slogs on into late spring. Severo and Gerry go bonkers trying to tie down locations. Crew people that have agreed to work on the film are turning down other jobs. Carolyn Beaver is overworked and underpaid.

"Why should I hang around waiting for this to happen?" she complains, "I could be earning three times the money doing commercials."

"How about a bonus when the film is finished," I blurt out. "How's about seventeen-hundred?"

"Well . . ."

"I promise."

I'm thinking fast. Carolyn is crucial; we can't afford to lose her. But it's a promise I'll never keep. With budget pressure at fever pitch, I don't have the guts to ask Eddie to cough up the extra dough.

Somehow, everything falls into place. Locations are set. Ninety of them, from palatial mansions to corporate offices, to stand-ins for Dallas streets and Dealey Plaza. We'll shoot in scuzzy motels, in a suite at the Ambassador Hotel and in a private railway car that travels a hundred miles to reach a remote siding. Harry Caplan is taken on as David Miller's assistant director. Bob Steadman, still green in features, serves as DP/cameraman. A grip, prop person, script supervisor, gaffer and assistants at every level are standing by; grumbling, because Gary and I have sharp-penciled every budget item and they are getting half their accustomed salaries. Of course, Eddie Lewis is collecting no salary at all. (In advance, that is.)

But producers have ways. With Lancaster and Ryan aboard, National General Corporation, now locked in as the distributor, shells out $25,000 for a ten minute promo film – that W/O associate Sid Galanty directs and that is produced for a third of that amount. It will be years, however, before I learn that Eddie has demanded from Gary (and received) a new Mercedes out of that budget.

At last, David Miller is reasonably happy. He doesn't have the grassy knoll he wants. We don't have the bucks to allow the fifty or more shooting days he's accustomed to. And though Miller can get down on people, even humiliating them sometimes, when Severo

EXECUTIVE ACTION

discovers that if he arrives right after lunch with a stiff vodka and orange juice, David turns into a pussy cat.

May 1973. The day before the shoot. Everyone has a call sheet (listing directions to the location, time to be there, the scenes to be filmed). Eddie has asked me to pick up Robert Ryan, who is flying in from New York. An honor. I've followed his work for years.

Ryan first impressed me as a detective in a sensitive anti-war film, *The Boy With Green Hair* (1948), but left me deflated when he showed up as a nasty Red in *The Woman on Pier 13* (1949).[4] I had happened to catch that flick (with subtitles) one afternoon in Kobe, Japan, in December of 1951, when I accompanied a young woman to a movie house after spending a most amiable morning with her. In a house of a very different sort.

Ryan deserves a limo. Instead, I arrive at LAX in my tinny Datsun. I'm to meet him at the gate. He comes off the plane with Robert Preston (*The Music Man*, 1962). Both are stewed to the gills and being fawned over by a bevy of giggling dowagers who the stars have clearly charmed on the flight. We claim Ryan's luggage then head for my car. He looks at the Datsun then down at me (he's tall) and asks, with a cynical sneer, "And where do you live, Reseda?"

"Woodland Hills, actually."

I don't tell him that I *had* lived in Reseda until recently and he certainly knows that Woodland Hills is the same sort of suburban enclave (though more up the market), with residents on a mortgage debt treadmill. I change the subject. "You know," I retort, with a cheery smile, "I really think this picture is going to be successful."

"It sure as hell better be, I've got a piece of it." Then, as we pass

---

[4] The title was later changed to *I Married a Communist*. Produced in the aftermath of the HUAC investigations, more than a few liberals such as Ryan decided they'd better verify their anti-communist credentials with a picture like this. Between 1948 and 1954 Hollywood turned out more than forty flag-waving films warning about Communism. (A framed advertisement for *I Married A Communist* currently hangs in my bathroom.)

a liquor store Ryan says, "Hey, pull over. Here's a twenty. Go in there and get me a fifth of Jim Beam, will you?"

Great. Just what we need, a drunken star. What I don't realize at the time is that Ryan is battling a lymphatic cancer that will kill him within weeks of completing his work on our picture.

Next morning, I pick him up at the Beverly Wilshire hotel. He's cold sober, but says he hasn't read the screenplay for weeks. So as I drive he reviews his lines briefly then closes the script and doesn't look at it again the entire day. He never drops a word.

Our first location is three days in a Bel Air mansion, doubling for the Virginia home of Ryan's character, Foster. It costs us a flat $7500 to rent.[5] Not satisfied with the fee, or with our feeding a dozen of his employees, who troop out of a home office every time the catering truck arrives, the mansion's owner later sues the production for denting a wastebasket. He doesn't collect.

That first day, Gary and I are on hand to greet Lancaster as he arrives.

"Hi, Burt, I'm Dan and this is Gary, we're producing." Burt stares down at me with a benign smile (he's also tall) and keeps on walking. Gary and I hurry to catch up. "Uh, we've got a dressing room for you over there beyond the

Burt Lancaster (L) and Robert Ryan, as conspirators planning the assassination of JFK

---

[5] Multiples of seventy-five seem to have been *Executive Action's* magic number: Ryan's fee, Pop's rewrite salary, my producer's fee and just about the cost of the film when finally completed.

swimming pool and -- " Not a word. Burt keeps moving. I'm about to try again when Gary puts a self-assured hand on my shoulder and says, "Let me talk to him."

"Hi, Burt. Listen; want you to know that if there's anything you need, just -- " Burt turns and withers Gary with another of his bemused "who the hell are *you*?" looks then heads for the dressing room. Gary turns to me and shrugs.

Burt stares down at me with a benign smile. . .

The crew is lighting for the first shot when Eddie Lewis arrives and gets together with Burt (who he's known for years). From then on, Lancaster is Mr. Cooperation, friendly and approachable. So friendly, in fact, that he sometimes strips to his skivvies in front of everyone when changing costume. Only problem, he isn't up on his lines. Which makes him seem to resent some of the other actors, all of who know theirs cold.

During that first scene, in the mansion's library, the conspirators are trying to convince Ferguson (Will Geer's character) of the need to kill JFK. Soon, Farrington (Lancaster), watching from a balcony, joins them. Then he asks Ferguson to accompany him to the next room for a slide presentation detailing the history of presidential assassinations. In dialogue created by my father, Ferguson (who notes that Farrington constantly pops pills for a heart condition) asks, "Why the next room?"

FARRINGTON
Just a short walk. Do you good.

FERGUSON
There's nothing wrong with *my* heart,
James.

FARRINGTON
(laughs, then)
Tell me sir, to what do you ascribe
your great good health?

Ferguson winks then elbows Farrington.

FERGUSON
Hard liquor and soft women!

Later, during another slide presentation, Farrington describes Lee Harvey Oswald's murky background. A black and white photo of a surprised-looking man in a rakish Panama hat flashes on screen. It's Pop! Posing as one Ralph P. Waterford, representing the Concerned Travelers Society, who meets Oswald in Texas on his return from the Soviet Union. Another conspirator asks Farrington (Lancaster),

HALLIDAY
Isn't that name familiar?

FARRINGTON
There's a Ralph P. Waterford known in
Taiwan as the secretary general of the
World Campaign Against Communism, Inc.

Anyone spotting Alvah Bessie and aware of his politics (nobody ever recognizes him), would have chuckled at the in-joke.

My father Alvah Bessie, portraying Ralph P. Waterford,
Secretary-General of the World Campaign Against Communism, Inc.

In that same presentation Oswald's correspondence is flashed on screen, letters indicating his unstable past. "Eddie," I tell my boss before the slides are prepared, "we can't use actual copies of Oswald's handwriting without paying big fees."

"Fine," replies Eddie, "you write the letters.

So, using photographic transcripts I recreate Oswald's letters. In one shot, Oswald writes to the Soviet embassy requesting a visa to the USSR. Since the writing has to match the other letters, my hand gets to star. Another seven seconds of fame (after my tiny stint in *Salt of the Earth*.) Is that my old high school drama teacher I hear applauding?

The Bel Air mansion filming complete, we're off to another mansion, in Pasadena, doubling as the exterior of Foster's estate. There, the conspiracy continues – within earshot of a black servant who appears now and then with coffee and hors d'oeuvres. This seems terribly incongruous, but nobody (including me) says a word.

Incongruity upon incongruity. As we're filming *Executive Action* the Watergate trials are taking place. Inside our Winnebago, anyone with a free moment is glued to the radio, while outside we are spinning a tale about a massive government cover up.

Next, rehearsal for the killing. The script specifies two assassination teams, A and B; one will get the assignment. Early on in filming, Lancaster has a scene in a Mexican restaurant. There, he goes over plans with Jeff Morrow (*The Robe*, 1953), playing the chief of team A. Next day, Burt calls Eddie to say he is "uncomfortable" with Morrow's performance. Too much of a nice guy, not convincing as a killer.

Jim MacColl, portraying Lee Harvey Oswold

Typical star power; Lancaster gets to veto Jeff, but I am assigned to do the dirty work. "Phone Jeff and can him," says Eddie. I call. Jeff's wife answers. I lay on the bad news. I hear a voice choking with regret, for Jeff hasn't worked much lately. Fortunately, Screen Actor's Guild rules demand that he gets a week's pay. Morrow is

EXECUTIVE ACTION

replaced with the suitably menacing Ed Lauter and we restage the entire scene a few days later.

There are more scenes: in upscale living rooms, and in the elegantly furnished private railroad car, where the crew spills oil on the red plush carpet and breaks a window when lights are placed too close. Then a scene in a billiard room, after which, Lancaster, Ryan and Geer have finished their stints. The first two weeks are a piece of cake compared to what lies ahead.

Now, the entire crew caravans to the desert outside of Los Angeles. Both assassination teams practice at remote locations, one at Vasquez Rocks County Park, landscape familiar to me as a kid from umpteen Gene Autry movies. The other location is private land near the town of Lancaster (no relation to Burt).

Hot. Roasting hot. A hundred and two in the shade on each of the three days it takes to complete our half-dozen sequences. For the first morning, David Miller has called for cherry pickers; big, clunky, mobile vehicles with man-sized baskets on long arms that crane up into trees so fruit can be picked. The gunmen are to ascend in these, simulating the height of rooftops from which JFK will be targeted. The vehicles travel at twenty-five miles an hour, so Severo, in charge of cherry-picker logistics, calculates that they need to leave their base in Burbank by 5 a.m. in order to arrive by eight. Assistant director Harry Caplan signs off on the plan. Slight glitch: the grade on Highway 5 out of L.A. is so steep that the pickers can only make seven miles an hour. When Severo and the machines finally pull in three hours late, David Miller is having kittens.

"I told you I needed those here at eight! It's eleven! The day is ruined! And besides, somebody just told me there are cherry pickers not twenty miles away, in Lancaster. What kind of an idiotic idea was it to bring them all the way from Burbank?"

So, while David scrambles to get his coverage, Severo goes to check out the local cherry pickers. Sure enough, there are "cherry pickers" in nearby Lancaster – migrant laborers with buckets, who hire out to pick cherries.

OK, we've jockeyed the awkward machines into position. Camera has framed the first shot. We're all set.

"You think you're getting me up in one of those? With *this* wind? No way," says Lee Delano, playing one of the riflemen. (The wind is a mild desert breeze.) I convey this unquiet news to my director.

"He'll never work for me again," David blusters.

He tosses out this line several more times during the shoot. Not a threat to lose sleep over as it turns out, since in the next nineteen years before his death in 1992, David will direct but five more films (four of them for TV) and none of them memorable.

The four actor/riflemen confer with AD Harry Caplan. They are adamant; too dangerous. Threats are hurled, promises made, flattery attempted. David stays on the sidelines, glowering. Half an hour later the "wind" dies down, the actors climb into the boxes, up they nervously go and we get the shots.

For the second desert day we've rigged a convertible with mannequins doubling for JFK, Jackie, and Governor and Mrs. John Connally, who will ride with the president in Dallas. Another glitch: no one has thought to equip the car with a device allowing it to be

Director David Miller directing car doubles for
Governor & Mrs. John Connally,
who rode in the JFK motorcade

steered by remote control. What to do? Prop man Romiro Jaloma has a solution. "I'll get in the convertible," he says, "and crouch down low so I won't be seen. I'll steer the car."

"How can you see to steer if you're crouched down?" asks David, amazed.

"No problem. I'll have a walkie-talkie. Somebody will guide me on another walkie-talkie. And we'll have the car towed. I've got a tow bar."

"Towed! We're going to *tow* the car? With gunmen shooting at it? That's insane. The driver of the tow car will be in the line of fire. These guys are theoretically practicing with live ammunition. What kind of stupid assassins do you think these are? Audiences will laugh the movie off the screen!"

"Well . . ."

David checks his watch. "I'm running out of time, let's do it!"

Instead of a short tow bar we opt for a long, thick rope, which at least creates a slightly safer looking distance. OK, it seems to be working. Sort of. The tow car is approaching. Directly behind comes the convertible with the dummies. And with Romiro out of sight.

"*Right*, Romiro, steer *right*," yells key grip Charlie McCoy, manning the second walkie-talkie. "That's it . . .no, no, no, too much, go left . . .OK, now back to the right . . ."

The convertible is getting closer, weaving back and forth across the road like a drunken hippopotamus. The tow car drops the rope and moves on past the grip truck, in front of which David and everyone else stands, watching. The convertible closes the distance. Closer . . . closer . . .

"It's going to plow into us!" yells David.

"Stop, stop, stop!" shouts McCoy.

"*Run!*" shout half a dozen voices.

REELING THROUGH HOLLYWOOD

With David leading the charge, everyone scrambles for safety just as Romiro applies the breaks, raising a cloud of choking sand. The convertible bumps to a stop two feet in front of the grip truck.[6] We do four more takes before David decides he's had a long enough run with the car in the middle of the road for him to cut the shot credibly.

The struggle to bring the movie in on time blunders ahead.

Eddie yells at me because I've budgeted too low. Gary Horowitz tells Eddie that it's David Miller causing the overruns. To some extent, he's right, for, like any good director, David adds touches which, though costing more money, give the film a richer look. And David and Eddie keep squabbling on the set because David takes longer to shoot scenes than Eddie thinks he should. Used to two-month shoots, David has to wrap this one in twenty-nine days.

We survive the desert; with sunburned noses. Now we need to duplicate the assassination itself. We've acquired TV footage of everything available from the day of the assassination. We have bootlegged copies of the Zapruder film, the Nix film and other home movies taken that awful day in Dallas. But to intensify the dramatic pace we need to fill in with additional shots. For these we need doubles for JFK, Jackie and the Connallys. Carolyn Beaver has located a passable JFK (in long shots), an excellent Jackie look-alike, and "close enoughs" for the Connallys (when seen in fuzzy focus).

The presidential limo is another matter. We've been unable to find a close match for SS100X, the custom-built 1961 Lincoln Continental designed by Ford that transported JFK. Next best is a 1962

---

6 Grip truck: a vehicle used by film crews to transport production equipment. Grip: a technician responsible for setting up and adjusting such equipment on a set. Several versions of the term's origin exist; from a valise or "grip" in which stagehands in theater carried their tools. Or from the need for a strong person who could get a firm "grip" on heavy stage equipment.

The term "gaffer," for a lighting technician, comes from the days when stagehands controlled natural lighting with large tent cloths on long polls. Beached seamen or longshoremen often worked as stagehands, and a "gaff" is a type of boom on a sailing ship.

184

sedan that I locate through an ad in the *L.A. Times*. The owner agrees to a $2000 purchase price. And agrees to buy the car back for $700 after we've chopped the top off and modified it for the film.

Finally, Gary and a second unit cameraman fly to Dallas for helicopter shots of Dealey Plaza. They film early, when few cars are on the streets. And we hope no one will notice that these are not 1963 (or earlier) models.

Done at last. Finished. I haven't been home before 10 p.m. for a month, then it's been up at dawn and off again. Same for everyone. The wrap party is appropriately lavish. Crab meat and cakes, delicacies galore. Well, I mean, Eddie has to do *something* to make up for all those skinny wages and bleary hours.

Now for the editing. Irving Lerner, a gifted and gentle soul – he directed *Studs Lonigan* (1960) and *Royal Hunt of the Sun* (1969) – brings in a long first cut. I never see it, but Eddie is less than thrilled; it drags, he tells me. With George Grenville taking over and with Eddie's two cents tossed in, the film is restructured and whittled to a releasable ninety-one minutes.

Randy Edelman, who goes on to score such films as *My Cousin Vinny* (1992) and *Dragonheart* (1996), creates music for this, his first theatrical feature. The almost eerie score utilizes snatches of everything from "The Eyes of Texas Are Upon You," to haunting themes of Randy's own.

Meanwhile, with graphic designer Bill Brown I create main and end titles. Stills for the main are images of corporate power with credits playing over them. For the end title, a startling piece of copy that rolls up just before the final credits:

> "In the three-year period which followed the murder of President Kennedy and Lee Harvey Oswald, eighteen material witnesses died – six by gunfire, three in motor accidents, two by suicide, one from a cut throat, one from a karate chop to the neck, three from heart attacks and two from natural causes. An actuary engaged by the *London Sunday Times* concluded that on November 22, 1963, the odds against these witnesses being dead by February, 1967, were one hundred thousand trillion to one."

Unable to acquire actual photos of these witnesses before the film's scheduled debut (plus the legal releases required), I create the rollup using photos of seventeen close friends. And when I can't find an eighteenth that seems right, I slip my own photo in.

We preview for the press at the Directors Guild of America. Days later, November 7, 1973, two weeks before the tenth anniversary of JFK's assassination, the film opens across the country. And is a big splash for six weeks. Soon after its release I catch it again in Berkeley with friends. Lines are around the block.

Reviews are all over the lot. Vincent Canby, in *The New York Times* calls the film "a shabby fiction," put together with "pious, unexciting, low-keyed professionalism." Joan Mellen, of *Cineaste*, while welcoming "any film attempting to penetrate and expose the tissue of lies presented to the American people as the report of the Warren Commission," is at the same time annoyed because "*Executive Action* subtly undermines the most powerful aspects of the evidence discovered by the historical analysts." Crediting the film with raising important issues, she then castigates it because it

EXECUTIVE ACTION

"indirectly absolves the government agency [the CIA] of all knowledge of the killing." Thus, she feels the film says "that the government was innocent of complicity in Kennedy's murder."

Like Mark Lane and Don Fried, authors of the book the film is based on, Ms Mellen didn't seem to understand that in 1973 a major Hollywood film would simply never have been distributed, let alone be made, had it fingered the U.S. government and the Central Intelligence Agency as being directly responsible for the assassination.

Ralph Gleason, in *Rolling Stone*, calls the picture "a remarkable piece of filmmaking," with "poetic truth"; the *Christian Science Monitor* concludes it's review with the assessment that "despite cinematic shortcomings and unresolved issues of taste" the film "largely succeeds on its own terms." A group of senators, including Lowell Weicker of Connecticut, Mike Mansfield of Montana and Ernest Hollings of South Carolina, are deeply moved after seeing the film. Weicker, who calls it "well done," is more concerned with censorship, implied in the initial refusal of some TV networks to accept ads for the movie.

While making *Executive Action*, Eddie Lewis has been buttering me up with hints that I'll produce other projects. *The Blue Bird* (cited above) is one. I never become involved; perhaps fortunately, considering the disaster it becomes. But I do go see the picture. There are maybe three people in a theater seating a thousand. There are maybe three people in every theater in which it plays.

Ishi, Theodora Kroeber's history of the last Native American found living in the wild, is to be a Wakeford-Orloff production, with TV commercial director Joe Hanwright at the helm. Based on Eddie's word that we'll be involved, Joe and I put unpaid weeks into the project. Ultimately, none of us work on the picture. Not Joe, not me, not W/O. The film is released in 1978 as a movie of the week, with Dalton Trumbo's touching script rewritten by his son, Chris, after Dalton dies. Though Eddie has forgotten any mention of involving Hanwright or me, or W/O, when released as an "Edward

REELING THROUGH HOLLYWOOD

and Millie Lewis Production" Gary Horowitz reminds Eddie that he's signed a letter of agreement for W/O to produce, and collects a wad from Lewis for reneging. I collect bubkas.

But why complain? Before Wakeford-Orloff is sold to Howard Brown, who drowns the company in a tsunami of debt and leaves me at the ass end of a small army of creditors, I receive almost $12,000 in royalties for my one third of four percent of the producers net share of profits. That, plus the $7500 producers fee isn't so shabby, considering.

Or is it? Soon after the picture opens, when Eddie asks me to zip out to Burt Lancaster's home and deliver an envelope with his first royalty check, ten percent of the distributor's gross, I peek – and note the figure: $870,000. At the door, Burt smiles and says, "Thank you." I have no idea what Eddie's share comes to. National General's full-page ad in *Variety* for January 22, 1974 thanks Eddie Lewis and announces an anticipated $30,000,000 world gross for *Executive Action*. (Even before the film opens, Eddie has negotiated a $5,000,000 deal for a release in Japan.)

Adding up my hours, my twenty grand probably comes to $10 per. Bummer! And pushing folks to work cheap, firing actors and popping Emprine codeine for weeks is certainly a drain on the creative psyche.

Perhaps there'd have been fewer sleepless nights if I'd hired on as an extra.

Time slips away. Within six months *Executive Action* is mostly forgotten. But seven years later Pop still sends clippings whenever the film shows up in some remote venue:

30 May 1980

This came from a friend in the German Democratic Republic. *Executive Action* was shown on their TV, he says, on 3 February. CALL UP ED LEWIS IMMEDIATELY & DEMAND YOUR SHARE OF ROYALTIES!

EXECUTIVE ACTION

I never do. My share is tied in with W/O's royalties and that company has fallen on bankrupt days.

But recall for a moment Eddie Lewis's excited, "Millie, he asked for *white wine*," on the day I came to his house to read the screenplay for the first time. Recall my reminder that "movie people grasp at shadows." If both the potential producer and director of a film appear to be in sync, this must be an omen. The film is going to make millions! And indeed it did. Pots of money. For Eddie. For Burt Lancaster. And for Wakeford-Orloff too, which, before Howard Brown ran it into the ground, sold its interest back to Eddie for a wad of cash. But no more for me. Nor for the crew that worked their asses off. We never saw another dime.

Still want to be a producer?

If you do, I hope it will be as a conscionable person. Not as one of those job-shifting, "musical chairs" execs who, failing to produce in one place, or having turned out a string of disasters, gets endlessly reborn at one studio after another. And I hope you won't let yourself fall for the "I'm the hottest thing since sliced bread" syndrome; the kind of man or woman who, within six months of entering the business, finds him or herself heading a major studio. Hollywood seems to do that to people, thriving on mediocre executive competence. Or it simply moves people up the ladder on the basis of glad-handing or sexy good looks.

Not a way to run a business.

189

TWENTY

henry who?

FLASHFORWARD TO:

A TV STUDIO. HOLLYWOOD, CALIFORNIA. 2002 — DAY

A TWENTY-SOMETHING PRODUCER is talking with Dan Bessie's friend and former employer, SID GALANTY.

> TWENTY-SOMETHING PRODUCER
> Oh, you're a director. Do I know your work?

> GALANTY
> Well, I made a whole series of Jane Fonda's workout tapes.

> TWENTY-SOMETHING PRODUCER
> Jane who?

> GALANTY
> Jane Fonda.

> TWENTY-SOMETHING PRODUCER
> Don't know the name. Is that Bridget's mother?

SID GALANTY. ON THE PHONE WITH DAN BESSIE

> GALANTY
> It was at that point I knew it was time for me to get out of the business.

I'm fifteen years into my film career when I first meet Jane, in 1971, at meetings of her Entertainment Industry for Peace and Justice. There is a lot of lounging around on giant pillows (provided by Jane) in the group's office on Sunset Boulevard in Hollywood. Don Sutherland, with whom she's been entertaining soldiers in her FTA (Free the Army or Fuck the Army. Take your choice) anti-Vietnam War show, and who is also at nearly every meeting, is an amusing guy who reminds me of a bloodhound. While we're trying to figure out how to rally artists to join the cause, while at the same time trying not to alienate those who feel they need to support the troops in the field, Donald sometimes falls asleep.

Set up to oppose the war and to champion other progressive causes, the Committee lasts only a year or two. After that, Jane, ever the activist, is off with new hubby Tom Hayden to find out for herself what's going on in North Vietnam. This is her second trip. On her first, in 1972, she'd been photographed in the seat of a North Vietnamese anti-aircraft gun, and had broadcast to American troops from Hanoi. (Incidents that would forever win her the enmity of a number of Vietnam-era soldiers.)[1]

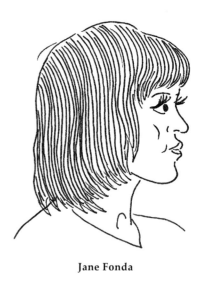

Jane Fonda

Spring 1974. Tom and Jane are back in Los Angeles. Along with Tom and Academy Award winning cinematographer Haskell Wexler (*One Flew Over the Cuckoo's Nest*, 1975; *Coming Home*, 1978), Jane has been mucking about in dank underground tunnels, and documenting the Viet Cong in action, the devastation of the North by American bombs, and the misery of average Vietnamese.

---

[1] For her own view of her Vietnam experiences, see Jane's heartfelt and thoughtful biography, *My Life So Far* (2005).

Henry Who?

She has called to invite me to a screening of this footage at the offices of her manager, major Hollywood player Mike Medavoy. I arrive with Kaaren, a close friend, probably expecting in the back of my mind to dazzle my companion with all the important people I'm acquainted with.

I never do ask Kaaren if she was dazzled. But do recall Jane saying how delighted she is that I've shown up. Then, as I rattle on she indicates a tall, graying-at-the-temples gentleman standing next to her, and interrupts my effusive blather with "Dan, I'd like you to meet Henry."

Henry Fonda in various roles

"Oh, hi, Henry," say I, with barely an acknowledging glance at him. And I go right on blathering.

Henry, one eyebrow significantly arched (I'm at least conscious of that), stares at me oddly. There's something familiar about that stare. Those sad, haunting eyes. That chiseled Nebraska face. I know it . . . Long pause . . . Of course: it's Tom Jode (*The Grapes of Wrath*, 1940); juror #8 (*Twelve Angry Men*, 1957), Norman Thayer Jr. (*On Golden Pond*, 1981); Mister Roberts, young Abe Lincoln, and a hundred other big screen characters my generation has come to know and love. It's Jane's dad! Henry Fonda.

Instead of groveling in apology and explaining to Henry that I've escaped from Miss Manners Asylum for Rude Behavior, I nibble hors d'oeuvres, schmooze and make small talk with Kaaren and Jane and a crowd of others waiting to see the footage. Then, seizing on a moment when he'd retreated alone to a corner, I trap Henry and mumble a fawning complement about how much I've enjoyed his performances over the years. Henry forces a stiff half smile, nods then gracefully glides away.

Perhaps, like friend Sid Galanty's revelation, I should have taken this brief encounter as a broad hint. Did I lack the character for building a life in the movie game?

At the time, I didn't think that way. Like my brief fantasy about Ms Playmate of the Year for 1964, I was probably caught up in the glamour of the moment; with the vague impression that by associating with the glitterati I might find their success rubbing off on me. Not that this was ever conscious. It wasn't. But as with ignorance of the law, failure to focus is no excuse. It takes strength of character to see beyond the tinsel, to understand that nothing succeeds like steady competence, learning to master one's craft, working hard and then hoping for the best result. Dropping famous names may draw breathless sighs from those whose interests rarely range beyond *People* magazine, but won't get you very far unless your skills are such that they contribute in some meaningful way to whatever art form, job or endeavor you chose to become involved in.

Yes, faking it and snuggling "close to the tit" (as it's often put in Hollywood) sometimes does bring fame and fortune. But more often than not the work such people turn out is mediocre or routine. I always hoped for more than that. Though I didn't recognize it at the time, I still had a lot to learn. And it would take me the rest of my career to learn it.

Book Five

changes

There is nothing permanent except change.

Heraclitus

You gain strength, courage and confidence by every experience in which you really stop to look fear in the face . . .
You must do the thing you think you cannot do.

Eleanor Roosevelt

TWENTY-ONE

the graveyard of good ideas

And some probably not so good.

Credit on a successful movie like *Executive Action*, I hoped, would be my ticket to play in the big boys sandbox. Because stressful as working on the production has been, I've definitely caught the feature film bug. And I've got a trunk full of projects.

Though Learning Garden has turned out several shorts, for me, educational distribution is withering on the vine. School districts, accustomed to free previews, take weeks to return a print. And most don't buy. With only four titles, not enough of a track record to attract more, and no real business plan, I'm unable to generate steady sales. So, what to do? The answer is obvious. Turn the four films over to another distribution company (which I do). And, since my name is up there on the opening credits of a big grossing and widely known movie, go knocking on doors. Which I also start to do.

INT. ROGER CORMAN'S OFFICE. SPRING, 1974 — DAY

ROGER CORMAN, graying at the temples, sits with his feet on his desk. He's smiling. In front of him sits an EAGER PRODUCER. He's pitching.

> EAGER PRODUCER
> It's about the Spanish Civil War, see. 1938. We begin with three men in a touring car, on a bridge in Barcelona. One is Ernest Hemingway. Suddenly, an airplane zooms into the shot and --

REELING THROUGH HOLLYWOOD

                    CORMAN
Airplanes? Hemingway? 1938? You're talking millions.
                    (sighs)
Look, you want to produce? Great. Bring me a terrific
script. Like *Swamp Women*, or *Premature Burial*. You
know the kind of stuff I do. I'll put up fifty thousand,
you get a few deferments, and we've got a deal.

Eager Producer gets up, in high dudgeon.

                 EAGER PRODUCER
Well, if I ever want to make that kind of movie I'll
let you know.

                    CORMAN
             (rising, his smile gone)
You do that. You just do that!

A stiff, formal handshake and the interview is terminated.

So too is my first chance to direct a feature.

This kind of behavior when someone offers to help you, even
with an exploitation quickie, is shortsighted and rude. While you
need to stick to your creative guns and aim high, recall that long
before *The Godfather* (1972) Frances Ford Coppola cranked out
Dementia 13 (for Corman, in 1963), as well as such fluff as *The Bellboy
and the Playgirls* (1962). Doesn't mean you need to do that quickie if
it offends your sensibilities, but tactful consideration and grateful
thanks are certainly in order.

No Roger Corman movie. So here I sit at my Learning Garden
desk, wondering what direction to take. And mulling over projects
I've dreamed up, talked about, developed and which have eventually gone nowhere since I walked into MGM some eighteen years
before. Everything from an idea for a national animation workshop
that I thought of pitching to the Ford Foundation, to a failed line of

The Graveyard of Good Ideas

greeting cards Rose and I designed, to screenplays I have no concept of how to write (since at that time I'd never written one). Well, I figure, Pop can do those.

Then too, he's developed screenplays of his own:

The Only Child: which finds a doctor in a moral crisis after he's called on to save the life of a crazed young man who has killed the doctor's daughter.

The S Bomb: a sexy stripper is the only one who can read telepathic signals from an alien sent to warn Earth about nuclear annihilation.

One For My Baby: a menagerie of oddballs populates a 1950s nightclub. (Based on Pop's gig at San Francisco's hungry i and on his 1980 novel of the same title.)

Bread and a Stone: an uneducated drifter kills a man while trying to find money to support his family. (Stay tuned. This one gets made.)

I keep trying to push all these. Plus, while working with Gary Horowitz and Les Goldman, *The Hostages* and *Mother Night* (Pop hates it, calls it "Motherfucker Night"). And more: *Bread and Roses,* a story of the Lawrence, Massachusetts textile strike of 1912; *Windmills in Brooklyn* (1960), a tender memoir about Spanish-American cigar makers in the 1920s; *Naked Among Wolves*, in which a tiny boy is smuggled into the Buchenwald concentration camp in a suitcase; *Mesada*, chronicling the defense of the holy land fortress by Jewish zealots in 72 A.D.; *A Cool Million*, Nathaniel West's great parody on the Horatio Alger stories (1934).[1]

And still more: Peter Begal's *The California Feeling* (1969), about a couple traveling the state in a VW bus called Lucretia Borgia; Bertolt Brecht's *The Threepenny Opera*, an animated feature transferred from Berlin to the American west; a film on abolitionist John Brown, one on jazz great Jelly Roll Morton, another on the *Enola Gay*, the B-

---

[1] Horatio Alger, Jr. (1824-99) was a prolific writer of dime novels for boys. His sales, beginning with his debut book *Ragged Dick* (1867) rivaled those of Stephen King's today.

29 that bombed Hiroshima. And we came close to optioning a book Spielberg later made into *Amistad*. Indeed, several of the above eventually got produced. By others, of course.[2]

Though projects die I keep trying, with —

You Might as Well Live (1970): a bio about Pop's longtime friend, writer Dorothy Parker. I take it to Eddie Lewis, who makes cooing noises. If Streisand bites, he says, John Frankenheimer will direct and we'll have a done deal. Barbra doesn't bite. (In 1994, Alan Rudolph directs *Mrs. Parker and the Vicious Circle*.)[3]

The Rebellion of the Hanged (1952): a horrifying yet valiant tale of a revolt by mahogany forest workers in Yucatan, from a novel by B. Traven (*Treasure of the Sierra Madre*, 1948). I negotiate a short free option (the book has been filmed once, in Mexico), acquire a copy of Traven's original screenplay and pitch it to Eddie. "Too grim," says Lewis.

Rip Van Winkle: a musical adapted from Washington Irving's tale set in pre-revolutionary America. Robert Wise (*West Side Story*, 1961; *The Sound of Music*, 1965) is grabbed by the idea, but his studio, Universal, is down on revolutionary war material. Mattel Toys also passes.

And, would you believe, a theme park concept: The Land of Oz. Brilliant (if I do say so). I envision the park in the shape of a gigantic donut. Groups of visitors, greeted by "Dorothy," enter a Kansas farmhouse. The house shakes, whirls about, rises in the air then lands with a thump. Visitors then exit (through another door) and follow the yellow brick road through Oz, meeting in turn, Scarecrow, Tin Woodman and Cowardly Lion. Each of whom, along with Dorothy, protects them as they journey to the castle of the Wicked

---

[2] For example: *Mesada* (1981) became a TV mini series, with Peter O'Tolle and Peter Strauss. To date, two versions of the Enola Gay story have been filmed (in 1980 and 1995).

[3] Based on the crowd that gathered during the 1920 and 30s at New York's Algonquin Hotel. The group included Parker, Harpo Marx, Harold Ross (founder of *The New Yorker*), critic Alexander Wollcott, playwrights George S. Kaufman, Edna Ferber, Marc Connelly and Robert Sherwood, humorist Robert Benchley and others.

The Graveyard of Good Ideas

Witch of the West. They vanquish her then leave for home in a carnival balloon (escorted by the Wizard, of course). Employment for a legion of Dorothys, Scarecrows and Wizards, since each party will need its own set of guides. And guests can enter the middle of the "donut" at any time for rides and refreshments then join another group on the continuing adventure whenever they want.

I write to the L. Frank Baum estate. They like the idea, but reply that unless I can come up with concrete backing they see no point in talking about rights.

Gee folks, all I need is forty million bucks! Too bad Michael Jackson is only sixteen years old in 1974.

While theme parks are little more than a dream, staying involved in features is uppermost. I continue thinking back.

In May of 1972 I had met author James Baldwin at a party in support of Angela Davis and her involvement in the Soledad Brothers case.[4] "You know," I said, after we shook hands, "I've just read *The Amen Corner*, and I think it would make a terrific movie." His eyes brightened. "I've always wanted to see that as a film. Write me. Here's my address in Paris." He scribbled it on one of my business cards. I wrote two letters. He never replied. Of course he didn't; I had no solid contacts, no option money. No funds to commission a

[4] See *Soledad Brother: the Prison Letters of George Jackson, Angela Davis: An Autobiography* (1970), or the 1977 film *Brothers*, starring Bernie Casey and Vonetta McGee (produced by Edward and Millie Lewis and by Sid Galanty)

screenplay. And only the fuzziest notion of how to get a feature off the ground. Nor were many of my ideas what Hollywood usually thought of as commercial.

Except perhaps, *World Without End, Amen.*

One of Gary Horowitz's TV commercial directors, Stan Dragotti, had optioned this novel by Jimmy Breslin (published in 1973). The story found a New York cop on vacation in the Old Sod getting mixed up in the "troubles," and falling for an Irish radical somewhat like freedom fighter Bernadette Devlin. With Gary and Stan, I had met to discuss the project at Stan's home in Beverly Hills, over a lunch served by his wife, the gorgeous megamodel Cheryl Tiegs.

Stan wanted to pitch the book to Jane Fonda, so I called her and set a lunch meeting at the Bistro on Canon Drive. Except that I had mistakenly told her the restaurant was on a different street. At the Bistro, with Jane running fifteen minutes late, I suddenly freaked. I'd given her the wrong address! So I jumped up, dashed out and raced one block over. And there was Jane, cruising Crescent Drive in her green Volvo station wagon. And doing a slow boil. I swallowed humble pie as I climbed in and directed her around the corner to the Bistro's parking lot.

All during lunch Jane ignored the gawks and chit chat from other patrons that always takes place when a star appears. After we finished and I walked her back to the Volvo, Jane chewed me out. "Jesus, Dan," she said, "how come you kept interrupting him all the time?"

THE GRAVEYARD OF GOOD IDEAS

"Did I?"

"You did. You kept trying to explain the story. Couldn't you have just let Stan outline the project without jumping in every two seconds?" I cut another slice of humble pie, mumbling apologies for my hyperactive attempt at deal making.

"That's OK," she replied, tossing me a killer smile, "I got the general sense of what he wants to do with the book." Then she gave me a big hug and was into the Volvo and away. I slunk back to Wakeford-Orloff and apologized to Stan, who brushed it off.

Soon after, Bob Young, who co-wrote without credit (so he claimed) *The Hustler* (1961) with Robert Rossen, was hired to do an adaptation of the book. Jane never did the project. In fact, its never been filmed. Stan Dragotti would later direct *Love at First Bite* (1979), *Mr. Mom* (1983) and *Necessary Roughness* (1991). And get divorced.

Cheryl Tiegs would never make lunch for me again.

Long sigh. Enough scanning inscriptions in the bone yard. How can I launch a project? If I only had something to show Baldwin... Or had optioned some obviously commercial property. Difficult, because my sensibilities constantly gravitate toward "small" stories and Hollywood mostly wants blockbusters. Maybe, I decide, it's time to create my own screenplays? And since I've directed second unit on *Executive Action*, along with one or two educational films, why should I keep hiring others to do what I ought to be able to do myself?

Time to a give it a shot.

TWENTY-TWO

wordsmithing

> I've always believed that you learn by doing. Not that school isn't productive, but there's no substitute for plunging in and getting your hands dirty. This is as true of the arts as with anything in life. The only thing that can hold you back is fear. Fear of not "getting it right." And that very fear makes learning more difficult. By doing, the fear usually dissipates. And while mastery may take a while, letting go of the fear and charging toward your goal is half the journey. That's what I learned as I began to write screenplays.

The Last Volunteer, the Spanish Civil War story I had pitched to Roger Corman, was my first. And that was a rewrite. Lacking confidence, I had Pop and another Spanish Civil War vet (also a writer) craft an adventure based loosely on the life of the last volunteer to join the Abraham Lincoln Battalion fighting General Franco in Spain (1936-38).[1] This was an exciting tale. Both political and historically colorful, *The Last Volunteer* was, I felt, an idea that with the right ingredients might have blockbuster potential.

In January of 1974, Gary Horowitz and I had lunch with Jane Fonda (before she went off to Vietnam for the second time), during which I mentioned the project. There would be a starring role for her as a nurse and ambulance driver, also volunteering in Spain. Jane was interested. So Pop and the other writer each wrote an out-

---

[1] The volunteer was James Lardner, youngest son of Ringold (Ring) Lardner (1885-1933), one of America's most famous sports writers and humorists.

Wordsmithing

line. Then, with my feedback, both wrote screenplays. But Pop's was overly melodramatic, the other, heavy with superfluous detail. So, having at least read a bunch of well-written scripts by now, I thought, well, maybe I should tackle this. It seemed largely a matter of taking what Pop and the other writer had done and, with cutting and adjustment, creating a piece that had stronger characterizations and a more up to date and compelling story. Two months later I had turned both screenplays into a new, but still far too long version: a hundred eighty pages. Then I trimmed it to a hundred fifty. Still too long.

As I rewrote, I fed pages to Jane. We met at the Santa Monica home she shared with husband Tom Hayden, and from which I pushed her daughter Vanessa, in a stroller, to a local café. There, we story-conferenced over lunch (Jane kept slim with a salad). She really liked the first act. But the more pages I handed her the more her enthusiasm faded. "The love story," she said, "gets in the way of the politics." Or vice versa, I wasn't quite sure what she meant. Unfortunately, she didn't offer specific feedback and I didn't know how to push her to do so.

Eventually, she moved on to other projects. I moved on with *The Last Volunteer*, pitching it everywhere. It raised important Hollywood eyebrows and was optioned twice, but somehow it still remained a rumpled bed: unmade. In the mid 1990s I rewrote it again, cutting twenty-five more pages. It still isn't quite there. One of these days . . .

Undeterred, I keep on writing:

The Chickenbone Special is based on a warmhearted book of the same name (1971). Essentially a series of non-fiction vignettes, the story follows four groups of rural blacks leaving for the North during the late 1960s. I take an option – for a mere $300; with little known works it's often possible to make such deals – and write a fair screenplay. But agent feedback indicates it will be an unlikely sale. Too "soft." And since its topicality soon fades, off it goes to the graveyard of good ideas.

In *Joaquin*, a bounty-hunting posse stampedes across California, tracking the legendary bandito Joaquin Murieta. Based on an idea I have and drawn from a number of books about Joaquin, Pop writes a respectable script (and, ever the ham, writes himself a part as a crusty reporter). Somehow it doesn't capture the flavor of the period or the main character, so Severo Perez and I rewrite it. A dozen copies go out. Mild interest comes in, but ultimately a dozen "thanks but no thanks" arrive in the mail.

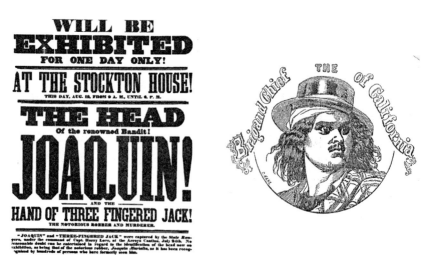

Period flyer (L) inviting the curious to come view Joaquin's head

But then an obviously commercial property lands on my doorstep. Donald Freed, co-author of the book on which *Executive Action* had been based, asks me to read a script he's written. Another assassination film about another Kennedy brother.

WORDSMITHING

Hey, this sounds exciting!

RFK Must Die finds Sirhan Sirhan hypnotically programmed to kill presidential candidate Robert Kennedy. And I'm asked to produce it. The script is political, which is fine with me, but it is also way too didactic. So I insist on doing a rewrite. Via Mike Selsman – partner with myself, Gary Horowitz and Michael Campus (*The Mack*, 1973; *The Passover Plot*, 1976) in a never-gets-to-second base company, Group Four Productions[2] – my rewrite goes to football great Jim Brown, who we want for the role of an FBI man. Orson Welles, who is to play the conspirator who programs Sirhan to kill RFK, also gets a copy. Meanwhile, Don Freed's executive producer, his sister-in-law Virginia, is hustling production money from Texas. And almost nails it. But then comes word that insurance carriers demand a $250,000 deposit against the possibility of legal action by Sirhan. The budget soars. By now, contracts have been signed with Welles and Brown. The investors are jittery. Then Virginia makes a deal with AVCO-Embassy, which insists on naming its own producer. So I am out. Then in again, because Virginia has a written agreement with me. Then Orson Welles decides to write his own script. Then everything falls apart. End of story.

Later, I create my first original. Initially called *Babyface*, when a film with that title appears it becomes *Working Girls*. And when that title is also taken, *Off the Ropes*. In this gritty, down home screenplay – on the order of John Huston's *Fat City* (1972) – a huge, tender-hearted African-American woman and her nervy and emotionally damaged white companion travel California's Central Valley wrestling circuit during the 1950s. The little one becomes the manager for the big one, who wrestles. As the story builds, all the women wrestlers, along with sympathetic truck drivers, get together to fight off a band of scumbag promoters and win the day.

---

[2] Group Four did produce one film, a pilot for a series to be called *The Interview*. John Wilkes Booth, who murdered Abraham Lincoln, was the first interviewee. We commissioned my father to write a second script: Jeanne d'Arc. He wrote in Jane Fonda as the interviewer. None of us liked it. And the networks had handled similar material in a more imaginative way.

Sam Arkoff at American International is interested. Jim Aubrey (who had, at different times, headed both CBS and MGM) is interested. But both want the other to pay for a rewrite. Stalemate. Five years later I will revisit it myself. No takers. Ten years later I'll rewrite it again. Roger Corman (who has perhaps forgotten our past contretemps) takes a look. And passes. As I write this, it gathers dust.

But wrestling continues to be a huge, crowd-pleasing draw. *Off the Ropes* is a story with soul, and in spite of its subculture aura is no exploitation potboiler. Nostalgia for the sweaty grunts of yesteryear should make for an attractive package. Any takers?

There will be other screenplays, and I'll eventually spend more than twenty years teaching the craft.

Looking back on how I learned by doing, I also realized that becoming a director involved much the same path. Indeed, the process had started years before, while I was little more than a fledgling animator . . .

It is highly unlikely that any three-and-a-half page coverage could do justice to this expertly written screenplay. This story was handled with true drama and characterization, backed by a solid story line and historically accurate events — brought together to create a fantastic read and potential for one hell of a picture.

This screenplay contains all the elements: love, drama, war, real people, and a strong sense of history. The characterizations are sharp and real, with Allan's quest for heroics and the cause not only gripping but entertaining. This is a page-turner like I have yet to come across.

This screenplay successfully captures the period of this era with its attention to detail and the politics of a segment of World War II that is little treated in films. As for the style, it is treated with a Hemingwayesque romantic sensibility, with these characters and their quests defined and believable. This team of writers obviously know what they are writing about and obviously know how to do it well.

I recommend this screenplay for purchase with no reservations whatsoever.

Reader coverage comment on *The Last Volunteer*, **first screenplay I had a hand in.**

TWENTY-THREE

flashback: directors' boot camp

As *The Last Volunteer* was my first screenplay (though a rewrite), so *High Blood Pressure* was the first live action film I directed all the way through. While the title doesn't have the cachet of *Harry Potter and the Sorcerer's Stone* (2001), to me the assignment was just as magical. All I'd directed to that point had been half a dozen shots on the consumer education film, *Buyer Beware*, and an empty hospital corridor for another film.

Animation had been a great training ground for live action, because the shooting ratio was invariably one to one. Every shot was planned in advance (often based on a storyboard) and editing consisted of simply snipping off spare footage at the beginning or end of a scene, then adding music and effects. You couldn't "save" the film in the cutting room. If the story wasn't there when you planned and photographed the art, it simply wasn't there. So by the time I started directing live action the skill had become second nature. I was able to pretty much think the structure out in advance and knew what the end product would probably look like.

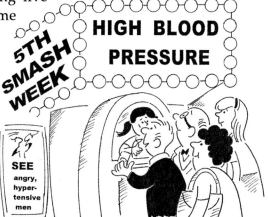

Even without having an animation background, acquiring the skill to direct isn't that

209

difficult. Paying close attention to the arrangement of shots as you watch films, then doing the same thing in your head before and during a shoot, will usually produce an adequate result. From there on it's a matter of practice. Working with actors is something else again. But even there, casting skilled pros is ninety percent of the job.

High Blood Pressure starred a hypertensive dad who jumped up, waving and shouting, to urge his kid on in a Little League game. As director, I hired myself. Though I too was a bit hyper, I quickly found it natural to edit in my head. As I choreographed the shots I could see the cuts: the kid smacking the ball; his dad jumping up; the kid racing the bases; dad again, purple with rage as his son slides for home and is called out by the ump. The actor pulled off his role so well that I was afraid he might keel over.

In fact, this wasn't precisely a medical film. "Patient-counseling" more correctly defines it. *High Blood Pressure*, along with a raft of other titles I'd eventually produce and direct, was made for doctor's offices.

This had all begun back in 1965, during my year on the *Marvel Superheroes* TV series. During coffee break one day, fellow scribbler Ed DeMattia announced that someone had phoned him, looking for animators to moonlight on a film.[1] None of the other animators were interested. Forty hours a week chained to a desk while penciling Iron Man or Captain America was enough to prepare the crew of older and often cynical guys to spend the weekend attacking crabgrass. Or hit the bottle. Or both. But I was game. (Thirty-three years old, mortgage payments and a hefty credit union debt.) So after work Ed and I dropped by an office near Beverly Hills where a gregarious middle-aged couple, Al and Barbara Williams, had set up shop to produce patient-counseling films.

As quickly became apparent, Al knew much less about making films than I did. Paunchy, with energy to burn, he spent the next

---

[1] Ed DeMattia's career began at Disney in 1938, and included stints at MGM, Walter Lantz, Warner and Hanna-Barbera, among other studios. He died in 1997.

Flashback: Directors' Boot Camp

hour explaining that he wanted us to animate a storyboard he'd created and taped to the wall. The subject? Pregnancy. Ed and I didn't say much, a lot of head nodding mostly. Then Al said, "OK, I think you've got it. We're going to dinner. If we decide not to come back, just lock up." Then he and Barbara were out the door.

Ed and I looked at one another. We had only a vague notion of what was expected, but we plunged in. And worked several more evenings and a long weekend to complete the assignment. "Great job," said Al. He and Barbara would take it from there, get the artwork shot and see the show through editing.

Two weeks later, Ed crossed to my desk as I was carving out a scene from The Hulk. "Al isn't happy," he said. "He wants everything redone right away." Not that he'd been dissatisfied with our animation. OK, then how come he wants it done over? Because it didn't work the way he thought it would. And he's got a new vision. Then Ed added, "Look, I've got stuff to do. If you want to take it on yourself, be my guest." So I did. Another few evenings, another weekend, and this time Al was satisfied. Almost. About half of it was OK. The rest he had me redo one more time.

Al Williams is simply one of several entrepreneurs I've come across during forty years in film who lack much ability to visualize. Until they see the final result they're often clueless about whether or not their concept will work.

But Al did have a unique idea. Most doctors, he reasoned, must spend huge blocks of time counseling patients, easing fears about an individual's disease or condition; unlike the harried clinician with a heavy case load who plunks a cold stethoscope onto your chest, squeezes your boobs or sticks an inquisitive finger up your wazoo and then prescribes.

Al realized that most patients had identical concerns. So what if, instead of doctors having to recite the same information over and over, a patient could walk into his or her physician's office and, before they were summoned to the inner sanctum, view a short film dealing with the general aspect of their condition. That way, Al figured, doctors could spend their valuable counseling time dealing with the patient's specific complaint.

Brilliant idea. How come I didn't think of it?

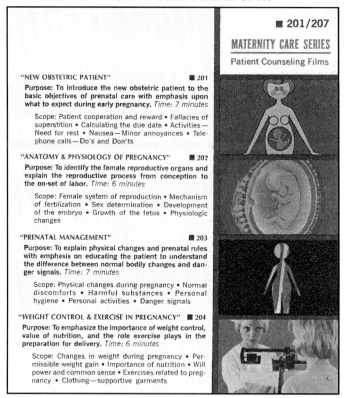

Al and Barbara formed Professional Research, Inc (PRI) then sold the concept to a major player in the health field, American Medical Enterprises, which agreed to back them.

The next clever part of the scheme was that instead of selling prints, PRI would *lease* each film to doctors, along with a boxy rear screen projector, kind of like a TV, on which the films would be shown. On a continuous, rewindable, 8mm loop. This was BVT (before videotape) of course. And everything was rented on a monthly basis. So, for example, an obstetrician who wanted the whole line of PRI films paid maybe $1000 a year for titles such as

Flashback: Directors' Boot Camp

"New Obstetric Patient," "Anatomy and Physiology of Pregnancy," "Prenatal Management," etc. A gold mine for PRI, a fat tax deduction for the physician.

Within months, PRI had moved to new offices on La Brea Avenue; from which location I received an urgent call every now and then to "come in and help us out, Dan, we've got to put a show to bed by the end of next week." Al was always down to the wire. Same story as in every business: "You want it *when*?" Yesterday.

Inariably, the process repeated itself. Along with a clever and flamboyant commercial artist and a fine medical illustrator, I burned the midnight oil to get the work out on Al's crazy deadlines. But always did. Fortunately (or perhaps unfortunately) he left us alone. Then, a few days after the animation had been shot, he'd announce that he wanted "changes." Which involved redoing a big part (and sometimes all) of the work, because Al now had a more interesting concept. And it drove everyone nuts, including his perpetually smiling wife, Barbara, who ran around like a mother hen, soothing jangled egos (especially Al's).

Although the films were eminently worthwhile I always got a squeamish feeling when I looked up now and then from my animation. On the shelf above were jars of formaldehyde Al had borrowed from a medical school; containing perhaps a human kidney, a fetus, or the eyeball of an ox.

"The eyeball," he said, holding up a jar, "will help you make sure it's accurate."

At the time, I was animating a pair of orbs floating in space that moved up, down and sideways, contrasting normal movement with that found in patients with strabismus (crossed eyes).

Working on these titles I learned more about the human

body than I had ever wanted to know. And about directing too, because everything had to be planned in advance. Except for Al's mania, the work was fairly satisfying, since my skills served a better purpose describing glaucoma than they did ripping off Bruce Banner's clothes as he morphed into the Incredible Hulk. Even though the films were rented mainly to doctors with thriving practices (they had to be thriving in order to afford the fees), at least they passed on valuable information; guiding patients toward a better understanding of what ailed them.

What they didn't produce was a wad of extra cash for yours truly. As usual, I lacked the funds (when advised) to purchase a fistful of PRI stock just before it went public. (Today, such advice would be considered insider trading. At the time the company went public it was a "friendly tip.") As the stock doubled from $20 to $40, then to $80, Al and Barbara cleaned up. So too did the medical illustrator. The flamboyant graphic designer wasn't on board at that time, and Dan Bessie was barely squeaking by.

Changeable as Al Williams had been, planning animation for those patient-counseling films was marvelous training for the day in 1972 when I decided to take on *High Blood Pressure*. And for the day, two years later, when I'd begin directing live action on an entire series of these titles.

And not only direct, but also straw boss yet another studio operation.

TWENTY-FOUR

remember to wash your hands

My friend Elaine Smitham (married to Thom, my former partner in Circus Films) once said, "When the sun's barely up and you look out your window and a big truck arrives and there are a bunch of people getting out of cars and everyone starts hugging each other, you know it's a film crew, right?" Such was a typical seven a.m. scene at the many homes we filmed at during the eighteen months I was in charge of Media Medical Films, turning out patient counseling titles for Professional Research.

Fall 1974. Learning Garden had moved from Westwood to North Hollywood. (My landlord needed the space.)

The previous summer, Rose and I, burned out on Smogtown, had sold our Woodland Hills home and moved the family north to the pleasant village of Aptos, near Santa Cruz. To a rental surrounded by eucalyptus and within a stone's throw of the Pacific. But I continued to camp in my North Hollywood office four days a week. Because that's where the work was and so I could continue visiting Lisa, who was now living in a Los Angeles board and care home.

That summer, Rose, Joe, Tim and I were just back from Europe. Our first time there; financed by royalties from *Executive Action*, plus the annual Culligan spots.

Another reason for the trip was that Marianne Meyerhoff, who had worked for me gratis for a year (and who had been chauffeuring me to Burbank airport for my weekly commute) was due her promised reward – my promised funding of her film about the legendary 14th Century German prankster, Till Eulenspiegel. The $10,000 profit from the sale of our house just covered her production costs.

Shiny foot, because everyone rubs it for good luck

When we returned, Professional Research (now no longer run by the constantly changing mind of Al Williams) wanted to make more films. A lot of them.

So once again I'm working with pal Gary, with whom I've arranged for PRI to negotiate a deal. With me as head honcho of the production unit.[1] A sweet deal too, because for the first time in my life I earn significant and steady money. Not the megabucks that son Tim will eventually pull in as a programmer during the boom years of the computer industry, but enough. With a producer's fee for each title, plus a separate fee for those I choose to direct (eleven of the seventeen we finally turn out), my salary that year tops $65,000.[2] Diddle squat to those who aspire to millions, but in the mid-1970s as much as we need. And the most I'll ever earn in one year. More important, it's for work I mostly enjoy.

Who needs to be filthy rich anyhow? You perhaps? OK, sincere good luck.

By now, I'm confident directing live action. No more Buck Penningtons to terrorize the actors. No more fretting over whether or not a director will bring a shoot in on time and within budget. I haven't blown one since assuming the director's chair. Actually, I

---

[1] Soon after, I gave up Learning Garden's North Hollywood headquarters, but continued to run the company out of an office in Wakeford-Orloff's big Hollywood sound stage on Seward Street.

[2] In today's dollars that $65,000 would be a bit over $200,000.

never use a chair. My style involves moving around the set, lining up shots, working with the talent close up then framing shots for the camera myself. That way, I know what I'll get. Directing like this demands constant motion. Besides, the process is too exciting for me to be sitting on my duff.

With a terrific support crew that includes Marianne, now a paid production manager,[3] we turn out an average of a film a month. And have a hell of a lot of fun doing so, because dealing with serious subject matter and having to adhere to tight schedules it's natural to release tension by fooling around.

Shooting a PRI film. Assistant camera Chris Mankofsky (L) Sarah Bleick, myself, Marianne Meyerhoff

"Always remember to wash your hands" becomes a kind of in-joke. "Wash your hands" because several titles mention body parts or functions, and the pesky reminder that cleanliness is next to godliness. The anxiety provoking *Vasectomy*, for example; the pedantic *Care and Protection of Your Eyes*, the always exciting *Urinary Tract Infections*, and the voyeuristic *Breast Feeding*.

[3] Sarah Bleick supervised graphics and animation. Mal Pearce animated. Lois Eisenberg (who I stole from Sid Galanty) was our main production assistant. And we hired freelance directors, crew people and others as needed. Severo Perez did a fine job directing one title, *Laser Light Therapy*

Breast Feeding is voyeuristic because we can't find a pregnant woman who is able to lactate on cue in front of a camera. (With half a dozen crew looking on.) But Marianne discovers a mom-to-be from El Salvador. She too is skittish, so we dismiss everyone except cameraman Isidore Mankofsky.[4] Izzy and his Éclair camera and I then crowd into the bathtub. Because in order to check that she's lactating properly the woman has to look in the mirror. And from every other place in the bathroom she sees our reflection. And she prefers we don't watch. Even though we are! (Go figure.)

In the bathtub with Izzy Mankofsky

Vasectomy is anxiety provoking for any man. Perhaps more so when it's seen on film. So we deliberately cast an Italian-American stud-muffin as the vasectomee. He disrobes on camera, exposes his genitals, washes them then lies on a physician's table, preparing for the procedure. After it's completed, he puts an ice pack on his testicles so they'll heal quicker. No PRI film shows blood and gore; graphics and animation describe what's going on internally.

---

[4] Isidore Mankofsky went on to a long and successful career as director of photography on such films as *Homebodies* (1974), *The Muppet Movie* (1979), *Somewhere in Time* (1980), *The Burning Bed* (1984), and *The Absent-Minded Professor* (1988).

(Though a fuzzy-haired fellow director playing the physician does have something of a Doctor Frankenstein look about him, especially as he hovers over the actor with a scalpel and the camera zooms in.) For the vasectomy wounds a urologist draws appropriately purple scars on the actor's testicles. This same hunk (the actor, not the urologist) has also been featured in a then current TV series, so a couple months after *Vasectomy* is into distribution, when he appears on location in a Washington, D.C. hospital, a horde of smirking nurses crowd in to take a peek at this guy, whose "everything" they're already familiar with from having seen our little movie.

Care and Protection of Your Eyes warns people to wear goggles while working with dangerous materials, shows how to apply eye drops and offers advise about putting on makeup. We spell out an elaborate ritual: keeping makeup secure in a drawer, detailing how not to get it into the eyes, and warning about other ways folks might mess up their vision. With everything in the can we do a couple gag shots. For one, a woman reaching into her dresser drawer for cosmetics, we restage it with her shaking hand reaching in to pull out a joint. (There is also a hypodermic syringe lying in the drawer.) We make this a practice on almost every shoot. Silly, but it cracks us up and helps lighten the load, especially after a tedious day of Dr. Rick Sternberg, PRI's melancholy minder – who always takes making the films just as seriously as he needs to – checking to see that everything conforms to medical accuracy.

In April 1975, Professional Research runs out of money. Temporarily, they say. But with no idea how long before they'll secure more, Gary Horowitz isn't about to maintain half a dozen people on staff. So Media Medical Films closes up shop. By then my crew has become something of a family and looks forward to each new project, so the termination is a huge letdown.

My own little family has also terminated.

The previous fall, I separated from Rose for the third and final time. I had simply "lost the plot" (as the Brits would say) regarding sex, love and marriage. I didn't have a firm enough understanding of what they were about. But I did know that my continuing attraction to the string of women (some as confused as I)[5] who popped into my life while I was also in a marriage that basically "worked," indicated that a bolt was loose somewhere in my psychic machinery. Unable to tough it out (since my understanding made little headway), I concluded that the best thing to do was to go off on my own and try to find that loose bolt.

Also, the helpless feeling as I watched Lisa sink deeper and deeper into a secret and semi-psychotic world of fantasy had me grinding my teeth. At the same time, I was trying, not very successfully, to be a part time father to sons Joe and Tim.

Lisa (L), Tim and Joe

---

[5] One, not at all confused, was the delightful Leslie Parrish, featured on film and in TV from the 1950s through the 1970s (e.g. *The Manchurian Candidate* (1962). We met around anti Vietnam War activities and went out a few times - though Leslie wasn't up for more than a friendship. On one date, when I accompanied her to a piano recital at UCLA, conductor Zubin Metta sidled up to us, took Leslie's hand and offered me a smiling "excuse me," then spirited her away for a chat. Leslie later married author Richard Bach (*Jonathan Livingston Seagull*, 1970; *Bridge Across Forever*, 1984), and with him decided they would find eternal life on the astral plane. (They divorced in 1997, so I suppose the astral plane business is out.)

Remember to Wash Your Hands

Before Media Medical folded, Severo Perez, who had been at work on his own projects in a tiny room in our Seward Street complex, came into my office one afternoon to announce, "Dan, I'd like to buy Learning Garden from you." I was stunned. Though cranking out short films had begun to get a bit old, I hadn't thought of throwing in the towel. "Let me think about it," I replied after a long pause.

With Media down the tubes shortly thereafter, and figuring I could continue making my own films without the necessity to maintain an office, and with most feature ideas six feet under – or with the embalmer waiting in the wings – Severo and I made a deal. For $6,500 the operation became his. Lock, stock and whatever good will Learning Garden had in its barrel. Which was at least some.

Then, tired of sleeping in a windowless and lonely as a tomb office, I relocated to a sunny second floor apartment near Third and La Cienega; steps from Fatburger, one of L.A.'s more delicious high cholesterol emporiums.

After twenty-two years of marriage I'm single again. No office to maintain. No staff to pay. Lots of friends. A comfortable bachelor pad. A little cash in the bank, some of which goes for cheap furniture and an expensive tiger-striped velour couch. Psychologically, if not exactly swinging from the rafters I'm at least hanging on.

And for a change, not every film I'll make or try to make from here on out has to do with the necessity to make a living ...

TWENTY-FIVE

meadowlark lemon and the king of the cowboys

> So, you've been hanging around Tinseltown for more than ten minutes, knowing you could get rich if you had a nickel for every project that hasn't taken off. And your thesis film hasn't landed you a directing gig on Nicholas Cage's next movie. What now? Whatever you do, don't give up. Keep creating. Creation takes the sting out of the frustration and makes you feel better. Write another screenplay. Design sets for a little theater in beautiful downtown Burbank. Or hook up with United Cerebral Palsy or The World Wildlife Fund, or whatever cause you feel strongly about, and talk your cronies into pooling resources to shoot an on-the-cheap public service TV spot for your favorite charity.

That's what I do off and on through the years, like when I produced those anti-nuclear testing commercials. With a strong empathy for exceptional children (coming out of Rose's and my experience with Lisa), whenever I have a chance to contribute in that area I'm up for it. In addition to *Meet Lisa* and *Tierra del Sol*, I find time to create several public service spots.

The first is for a school for exceptional children on L.A's eastside. They have no budget. But they do have contact with a man in Apple Valley, California, who knows Roy Rogers. The Roy Rogers Museum is nearby, in Victorville. Roy and his wife Dale Evans are champions of orphaned and disadvantaged kids, so they seem ideal spokespersons. The Apple Valley guy says he'll handle logistics. All I need do is get Roy's agent to agree. I make the call. A freebie? No problem, "Roy and Dale are happy to do anything for kids." And rounding up a crew is a snap. Several folks from *Executive Action* agree to donate their time and talents.

Putting together every project should be so easy!

A week later everyone piles into the school's bus. Me, a teacher, a dozen mentally challenged children, our production manager – who has previously gone ahead to line up locations – and the crew, which includes cameraman Allen Daviau, always impeccable in silk shirt and gabardines.[1]

Digression: driving around Hollywood at the time is a fellow who calls himself "Nudie." Actually Nudka Cohen, from Kiev, Russia. Tailor to the stars, he creates custom outfits for everyone from Elvis Presley to Roy Rogers. He drives a Cadillac with six-guns for door handles; carbines mounted on the front fenders and Texas Longhorn steer horns as a hood ornament. Inside, the leather dashboard and seats are inset with silver dollars. And, of course, he dresses the part: boots (with gleaming spurs), string tie and a ten-

---

[1] Allan Daviau shot Steven Speilberg's first film, *Amblin'* (1968), and would later serve as D.P. on *E.T.* (1982), *The Color Purple* (1985), *Empire of the Sun* (1987), and *Van Helsing* (2004), among many other credits.

gallon hat. Our Apple Valley contact is not *the* Nudie, but an exact replica, down to the string tie and outlandish Cadillac.

By eleven a.m. we arrive at the Roy Rogers' museum. "Nudie" meets us. We've got limited time, so I rush to scope out locations. My production manager takes me on a quick tour. Everything will work fine. And next door to the museum is a small real estate office with a western facade, hitching post and all. Terrific! I'll stick Roy in front of the place and have him deliver his spiel.

Roy Rogers and Dale Evans

"Oh, he won't go over *there*," exclaims Roy's secretary, "he's got a feud going with those folks."

OK, we'll film Roy in front of the museum instead. Then, I figure, we'll zip around to the other locations and wrap by 4 p.m. So, with a few minutes before the King of the Cowboys is due to appear, I slip into the museum. There is Roy's famous horse, Trigger, along with his dog, Bullet, both stuffed and mounted. Other patrons raise their eyebrows when I start to laugh. Because I am immediately reminded of the old joke about the guy who brings his two recently deceased hunting dogs to a taxidermist. The taxidermist, noting the guy's sad face, says, "I understand, sir, you want them mounted." "Oh, gracious no," says the man, "just side by side; they were only good friends."

I wander back outside. The Nudie look alike tells us to get ready; Roy can only give us twenty minutes. Our kids pile out of the bus and we set up equipment. Ten minutes later, Roy and Dale appear – dressed in natty western style street clothes. Then Roy spots the camera. And the lights. And our dozen kids and crew of five. I sense trouble. He turns and heads back toward the museum, but Dale hustles to catch his arm.

"I thought this was a still shoot, mother," Roy complains, "I didn't expect no camera crew."

"Now, Daddy, it's for the children," scolds Dale.

"I didn't expect some crowd of kids. I though it was just a still shot."

"Now, daddy . . ."

Roy bites his lip then reluctantly lets Dale lead him back toward the camera. I quickly introduce myself, select a spot for him to stand, and before he can protest further hand him the script page for his intro. As he scans it he keeps mumbling under his breath, "I thought this was a still shot." Then, after a moment, he says, "Ok, I've got it," and hands the script to Dale.

Before he has a chance to change his mind I hand him six-year-old Wilbur, a cherub of a kid with Down Syndrome. Wilbur, who weighs at last eighty pounds, is delighted. Roy is nonplussed.

"Roll camera," I shout. Then, "Action!"

Consummate pro that he is, Roy immediately slips into the role, delivers the lines, then ends, off the cuff, by asking Wilbur if he agrees with the statement he's just made. The lad beams broadly and shakes his head. Great! But not quite right. Roy has trouble holding the kid and looks as if he's straining.

"Once more," I say.

This time, Roy, grunting under the boy's weight, almost lets Wilbur slip to the ground. We run through the scene seven times before we have what I considered a decent take. Each time, Roy looks as if he's about to pack it in – and each time a reproachful look from Dale snaps him back. As we finish, Roy wipes his brow, smiles obligingly to one and all and ducks back into the museum. Dale graciously hangs around to thank us for doing this series of spots "for the children."

Our twenty minutes with Roy has taken an hour. By now it's one p.m. We have three hours left to film five more locations. So we all pile into the bus and race around Apple Valley. We don't make four p.m. Six o'clock instead. By then, everyone is wiped out.

As we wrap, "Nudie," who has been standing off to the side all day with a benign smile, announces, "Now, boys and girls, I'm'a gonna take y'all t' dinner t' the Apple Valley Inn."

We look at one another. I've promised the crew sandwiches and sodas. But nobody complains. True to his word, "Nudie," his Cadillac in the lead, guides us to the Inn, where he's reserved a banquet table. And there, a crew of five, a teacher, a haggard director and a dozen kids enjoy "Whatever y'r l'il hearts wanna order."

As we climb back onto the bus for the long haul back to L.A., "Nudie" stands just outside, with a personal goodbye to each child. Then he tells me "If'n y'all ever need anythin' else out here in the Valley, j'es gimme a call." With that he turns, grasps the six-gun handle on the driver's side door, opens it, climbs into his arsenal and drives off into the sunset.

And as our bus climbs through the San Bernardino Mountains in the gathering dark, I stare out a window. Moments later, I burst out laughing. Wilbur hears me and joins in. But I don't tell him about the bizarre image carousing through my head: Roy and Dale, years hence, standing beside Bullet and Trigger in the museum – stuffed and mounted.

From the Wild West to the world of sport. The Harlem Globetrotters, to be precise.

MEADOWLARK LEMON AND THE KING OF THE COWBOYS

It's 1977, and by now Severo Perez has bought Learning Garden from me. Though I've about had it with L.A., I continue to direct and animate several films for him. Along the way, he hustles $2500 to produce a one-minute TV spot for the Los Angeles's Exceptional Children's Foundation. And someone there has contact with the Globetrotters organization. So Severo calls the team manager. Yes, the Trotters will give us twenty minutes. (Same as Roy Rogers.) Since we'll be shooting inside, this is barely time to set up lights. And only D.P. John Morrill will be paid, most of us are volunteers, and the rest of the budget is for lab work.

When we get to the court where the team is practicing, a fair amount of light is streaming in through windows high above, so we decide to dispense with the lights. Morrill readies his 16mm Eclair. The half-dozen kids we've brought along are wide-eyed. They're meeting the Harlem Globetrotters! And it's equally clear that the mere sight of the kids moves the Trotters emotionally.

"We gonna talk to 'em on camera, right?" asks the six-foot-nine center, Mel Davis.

"Right."

"And they're gonna understand what we say?"

"Sure. They're no dumbbells. But give them a bit longer for the question to sink in before they answer."

OK, we're set. And somehow I've got it into my head that one of the players is Meadowlark Lemon (one of their greats, a legendary "clown prince" of basketball.)

So the team gathers around me, all these gigantic guys. Except one, a bit taller than me and with a shiny bald head, who I think is

Meadowlark. I start giving directions

"OK, now first, Meadowlark has the ball and he dribbles down the court . . ."

"Curly," says the bald guy.

"Whatever," I reply, not comprehending. "So Meadowlark takes the ball, dribbles toward the basket and goes in for a lay-up."

The bald guy frowns at me then grabs the ball. The rest of the team take their places and as the Trotters move toward the basket John Morrill, brilliant at hand held camera work, perfectly captures their perfectly executed shot. Great start! The kids applaud like crazy. The Trotters all grin, and two or three began interacting with the children.

Then we set up for the next shot. This time, I want "Meadowlark" to steal the ball from another team member, race around their huge center and make a backhand shot.

"Got that, Meadowlark?"

"Curly."

"OK, the curly shot, that's cool."

"Curly, my name is Curly. Curly Neal."

I stare blankly for a beat then apologize.

"We all look alike to you?"

"No, no, sorry, I thought Meadowlark was still with the team and -- "

But Curly is already dribbling down the court so John hoists his Eclair and once again both shots are executed with precision.

"Time!" yells a voice off to the side.

We turn to look. The team's manager, pointing at his watch, is striding toward Severo. "These guys gotta practice," he says, frowning. "We have a game tonight!"

MEADOWLARK LEMON AND THE KING OF THE COWBOYS

"But . . . but we've only got two shots, we need at least a dozen more to make a decent sixty second spot," Severo implores.

"Of course, if you're budgeted for it, there might be something we could work out," says the manager.

"We have a very limited amount for this . . ."

The manager notes Severo's plaintive look then turns and starts back toward the stands, waving a dismissive arm. "You can have fifteen more minutes and that's it." Severo swallows hard then announces loudly, "OK, folks, we need a dozen more shots. Let's hustle."

John Morrill looks at me. I look at Severo. The sound woman and the grip shake their heads. I'm thinking fast: fifteen minutes? No way.

The huge center, Mel Davis, who has been squatting down and talking with one of our kids, suddenly rises, glances toward the manager then ambles over. He stands towering over us, indicates the manager and says in a low, rumbling voice, "He's an asshole. You folks take just as long as you need."

From Severo, "But it could take an hour or mo -- "

"As long as you need," says Mel. "For these kids . . . anything."

We do take another hour. And twenty minutes beyond that. One of the Globetrotter forwards (he has as much trouble remembering two lines as I do the names of the players) needs to interact with one of the kids. The shot takes twenty minutes, but we get it – as the manager sits in the bleachers, steaming. And by the time we finish we know that when everything is cut together we'll have a decent commercial.

As we wrap, the Trotters shake hands with each kid. Most of these giants aren't about to let their emotions loose, but as the kids wave goodbye and head for the door, back on the court there is more than one moist pair of eyes looking on.

229

This kind of filmmaking is tangible. It has meaning. It's something to hold on to through the angst that often accompanies trying to get projects off the ground. You may never get to write or direct or produce *The Wizard of Oz, As Good as it Gets* (1997), or *The Lord of the Rings* (2001-03), but if you have days to look back on like those I had with Roy and Dale, or Curly Neal and Mel Davis and the rest of the Globetrotters, then you've won. This is as good as it gets.

PS: Meadowlark Lemon actually was a member of that 1977 team. But wasn't around on the day we filmed.

TWENTY SIX

cutting the cord

Though it will take three more years, I am on my way out of Oz.

It's not easy to step off the Yellow Brick Road. You plod along because you're sure you will eventually reach the Emerald City. Because you know the Wizard will grant the rewards you so richly deserve. And mostly because it will be, you tell yourself, tulip time at the South Pole before you ever go back to Kansas.

Working with Severo at Learning Garden, I'm still turning out short films. And, at the same time, planning to exit Hollywood. But that's hard, because Lisa is still in Los Angeles and regular contact with her is important for both of us.

Meanwhile, my heart is thumping over a new flame: Ann. Funny, energetic, a determined wannabe actress – and eighteen years younger than me. We first meet at a Sunset Boulevard eatery while I'm dining with friend Marilyn Katz (who, along with Dr. Rick Sternberg, is co-producing several of the patient-counseling films.) With Marilyn's prodding I "pick her up." We get to know one another, and though we hang out together for two years, in the romance department I am never the icing on Ann's cake.

But we work on projects: *John Henry*, a screenplay about the folk hero steel driving railroad man. A short on divorce (appropriate) and another starring an orthodontist whose office is set up like a magic shop. (He does tricks to distract the kids.) We travel to Honolulu, Chicago, New York and Boston to research and film artwork by the great Edo period artist, Katsushika Hokusai (1760-1849).

(His *Great Wave* is reproduced on everything from T-shirts to coffee mugs.) But my attempts to fund the project get nowhere.

So I plug away at more feature ideas.

Danny Deever: from a long poem by Rudyard Kipling. Agent Richard Brand pitches this, along with a half dozen other projects of Pop's and mine. He moves none of them.

The Queen Against Defoe: Director Irving Lerner and I put up $750 to option this remarkable short story. Set in 1703, it finds author Daniel Defoe (*Robinson Crusoe*) tossed in jail for penning a satire on the Church of England's treatment of Protestant dissenters. We hope to interest Robert Shaw (*The Sting*, 1973; *Jaws*, 1975; Pizarro in Irving's *Royal Hunt of the Sun*, 1969). He likes the idea, hems and haws for a while, but finally has too many other commitments.

Sleepy Lagoon: about the L.A. "zoot suit" riots of 1943, in which Orson Welles and Rita Hayworth were among many involved in defending the "Sleepy Lagoon Boys," twenty-one young Mexican Americans convicted of murder.

Which reminds me. My pal Severo also tries to launch this project. He brings together Luis Valdez and Gordon Davidson (artistic director of the Mark Taper Forum, where Severo has previously put on a play). And sets up a meeting with Universal. They "love the idea." But "who is this guy Perez? Why should we let *him* produce?" Instead, they hire him to write an original screenplay. Pay him $35,000 for it too. He spends a year at it, then hands it in. "Thank you very much, Severo," says Universal. "See you around sometime. Bye bye." So much smoke and mirrors.

How come I keep forgetting? This is Hollywood.[1]

Are you getting the idea that my life (and maybe Severo's) has been one big barrel of sopping failure and frustration? Not so. On the other hand, anyone who wants to do their own thing creatively in film should expect a chunk of disappointment, know that many projects will poke along and get nowhere, and understand that lots

---

[1] In 1981, Luis Valdez wrote and directed the film, *Zoot Suit*.

CUTTING THE CORD

of promised deals will never materialize. It's the same with everything in life: work, love, managing money, keeping healthy. Survival means learning from past mistakes then picking up the pieces
and moving on.

With everything else, I also try to squeeze in time for Tim and
Joe. Unfortunately too little for Joe, who is now in college at UC
Santa Cruz. Though by shining on the IRS over how much I need to
pay in estimated taxes, I manage enough for his first term's tuition
and books. With Tim, I escape to Anza Borrego desert. He hunts for
snakes. The snakes clearly knew, because they never appear.

Around the same time, Lisa is kicked out of the board and care
home she's been in for two years. Her behavior has become too
bizarre for the kindly provider to handle. The State of California
transfers her to an end-of-the-line facility, run out of a decaying
motel and managed by caring but unskilled people. Desperate to
rescue her, and with the idea of setting up a group home in Santa
Cruz for young people like her still a fantasy, I push forward.
Friends are open to funding a property, so long as I can find one we
might sell at a profit down the line. On trips north, I start looking.

By late 1977 the Southern California housing market is heating
up. My lease (with option to buy) is about to expire on a modest
home I'm now renting close to Beverly Hills. I want to exercise the
option but have little money. So friend Thom Smitham buys it, we
immediately resell, and my $2000 profit share is enough to move
to a funky apartment in Venice (California), stave off the IRS for a
while, and think about a jaunt to Europe.

Desperate to help Lisa escape, I am also burned out and in piss-
poor shape psychologically. And realize it could take two more years
to find a way to meet my dear daughter's needs. For the moment,
Europe seems like a way to recoup energy.

My former assistant, Marianne, is living in London now. So in
January of 1978 I find myself bunking at her Marble Arch flat, visit-
ing museums and taking a day trip to Stratford-Upon-Avon. Then
Amsterdam, where I get all choked up on seeing Van Gogh's actual

paint box and palette in a glass case at the museum holding the bulk of his work. On by train to Barcelona, where I stay with Pop's friend, director Jaime Camino, whose apartment adjoins a church, the bells of which rattle me from sleep every fifteen minutes for five nights in a row.

Then I'm back from Europe. Back to hanging on in Oz.

March 2, 1978. A day of pounding rain. I've just returned to my apartment after a meeting on another film project. The answering machine is blinking. I pick up.

"Hello, Mr. Bessie, this is Mrs. Williams at Solubrium (the place where Lisa is staying). You need to call me right away, we have an emergency!"

Even as I dial I know that Lisa has died. I can sense it. But when it's confirmed, and I learn the details, I hold in my agony. I call Mom to say I need to come see her. Like me, she is perceptive and can tell something is amiss. I drive through the rain to her small apartment, and there, collapse in tears.[2]

Not diminishing my deep love for Joe and Tim, the most precious person in my life is gone. Rose and I have been through so much with Lisa that our feelings toward her have had a special quality. Though time will gradually soften the pain, my anguish over my inability to help my daughter when she really needed me will crop up again and again. Every time I think about her. Those feelings have never left.

Work becomes my salvation. More films for Severo. Another patient-counseling series, for he has picked up contracts on the PRI titles. And *Astronauts and Jellybeans*, a live and animated film about language and writing, script by Severo's wife Judy and me.

And it's at their home one evening in April, weeks after Lisa's death, that I meet an old friend of Judy's, a former officer of Stu-

---

[2] Lisa's death resulted from bronchial aspiration. She was alone at the time in her room at Solubrium. The Los Angeles County Corner's office ruled her death an accident.

CUTTING THE CORD

dents for a Democratic Society (SDS), the main radical student organization of the 1960s. Before the Soviet revolution of 1917, Helen Garvy's grandparents had been in a study circle with Lenin. Before reaching the States they had fled the USSR, then Hitler's Germany, then about-to-be-occupied France.

I am intrigued.

Helen is thirty-six, ten years younger than me. Dark brown hair starting to gray. Harvard 1964. And a Jill of All Trades; having built her own mountain getaway house with hand tools (and written a book about it), owned a bicycle repair shop (and written a book on bike repair), been a carpenter, a community organizer, and helped found an alternative school. Plus which, she has a smile that won't quit. And she seems to be taken with me. Soon after, I drive to San Francisco for a visit. We immediately began a romance. For the next six months she hitches to L.A. to visit me, or I drive north.

In August, Tim and I head for Missouri for a week to visit my cousin Phoebe, the world's preeminent birder.[3] By September the IRS has me by the cojones. Eight and a half thousand behind in taxes, I make an agreement to pay it off over two years. At almost the same time, my father's financial fortunes are resuscitated with a $7500 writing grant from the National Endowment for the Arts. He is purring, and doesn't need to pester me to find him work.

By mid October, I've made a decision: time to be closer to Joe and Tim. Time to be closer to Helen. Time to split Los Angeles smog, traffic and failed attempts at launching a feature. Time for clean air and a gentler lifestyle. Freelance animation is coming in from Bandelier Films and the Culligan spots are good for several more seasons. For Severo, I'm writing and directing a TV special, *The Notorious Jumping Frog of Calaveras County*, based on Mark Twain's waggish tall tale. So I drive north to collect Joe and Tim, return to L.A., rent a U-Haul, we pack up my Venice apartment and the following night are back in Santa Cruz by the sea.

---

[3] See my book *Rare Birds, An American Family* for a chapter on this remarkable woman. Or her posthumously published, *Birding On Borrowed Time* (2003).

Reeling Through Hollywood

The Learning Garden crew, after I left. (That's me on the right, sneaking off to Santa Cruz.) To the left, with big scissors, is Ruth Lee, editor *extraordinaire*. The fellow with giant hair to her right is animator Mallory Pearce. Severo Perez is in the director's chair in the middle. His wife Judy is to his right. And to my left (holding the sheet of paper) is the immenselty talented designer and animator Bill Davis, whose caricature this is.

After a couple months of wishy-washy angst over commitment (typical of the male species), Helen and I hook up. Soon after, we purchase (with Helen's down payment) a modest early 1900s one story frame house that Helen will saw at and nail onto and tear apart and add to, until we have a roomy two story, four bedroom and den, combination home and workspace. Close enough to downtown for me to stroll to one of Santa Cruz's ubiquitous coffee shops.

We have also launched our own company, to produce films on which we'll have creative freedom. Films that promote positive cultural values, that will suggest that folks can have greater control over their own lives, and that will say something about making a better world. Even with the inevitable flare-ups between strong-willed partners working and living together twenty-four hours a day, even with occasional regrets, recriminations and misunderstandings, the seventeen years that follow will be the most satisfying and rewarding I have known until that point.

And while Santa Cruz isn't exactly the Emerald City, it sure beats Hollywood.

In Missouri, not Santa Cruz. But the photo says everything about having escaped tinseltown.

Book Six

mini-moguls

If you practice an art, be proud of it and make it proud of you . . . it may break your heart, but it will fill your heart before it breaks; it will make you a person in your own right.

Maxwell Anderson

You will do foolish things, but do them with enthusiasm.

Colette

Never invest your money in anything that eats or needs repainting.

Billy Rose

TWENTY SEVEN

movies in the shire

February 1981. Son Joe is now at the University of Minnesota, in their graduate program in philosophy. Tim is living with Helen and me (Rose has had enough of adolescent angst). I've started to teach screenwriting. And have directed a joyful and poignant play, *The World of Scholom Aleichem* by the great Yiddish writer whose works had been adapted for *Fiddler on the Roof* (both the play and the 1971 film). Standing room only for much of its three weekend run. Pop and I have had a knockdown drag-out (through the mail) because he and wife Sylviane won't make time to travel two hours to see a performance. I am hurt, mostly because instead of simply saying they don't want to interrupt Sylviane's Bridge night, or alter their daily routine, they detail a list of picky rationalizations.

And Helen and I have been making films. Shire Films, we call our modest little company, run out of our home. Her self-published books bear the Shire Press logo, and the kids in the alternative school she helped to start had named it Shire School, after the place where the Hobbits live. So Shire Films seems right.[1]

The new kid in town (most other film folks are making wedding videos), Shire Films already has six titles under its belt in the first year and a half. Including one patient counseling title, two dealing with teen pregnancy and another on child abuse. Barr Films, an L.A. distributor, has put up money for the last three, out of which we make a small profit, plus royalties that will come after the advance is (we hope) recouped from sales.

---

[1] A year or two into Shire Films' existence, someone at actress and producer Talia (Coppola) Shire's company called, curious to discover if we were infringing on her company name. (We weren't.)

REELING THROUGH HOLLYWOOD

Running a two-person film company in Santa Cruz means doing things vastly different than in Hollywood. You scout locations, cast talent, organize production and raise the money yourself. You plan far more carefully, and since studios with fat wallets aren't picking up any overage, learn to do things economically. But doing so can often lead to quality as high as that produced by studios with cash to burn. Not surprisingly, small town folks are eager to help. And almost any resource you need for a shoot (as the next chapters will demonstrate) can be found in Middle America.

Our most challenging early work is the live portion for Severo's *Notorious Jumping Frog of Calaveras County*, which I direct. For that, we recreate Mark Twain's billiard room in a classic Santa Cruz Victorian. And have to talk fast to secure it, because the mini-series *East of Eden* (1981), which used the same neighborhood months before, has infuriated the locals by blocking residential traffic, covering a street with dirt in order to achieve a period look, then folded their Winnebagos and snuck off into the night before a thorough cleanup. So another film company is persona non grata.

We cast a local high schooler as Twain's "angel fish." (In his dotage Twain had a peculiar though apparently puritanical fascination with young girls; sort of like Lewis Carrol (*Alice in Wonderland*.) As Twain and the girl play billiards, a cub reporter shows up to interview the author. Twain befuddles him with a string of outrageous lies then relates his tale about the jumping frog.

The shoot comes in on time and on budget. And we do a conscientious job of putting everything back in place. Except that as we're wrapping the homeowner decides to blockade the drive with her car. Because, she says, we haven't emptied the wastebaskets! Dumbfounded, we call the police. A pair of puzzled cops shows up and promptly tells her that such behavior is a major no-no.

While picked up by Home Box Office for a modest sum, the *Jumping Frog* doesn't exactly leap tall buildings at a single bound. With no star, Severo has relied on the story itself, along with animation, to sell the show. Sales are disappointing. But since Helen

242

Movies in the Shire

Scenes and publicity from various
Shire Films productions

Wayne Hefley (top R) as Mark Twain

and I plan to move beyond educational film, we hope to learn from Severo's experience. And from my own.

Flashback to Circus Films (1961): a noble effort but a crunching failure.

Flashback to Learning Garden (1971-75): a modest success, even with the inability to get my own feature off the ground (*Executive Action* was a for hire gig.)

Third time has to be a charm. Looking ahead now, I realize that "fly by the seat of your pants" is no longer going to work. Any project has to be approached with a solid plan. Fortunately, I've hooked up with a smart, organized and creative partner. After six films funded by others, Helen and I are ready to go out and raise money for our own independent production. We have a filing cabinet crammed with ideas.

Which one should we choose?

TWENTY-EIGHT

peter and the wolf

> For those of you aspiring to a career in media: OK, you've served your apprenticeship. You've slaved away as a PA on commercials, or been second assistant to the associate producer on a daytime soap. Or sorted mail at CBS while the sun shines then propped your eyes open with toothpicks until 3 a.m., laboring over a screenplay that will set Hollywood on its ear. Or you're a month out of film school and Aunt Trudy and six friends have put up a thousand bucks each for you to make your first video.

There are a dozen other ways to edge away from just earning a living into the chancy yet magical world of creating your own movie. And if that's your ambition, live the dream.

But even if you're not a filmmaker, I suspect you'll also enjoy what follows.

Nineteen eighty-one. Helen and I have produced films on physical fitness, teen pregnancy, child abuse, and nutrition. Worthwhile and fun to make, but bread and butter potboilers nevertheless. Now we are looking for a dream project. Searching my files, I pull out a forgotten folder. Back in the mid 1970s I had helped a Hollywood friend develop her idea to put *Peter and the Wolf* on film. Not a duplication of Disney's snarling menace. Live action instead. How, I wondered, would she get real animals to perform as Prokofiev's famous intro to the orchestra evoked them? You want hippos and alligators in tutus? Use animation, ala "The Dance of the Hours," in *Fantasia*.

Peter and the Wolf seemed just as unworkable in live action: a hungry cat spots a tiny bird and stalks it. The bird flits to a tree. The cat follows. A wolf appears, chases then devours a stupid duck. Peter, with the aid of the bird, lassos the wolf, binds him and turns him over to a trio of hunters. The tale needed to be told to precisely timed music. And in 1981 it would be a decade before digital effects made it possible to have the *Titanic* mambo across the screen while belting out something by Tito Puente. (If anyone wanted to, that is.) Standard advice handed down through generations of filmmakers: never work with children or animals. But rules are made to be broken, right?

My friend's project never happened. Maybe, I reason, we could attempt it. We're organized, efficient, know how to control a budget

Jeff the Chimp

PETER AND THE WOLF

and have discovered that talent is everywhere, even in Santa Cruz. Our films so far have featured high school students and amateur but talented actors. And a frenetic chimpanzee. And we've discovered nearby crew people. So we begin. With Helen peeking over my shoulder (she knows music, I don't), I write a shot by shot script keyed to the beats in Deutsche Grammophon's version of *Peter and the Wolf*. The story itself, plus time for an on-camera narrator, will bring the show in at almost half an hour, ideal TV length.

But can we get animals to do the things the story calls for? That's where the frenetic chimp comes in. His name is Jeff and he lives with Lou and Betty Egan who run an animal shelter in the Santa Cruz Mountains. Lou and Betty take their critters around to schools to familiarize kids with wildlife, and we've used them in a previous film dealing with nutrition. They are also perpetually broke keeping the menagerie fed. They own a tiger, lion, cougars, Jeff the chimp (their baby), llamas, a bear and other creatures. Many of these have been rescued from abusive owners and turned over to the Egans to protect. Most important, they also have three wolves. The big male they call Beetle Bailey.

So, a trip to the mountains with our script. We go over it page by page. Lou and Betty review each shot, nodding, smiling and scratching their heads. Then . . .

"Yeah," says Lou, "our guys can do this stuff."

"And how will you get them to do it?"

"Kindness," Betty chimes in. "With rewards of food. They mind us." Then, from Lou, "We won't do anything to torment or tease the animals." This we appreciate, because when we had approached a trainer in L.A. he had shown us a piece of film demonstrating how he got his wolf to snap and snarl – by poking a long stick in its face.

Helen and I drive off much relieved. First problem solved. (We hope.) And even though the Egans have assured us their charges will "work," that old adage about children and animals is still rattling around in my head. As is Murphy's Law:

Now for the money. We need a bigger budget than for any of our previous films. We mull. While directing the play, *The World of Sholom Aleichem*, an actress in the cast had come up to me after rehearsal one evening to whisper, "Dan, if you ever need money to make a film, just let me know." (How often does *that* happen?)

Within a couple weeks Helen and I have put together partnership papers. The actress invests $7500. Great start toward our $45,000 budget. Next, I contact an attorney who years before had purchased my collection of political campaign buttons. He loves the idea and is good for $2500. My L.A. accountant invests $1000 and gets another client to add $5000. Several dozen phone calls, letters and meetings later we are still $10,000 short, but figure we can raise it. Time to look for a star.

A star, because *Peter and the Wolf* has crossover potential. While the story introduces the orchestra and is thus educational, it might also be sold to TV and home video. And a star will make that easier. We've also promised investors that in order to protect their money we won't make it without a star. So the search begins. I draw up a list that includes Henry Winkler, Danny Kaye, and Victor Borge. But our first choice is Bill Cosby – funny, engaging and with family appeal. I send a letter to his agent then follow up with a phone call.

PETER AND THE WOLF

"Great project," says the agent. "How long would you need Bill for?"

"Just two days."

"Sure, we can make a deal.

My heart is thumping. Bill Cosby! Wow! The show's a winner.

"Say, seventy-five thousand a day," continues the agent. "Hundred fifty total. Plus airfare, hotel and per diem, of course."

"Uh . . . I'll get back to you," I mumble.

Henry Winkler likes the idea but doesn't have the time. Danny Kaye is also committed. More names are suggested: Dudley Moore; an odd choice, I think. Lorne Greene (of *Bonanza*). "Sells dog food," says a sales rep advising us. (Green is doing Alpo commercials at the time.) I phone International Creative Management in L.A., where I have contact with the head of the place. He puts me through to a minor agent. "We can afford $5000 for the two days," I say, apologetically. Who's available?"

"Here's an interesting name, Van Johnson."

Van Johnson? An interesting name during the 1940s, but mention him to anyone under fifty and you'll draw a glazed stare. The agent rattles off more dim or fading stars.

"Uh . . . I'll get back to you."

By now, we've raised nearly all the budget. But without a name to perk up network ears the project is destined for the shelf. So I'm in a melancholy funk when I stroll into the Santa Cruz library to scan the LPs in the children's section. Maybe someone I haven't thought of will pop up. And so he does. Among the LPs is *Queen Zixi of IX* or the *Story of the Magic Cloak*. Narrated by Ray Bolger. Perfect choice: the beloved scarecrow from *The Wizard of Oz*. But then, my heart sinks; how much will he want? Oh well, nothing ventured and all that.

Ray Bolger, in an intro to *Peter and the Wolf*

I phone the Screen Actors Guild. Bolger's agent, they tell me, is William Morris. The biggie. I call and am transferred to a pleasant young fellow who says, "Well, Ray isn't doing much these days. Frankly, there are few projects he finds interesting. But send me a script." Which I hasten to do. A week later the agent calls back. As it happens I'm in L.A. at the time and, says Helen when she phones to relay the message, "Ray wants to meet you."

"Can you come right over?" says Ray, when I call him. Absolutely. Within half an hour my oil-guzzling 1965 Peugeot is pulling up in front of his huge Beverly Hills home. He's told me to come around back to his studio, where he greets me with the same engaging smile I recall from the Scarecrow of Oz. His eyes tell me he's cautious but interested. He still dances a few minutes every day, he says, "to keep in shape." I look around. Signed photos of Ray dot the walls. With Judy Garland, Jack Haley, Bert Lahr and the rest of the Wizard gang. We discuss the script, go over suggestions he has for small changes, most of which I agree with. But I don't have the guts to ask if he'll do the movie.

"Of course," he goes on, "I'd like to see what you've done."

Of course. A week later Helen and I return, bringing along a copy of the *Jumping Frog*. We meet Ray at the Morris agency. He loves the show, except that I had used a fog filter over the live action (for an old fashioned look), that he finds disconcerting. I promise no fog filter if he agrees to star in *Peter and the Wolf*. Then back to his house to talk over the script some more. We get along famously and he's intrigued with Helen's smiling good looks. He agrees to do the film. And we leave with a handful of plump avocados from his backyard tree.

At this point we don't think any star will tumble for $5000. (Except Van Johnson.) So we've doubled our offer, knowing we'll have to scrounge for the additional money. Through his agent, Ray has agreed to $10,000, plus a percentage. Problem two is behind us; we've hooked a star.

We schedule the shoot for July. Clear weather anticipated. Now to scout locations, hire a crew, organize the zillion details and, most important, tell Lou and Betty Egan they can get to work training the animals. The Egans already have three wolves. We've cast Beetle Bailey, even though he's nervous around men (except Lou). For a duck, they borrow a neighbor's. For cats they'll use a stray tabby they've found, plus (since the tabby is skittish) a calico belonging to another neighbor as backup.

"How about the birds," I ask.

"We don't have any birds, but we'll find some."

I bite my nails. Days later Betty calls. "We found the birds," she says. "Couple baby blackbirds fell out of a nest in the big oak next to the bear pit. We'll train 'em."

Gad, I think, how does one "train" blackbirds? Or a duck? Or a cat?

Now for the rest of the actors. Peter is the human star. We call local schools, the main resource for our previous films, and set a casting call. A dozen boys ages eight to twelve show up. We herd them into our big kitchen, where we do nearly all the casting for the twenty-two films we'll ultimately produce. (This is tightwad film making, folks. Why rent fancy offices and incur huge overhead if you don't need to?)

Only one boy is a contender, a sturdy blonde who's had gymnastic training. Helen favors him. I don't. We call a school for gifted children. Four more boys appear. One, Jake Hathcock, could pass for Huckleberry Finn. A shaggy haircut, and freckles that won't quit.

Fortunately, Peter doesn't have lines. The key is how the boy moves and how he'll take direction. With our wardrobe person and art director on hand, we turn the finalists loose in our overgrown back yard. I call out specifics, having them duplicate action they'll need to do for the film. "Don't look at me," I instruct them, "just listen to what I say, and pretend." The blonde, in spite of his gymnastic training, is stiff and awkward. Jake listens exactly, doesn't look

Jake and Beetle

PETER AND THE WOLF

at me, and follows directions to the letter. Helen and I exchange glances. We check out the others. Everyone agrees. Jake will be Peter. "Thanks so much for coming," I tell the gymnast, "we'll let you know." Next day I call to tell him that he'll replace Jake if he happens to fall out.

Tip on casting children: don't rely on agencies; you can find talented, engaging kids anywhere. Just look for focus, intelligence, and children who aren't being pushed into the profession by parents living vicariously through their kids.

Next, the hunters. In our backyard tryouts every candidate seems like a klutz. Of course, we want them to be klutzes, but with the panache only fine acting can deliver. So we arrange a session with a San Francisco agency and quickly line up three great guys: Luis Oropeza, a short, comically intense Latino; Alan Blumenfeld, a comic with a fine rubbery face; and Bingwa, tall, gawky and black. An All-American trio who, in rehearsal, seem as if they've been stalking wolves all their lives (and are terrified of finding one.)[1]

For Peter's grandfather, who warns the boy to stay close to the house because "the woods are full of wolves," we discover a Hollywood retiree living in Santa Cruz: Ray Dawe, big, heavy and with just the right amount of grumpiness Peter's gramp should have. (He had been a stand-in for gravel-voiced movie funnyman Andy Devine.)

One more important ingredient: the orchestra. In the script, Ray Bolger, strolling through the woods, hears music then finds an orchestra tuning up in a shady glen. He joins them. Then, after introducing the tale and describing how each instrument plays a part, he begins the story. Which moves back and forth between Peter and the animals as Ray continues. For an orchestra we want the Oakland Symphony, conducted by the gifted Calvin Simmons. They are agreeable, except that musician's union fees and residual

---

[1] All three went on to film and television careers. Alan Blumenfeld has appeared in more than a hundred and fifty films and TV shows.

payments will blow the budget sky high. So we turn to the Santa Cruz Chamber Orchestra, whose conductor is, coincidentally, in charge of the school for gifted children where we found "Peter." Eager to participate, they work out a deal with the musician's union that satisfies our budget. And that's it; the major components. A week from filming, and with our careful organizing having paid off, we double check everything:

• Locations: we've tied down a pond where Peter first meets the duck. And Grandfather's house, a Seven Dwarfs-like cottage along a rural road, owned by brothers who run the county's biggest lumber operation. Their ninety-year-old mother, Mrs. McCrary, is in residence. Just the right amount of green moss clings (to the roof of the house, not to Mrs. McCrary.) With a garden gate and a crude fence facing the woods, both of which we've had built, the setting is ideal. The other main location is a downtown street, along which Peter, Grandfather and the hunters will parade triumphantly after the wolf is captured. San Jose has recreated such a place, an old section of town with wood frame houses, ice cream parlor, print shop, hotel and a park. No need to scatter dirt along the streets, it's already there. I only have to make sure the camera doesn't include the high voltage tower in the background.

• Costumes: the show will be period, early 1900s in California. "*Peter and the Wolf* was originally set in Russia," says Bolger in the narration, "but it could be anywhere." Our wardrobe person has haunted thrift stores and sewed and stitched and come up with great outfits for Peter, Grandfather and the hunters and for the forty extras we'll use in the parade. The orchestra supplies its own, and Ray will wear my tan corduroy Salvation Army-recycled sport jacket.

• Props: our property man, who teaches set construction at the local junior college, has everything ready. Even a big wooden cage in which the hunters will transport the wolf to the zoo. We test the cage by putting Beetle Bailey inside a day before filming. Fortunately! Because he smashes through the bars in twenty seconds. So another (and stronger) cage is built overnight. And Beetle can tell; he doesn't even attempt another breakout.

One last agonizing detail: how to raise the $10,000 committed to Ray? Investors have put up $45,000 by now, but with an eight-day schedule, with Peter and the hunters on Screen Actors Guild wages and with Helen having whittled the budget to the bone, we need every nickel for production. New investors might be possible but we're heavy into last minute details and have no time to beat the bushes. We discuss getting a loan to pay Bolger's salary. Or maybe try to sell the show at rough-cut stage then pay him.

Days before Ray is scheduled to fly to Santa Cruz, the phone rings. It's him.

"Look," he says, "I have to tell you something. Normally, I wouldn't walk across the street for ten thousand dollars." My heart sinks. Is he going to pull out? "But I see how hard you folks have been working to get this together and I'd like to help," he continues. "So here's what: just pay me SAG minimum for the two days, plus 10% of gross sales. Put the extra ten thousand into the show. Let's make it as good as we can."

Saved! Thank you, Ray. SAG minimum in 1981 is $250 a day for an educational film. (That's all we need to pay until a TV or theatrical deal is concluded.) So we have enough to produce the show. Barely. What we don't tell Ray, of course, is that no extra $10,000 exists. Just the same, we intend to make it as good as we can.

On to the filming.

Our first shot on the first day is the exterior of Grandfather's quaint cottage. But when we arrive, the lovely moss-covered roof is gone! Replaced with a brand new one with shiny wooden shingles. "No problem," says cameraman John Morrill, "we'll just wet it down, it'll be fine." Which it is. That shot accomplished, we move inside. Peter's upstairs bedroom is already furnished à la the early 1900s, so all we need to prop it is a washbasin. The whole sequence is simple and smooth. As planned, Peter wakes, washes then looks out the window and waves to the duck.

Next he's in the living room, stroking Grandfather's cat. Until surly Gramp tosses the cat out the front door. But the stray Tabby selected by Lou and Betty Egan is edgy (as they've told us), and since we didn't know which would work best we've been doing alternate takes with the calico. Fortunately. For when Grandfather tosses cat number one out the door she skedaddles; with Helen racing after, down an embankment, splashing across a stream and fifty yards up the side of an adjacent hill – through California's heaviest thicket of poison oak, in full, deadly bloom. The next day Helen's arms and legs are oozing, and it doesn't go completely away for a month. (Cortisone helps.)

Next, we film the hunters galumphing through the woods. Working with the actors, we create a burlesque in which they bump into one another, pop out from behind trees, ignore a prominent "no hunting" sign and generally bumble along like the three incompetents they're supposed to be. Great job. They complete their romp that first morning and will return for the parade a few days later. Day one is in the can. Days two and three will be devoted to Bolger.

After filming on that first afternoon I meet Ray at the San Jose airport and drive him to the Dream Inn, Santa Cruz's biggest hotel – where he happily signs autographs for staff and guests. And that night we take him to dinner at a Chinese restaurant.

PETER AND THE WOLF

The next day we drive him to the woodland location. Though he forgets his lines off and on (at seventy-eight a little fogginess is allowed) and though several takes are necessary, Ray is a delight. He trips through the forest humming Prokofiev's theme, hears the orchestra, moves on, discovers the musicians, then introduces the characters and the instruments they represent: Peter (violins). The bird (flute). The cat (bass). The duck (oboe). The wolf (French horns). And finally the hunters (kettle drums). As each character is introduced we cut (later, in editing) to scenes we'll shoot after Ray's stint is complete: to the duck in the pond, the bird greeting Peter, the clumsy hunters tracking the wolf, and so on.

Even the blackbirds perform on cue. Right after they fell from the nest the Egans had begun to train them – with mashed bugs as a tasty reward. The birds are virtually identical. One flies, the other perches. So, when the flyer lands on the flute player's flute, for example, or on Ray's shoulder, Lou or Betty are just off camera, tempting their avian actor with "bug butter" at the end of a matchstick. But on our first take with the flyer it won't perform. Seems lethargic. Helen goes into Mrs. McCrary's house (where the birds rest up) to ask if she knows anything about this. There, she discovers the sweet old lady feeding tidbits of her breakfast toast to the percher bird. Mrs. McCrary look up, smiles and says, "They looked so hungry." An hour later the flyer is ravenous, so we get the needed footage.

Bolger's part winds down with a last minute shot I dream up to end the film. In the original story the wolf swallows the duck. Small kids, we feel, might have anxious dreams over this, so we decide to resurrect the creature. In our version, just as Ray finishes his story he hears a loud quack. He turns and spots the duck, standing awkwardly next to the oboe player. Then, to camera, he says, "Oh, the duck! Well, do you know what? When the wolf swallowed that duck he got a duck feather stuck up his nose. And by the time the hunters got the wolf to the zoo, it was itching and tickling so much that he just sneezed; a big achoo! And out came the duck." With that, Ray, with the duck on a leash, ambles off down a sun-flecked forest path.

The following day, we record Ray's narration. And the next day, shoot the last sequence in Peter's adventure, in which he leads the hunters, carrying the wolf between them in the cage, in a grand celebratory procession down the old time San Jose street. Grandfather (holding the cat) and a band of excited kids tag after, as townsfolk wave shouted congratulations or gawk in amazement. Above it all flies the bird. Well, we can't risk releasing the flyer bird over the town, so we grab some wild bird footage. Of a crow.

Before taking off to the airport, Ray shows up at the parade location and spends half an hour chatting with the forty thrilled extras. Good day. We finish the sequence on time. So far so good. Now back to the country to shoot the rest of the film, of Peter interacting with the animals.

Remember Murphy's Law? Murphy was right. Anything that can go wrong will.

- Jake Hathcock (Peter) has a strong ragweed allergy, and during the first few outside shots, as he skips happily through the bright morning meadow on his way to find his friend the bird, his eyes begin to itch. Then his nose starts to run. Within minutes he's into a sneezing fit. Minutes later he's a wreck. But like a trouper he gets through the sequence, we give him an hour to recoup and he's raring to go again. And does exactly what we need, listens carefully

Kid "wrangler" Keith Kelsen comforts Jake Hathcock

without once looking at the camera, and carries out each piece of business perfectly.

The animals are another story. Did Lou and Betty tell us they could get their critters to do everything I had spelled out in the script? Well . . .

• Our flyer bird much prefers flitting around in the oaks and pines. Takes Lou Egan half an hour to coax it out of the trees. Twice. After that Lou provides insurance: black string tied to its legs – invisible on camera (unless you look closely). But that also reveals a disconcerting ritual at several places in the final cut, with the bird pecking furiously at its feet. Fortunately, most of the time it looks as if it's probing for bugs.

And how about that crow flying above the parade? In the completed film it's so outrageously big that no way will anyone accept it for the blackbird we used earlier. So our production manager borrows a Bolex and captures usable footage. Of a starling, not a blackbird, but close enough. Also, our hero blackbird had pooped on the shoulder of the orchestra conductor's black tuxedo jacket. This goes unnoticed as we assemble the footage. No such thing as poop remover in film, and digital hasn't come in yet. So, a little recutting.

• During the sequence at the pond, where the duck swims, the duck and bird are supposed to squabble. The duck won't stand still so I lie flat on the ground, holding its legs, while the camera frames its upper torso. The perching bird, on the other hand, stays on its mark. Then we film from the boat toward the bank, and I climb into waist-deep water to act as a dolly grip, pushing the boat slowly along as the camera turns.

• The cat cares beans about the bird. We film her ambling toward it. She's supposed to stalk, but try getting a cat to do anything it doesn't want to. Then she catches up to the bird, now perched on an overturned rowboat next to the pond. She is scripted to eye the bird then pounce. She won't pounce. I plead. She eyes me, yawns, then rolls over and stretches out in the sun. Frustrated, I pick up the cat and toss her (as the camera rolls) at the bird. Which cooperatively flies away just as the cat lands.

• Beetle Bailey (the wolf) gets lonesome for his mate whenever they are separated, so the Egans bring her along too. Whenever Beetle is away from her, working, mournful howls between them echo up and down the canyon. And since Beetle is skittish around men we use women production assistants to move reflectors around and do other chores. Cameraman John Morrill and I are the only males in the wolf's range of vision.

• In the script, the wolf comes roaring out of the woods and chases after the duck. Except that Beetle doesn't give a damn about the duck. (The Egan's menagerie is one big happy family. As it should be.) The day is hot, and Beetle decides to trot down to the stream for a drink. So, like our lost tabby, he's off at a rapid clip, with Lou Egan after him. This happens three times. It takes Lou ten minutes to bring him back each time and, like Helen, Lou is also soon popping out with poison oak blisters.

• And the duck won't "chase." I run at her. She sidesteps; then begins pecking for grubs. Helen races at her. Same thing. Three people race at her. Confused, she simply stands there, looking cock-eyed at each of us in turn. What to do? Fortunately, Lou and Betty have brought along Jeff, their chimp. (He's unhappy in his cage at home, their bedroom closet with a door made of iron bars.)

"Go get her," commands Lou. Instantly, Jeff is after the duck, hooting in chimpanzeeze and scraping his hands along the ground. The duck panics. John Morrill aims his Eclair. We do three quick takes. The footage is perfect: a duck waddling crazily through the brush, with a big hairy chimpanzee loping into the shot after her. Jeff, of necessity, ends up on the cutting room floor.

Then Jeff escapes into a giant eucalyptus. He has a blast, swinging from branch to branch and hollering at us below. More time spent coaxing him down.

• When it comes to the wolf eating the duck, we know that isn't going to happen. We don't want it to happen. But how to make

Peter and the Wolf

Scenes from *Peter and the Wolf*. Helen (L) on Ray's lap

Jake Hathcock as Peter
Beetle Bailey as the wolf

it look real? Fast cutting and a frenetic back and forth, timed to music, make it seem as if the wolf is actually after her. As the wolf races out of the last shot, apparently to gobble the duck, we –

Cut to: Peter (who is watching), covering his eyes with his hands. Then –

Cut to: the wolf, under the big oak where the cat and bird have fled. He needs to look as if he's munching the duck. We try a hunk of beef. Beetle "wolfs" it down faster than John can film. We need Beetle to chew then smack his lips. Too fast. Another take. Same thing. One more.

Cut to: the wolf, smacking his lips after supposedly munching the duck. Perfect this time! Lou has found the solution: half a jar of peanut butter.

• Now the wolf is snapping and snarling at the cat and the bird, gazing down, terrified (not!) from separate tree limbs. That's easy; same way we got the action earlier when the cat eyed the bird after it had flown to a branch in the oak: yummies. For the cat, cat food, dropped down bit by bit by me, standing on a ladder, so she keeps looking up for more. But when cut together it seems as if she's figuring out how to get to the bird. With Beetle, we swing a leg of lamb high above, on a rope. He jumps for it, snaps, snarls and salivates. And yes, after his outstanding performance he does get to eat it.

• Peter figures out a scheme to catch the wolf. After watching Beetle swallow the duck, he sneaks off and grabs a length of rope from Grandfather's house. Then up into the tree, and while he prepares a snare he has the bird fly down from the limb and distract the wolf.

Another impossibility; except for one brief take, we can't get the bird to fly past Beetle. It flies in the opposite direction. Or it won't move off the limb. Or it flies off Lou's finger then back again. Or it lands on Beetle's head. (Which fazes the wolf not at all.) Finally, we swing the bird (attached by strings to its legs) back and forth over Beetle's head a few times. And it doesn't even get dizzy. A little bug

REELING THROUGH HOLLYWOOD

butter and it's ready for another ride. John Morrell catches it all on film, and fast cutting makes it real. (Unless some joker plays the video in slow motion.)

When the hunters appear they are appropriately dumbfounded that a small boy has captured the wolf. Then, with the previously filmed grand procession, Peter's story concludes, followed by Ray strolling off with the duck. Mission accomplished. Two extra days over schedule because of the animal work, but the show is in the can.

A day to record the orchestra. Then three weeks in Los Angeles with Ruth Lee, editor extraordinaire, taking material we are sure won't work and cutting it together so skillfully that only those on the shoot know it didn't happen exactly that way. Then mixing and off to the lab and our little movie is complete.

Even at rough-cut we had begin screening *Peter and the Wolf* for prospective buyers. Three educational distributors want it. Each offers an advance against royalties. We need time to consider options.

Meanwhile, Santa Cruz Planned Parenthood has contracted with us to produce a film on birth control. A local investor springs for most of the budget. Helen creates a novel idea: a classroom of high school kids taking on the subject of birth control, and making a short film. They'd call it *The Birth Control Movie*, so that becomes the title. Featuring local teens, an actor from San Francisco to play their teacher (he has a fling with one of the "students," a woman in her early twenties, who, we later learn, has faked her age) and with a high school jazz combo included, we turn out a twenty-minute flick that delights Planned Parenthood.

By now, we are burned out and itching to escape. With a few thousand in profit from the birth control movie and with Helen's long felt desire to revisit her mom's side of her family – most of whom live in one small village in France – a vacation is on the agenda. Before leaving we call Home Box Office and pitch Peter and the Wolf. "Send us a tape," they say. We send it. Two weeks later we're in New York, on the way to two months in La Belle Europe. We haven't finalized who will distribute *Peter* to the educational market. But Pyramid Films, in Santa Monica, has offered a $15,000 advance. So has another company. We settle on Pyramid, since they have a better track record distributing films that are simultaneously educational and entertaining. We phone L.A. to cement the deal. Then, since we haven't heard from HBO, we call and tell them we'll stop by to pick up our tape. As we walk in, Lucy Chudson, director of family programming, greets us, ushers us into her office and before we even sit down says, "I love the show. I can give you twenty thousand for three runs."

Gadzooks!

The two extra days getting the animal footage have put us $7500 over our $45,000 budget. But less than a month after completion we've recouped two thirds of the total. Damn good we think, for a half hour film by a couple filmmakers from Podunk. Ultimately, *Peter* sells to Showtime, CBS and the Disney Channel, to TV in England, Denmark, Norway, Australia, Germany, the Netherlands and a flock of other countries. Even to Saudi Arabia. We also close a home video deal. In the educational market alone it grosses $200,000. With TV and home video sales the total take (including revenue from two companion films produced later) approaches double that. Distribution deals being what they are, and with investors involved, we end up with maybe a quarter of the total, over five years. But who's complaining? Not Helen. Not me. We're happy as clams.

With careful organizing, doing most of the prep work ourselves, and ignoring the "conventional" wisdom of hiring a flock of people at high salaries and hoping for the best, we wind up with a major success instead of a creative disaster. And begin to wonder if we can do it again.

TWENTY-NINE

a duck, a jabberwock, and uncle milty

Compared to jabberwocks, ducks are easy to tame.

I'll elucidate: May 1982. Ray Bolger has returned for two more films; "following the Yellow Brick Road to Santa Cruz," as a local paper headlines it. Helen and I are shooting *The Ugly Duckling* and *Beware the Jabberwock* back to back, over ten days. Along with *Peter and the Wolf*, these are the first in a planned series of thirteen, introducing the arts to children. As *Peter* introduces the orchestra, *Jabberwock* introduces poetry, and *Duckling*, the dance. Soon as these are in the can I write two more scripts, introducing literature and theater. And we have concepts for titles dealing with other arts as well.[1]

The Ugly Duckling begins with Ray strolling by a duck pond (naturally). Now, almost a year after filming *Peter*, he's a bit fuzzier around the memory edges with his lines, but still turns in a classy job. After some nifty moves to illustrate how dance can express emotions, he introduces the Hans Christian Andersen story.

But this ugly duckling is no duck. Charlie Duckling is the oddball son in a family of straight-laced small town Philistines who work together in Papa's dry goods store, circa 1910. The script follows Charlie from the store, where he clowns with customers, to a birthday party for his grandma. And from there to the lonely streets; after turning a stately waltz into his own free form ballet and being ostracized for doing so. Discouraged, and terrified of

---

1 Ray Bolger died in 1985, and after the initial three we produced no further titles.

A Duck, a Jabberwock, and Uncle Milty

returning home, Charlie moves on to find his place in the world with a colorful troupe of carefree theatricals, Swan's Magnificent Dance and Acrobatic Society.

Our dancers are home grown. Little theater is big in Santa Cruz and classes in drama and dance proliferate, so locating skilled talent is a snap. Except for Charlie, who we cast in San Francisco. Our choreographer works out steps the dancers can master in a few rehearsals, we take over an entire street for a parade (where Charlie first spots the performers), and then stage the finale on an elementary school stage doubling for a theater. There, Charlie's parents, unaware he's part of the troupe, come to take in the show. When she recognizes him his little sister jumps up to applaud, ignoring stuffy Papa's admonition to "sit down!" As the performance concludes, one of the dancers presents Charlie with a certificate honoring his talent, a certificate speaking to the idea that each person is special and needs to do their own thing. Suggested by Bolger, the award comes out of his vaudeville background, recognition by producers of how much they value their performers. "You are unique and extraordinary and cannot be duplicated," reads the inscription.

And Charlie lives happily ever after.

Piece of cake, the *Duckling*. Great to work with dancers, a choreographer, costumer and the forty-five extras who relish taking part in a high quality but low stress, down home production. And a special treat to work with Hungarian born composer George Barati. In his seventies, tall, distinguished and with a bit of an eye for the ladies (but only an eye) Barati is a lesser known but highly regarded world-class musician. He's been conductor of the Honolulu Symphony and Opera, the Santa Cruz Symphony and has guest conducted more than eighty-five orchestras around the globe. Intrigued with the duckling idea, he agrees to a modest $1000 fee. His music perfectly dovetails with the choreography and stands on its own as a fine classical piece. All in all, a joyful experience. The way filmmaking ought to be.

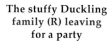
The stuffy Duckling family (R) leaving for a party

And then there's the jabberwock.

Picture a large, petulant man sweating profusely inside an uncomfortable rubberized costume that looks like a mini stegosaurus, and built around a backpack frame. Weighs seventy-five pounds, not including the ten-foot-long double tail. Takes half an hour to get out of the damn thing and in again whenever he needs to take a leak. And though the redwood glen we film in offers ample shade, mercury is in the nineties. The getup is so bulky it won't fit into a car, so Helen has to stand in the back of a pickup, the costume draped over her, as we drive slowly to the set. The imprisoning rig is my cockamamie design for Lewis Carroll's mythical creation. The man suffering inside is Michael Griggs, co-star of *Beware the Jabberwock*.

Day one of nine, during which we shot both films, has been devoted to Bolger's intro for *The Ugly Duckling*. (We shoot the bal-

A Duck, a Jabberwock, and Uncle Milty

ance of the film after he leaves.) On day two he meets a young girl (Juliette Tanner) walking through the woods with a huge butterfly net, while she recites a poem. When she encounters Ray he spots the net. "Looks big enough to catch a jabberwock," he says.

"A what?" the girl exclaims.

"A jabberwock."

"What's that?"

"Well, if you catch one, you'll know it," says Ray.

He scans the tulgy woods with binoculars and tells her he's looking for a jub-jub bird. Deciding he's cracked, the girl takes off. Then, concerned about her traipsing into the forest alone, Ray decides to follow.

Good thing, for she's soon captured (with her own butterfly net) by the lumbering, gruff-voiced jabberwock (Michael Griggs), who marches her to his lair, a redwood clearing that we've propped with a gigantic metal cooking pot (culled from a long ago ranch cookhouse), an ancient kitchen stove, a mirror, sword, swing, collection of fancy headgear on a rack, and other jabberwockish paraphernalia.

The sylvan glen is idyllic. Except for Michael inside the bulky costume. And except that sunlight through the redwoods changes constantly. We'll rehearse a shot and be ready to film, then "Hold on," cameraman Dave Myers will cry. He has to reset everything.[2]

And what does the scary yet pitiful jabberwock want of the girl? Seems his previous baker has run off and he needs someone to bake him chocolate chip cookies. Which the girl finds ridiculous. So she asks to be set free. He refuses. She insists. He's adamant. Meanwhile, Bolger, watching from behind a tree, points out that this is one clever girl. She'll figure a way out, he says.

---

[2] David Myers, who died in 2004, had feature credits that included *Woodstock* (1970), George Lucas's *THX-1138* (1971), *Welcome to L.A.* (1976) and Luis Valdez's *Zoot Suit* (1981).

Also meanwhile, as I argue with Dave Myers over the shots we lose every time he resets the reflectors, the rest of the crew is sniggering in the background.

In the jabberwock's lair, the girl prepares batter for the cookies. "Gosh," she says, as she puts them in the stove to bake, "isn't there any way I can get out of here? "Well," replies the jabberwock, there is one thing I like better than chocolate chip cookies . . ."

"What's that, what's that?" exclaims the hopeful girl.

"Entertainment."

She's crestfallen.

And so shortly is Michael Griggs. His third day on the shoot he wants out of the jabberwock costume. He's developed a bad case of poison oak. Itching like mad. He can't stand it. He calls from home to say he's through. What can I say? I know how he feels. Should I threaten? Cajole? Plead? Finally, appealing to his theatrical background, I remind him that we have thousands of dollars worth of talent and equipment sitting around in the woods, that without him the film will be a disaster and "Remember, Michael, the show must go on." The old saw does it; within an hour he's back on the set. Itching, and groggy from lack of sleep (the poison oak has kept him up half the night), but available.

Back to the shoot. The girl protests that she can't sing or dance. How can she possibly entertain the jabberwock?

"But you have a lovely singing voice," says the jabberwock, "I heard you." And he sings, "One misty moisty morning, when cloudy was the weather . . ." (Which she is reciting when we first meet her.)

"That's not a song," says the girl, "it's poetry."

"OK," replies the creature, "I'll let you go if you can dazzle me with a really great poem. But none of your run-of-the-mill stuff."

And so she begins. One poem, then another.

A Duck, a Jabberwock, and Uncle Milty

Scenes from *Beware the Jabberwock* and *The Ugly Duckling*

Director in the Jabberwock costume as it's being constructed

Michael Griggs
(The Jabberwock)
with Juliette Tanner

With cinematographer
David Myers (R)

A Duck, a Jabberwock, and Uncle Milty

Then our generator burns out and we wait half a day for a replacement from San Francisco. While I sweat bullets over how to complete the show on time. Finally, the generator arrives. But by now the sunlight has shifted again, so another readjustment.

From here on the story becomes an exercise in explaining poetry, with the girl reciting selections from Robert Louis Stevenson to Emily Dickinson to Christina Rosetti. Though his monster's brain is slow to fathom the concept, the jabberwock eventually "makes up" a poem himself (by Gelette Burgess):

I never saw a purple cow

I never hope to see one.

But I can tell you anyhow,

I'd rather see than be one.

Swelling with pride, he decides he wants more poetry. In fact, he likes it so much that "I can't possibly let you go," Any hope the girl has had, vanishes. Looking on, Bolger too is appalled. But he knows she's a smart girl, so "let's watch," he says. Finally, the girl distracts the jabberwocky with Carl Sandburg's comic masterpiece, "Arithmetic:"

Arithmetic is when numbers fly like pigeons in and out of your head.

Arithmetic tells you how many you lose or win if you know how many you had before you lost or won. Arithmetic is seven eleven, all good children go to heaven.

Or five six, pick up sticks . . .

To the creature, this is gibberish. But it's given the girl time to surreptitiously stoke the fire in the stove, which creates billows of smoke – and cinders the cookies. Then, while the jabberwock rushes to rescue his cookies, she grabs a sword and confronts him with –

'Twas brillig and the slithy toves

273

Did gyre and gimble in the wave;

All mimsy were the borogroves,

and the mom raths, outgrabe . . .

And it's this poem that gets to him. As it unfolds he chokes up. "All my friends are in it," he blubbers, "jub-jub bird and bandersnatch . . ."

The poem gets to me too. Because I've scheduled half a day for this encounter, light is fading and we have forty-five minutes to get the half dozen shots we still need. Racing like mad, we roll the final take as the last rays of sun filter away through the redwoods.

Backing the jabberwock against a tree with her sword (something I fantasized doing to cameraman Dave Myers), the girl extracts his promise to release her. "All right, all right," he pleads, "but if I ask very nicely . . . could you bake just one more batch of chocolate chip cookies?"

"Well . . . " says the girl, mulling it over.

Bolger guffaws, then hurries back to where the girl originally found him. When she shows up again Ray asks if she's found a jabberwock. She equivocates. Then, spotting a bag she's carrying, he asks what's in it. She opens it, producing a cache of giant cookies, and hands him one.

"Now where did you get these?" he demands. Embarrassed, and sure that if she tells him what's actually happened he'll think she's off her rocker, she rushes off. As Bolger laughs, he hears a loud squawk. He turns. On a tree limb next to him perches a large, colorful, blue and yellow bird.

"Waddya know," says Ray to camera, "a jub-jub bird! (A macaw we've borrowed for the day from a local pet shop.) Then, as he's about to offer a snippet of the huge cookie to the bird, the macaw takes an enormous bite out of it. Totally ad-lib. Ray too ad-libs. "Not the whole thing," he exclaims, "Here, I'll show you how we do that." He breaks off a tiny piece and feeds it to the bird.

A Duck, a Jabberwock, and Uncle Milty

How Bolger managed not to crack up when the bird gobbled half the cookie, I'll never know.

The film is in the can. Except that the laboratory dumps ten minutes of footage into the developing "soup," so Michael Griggs has to return for six more agonizing hours inside the torture chamber of a costume.

While the show "works," and is even a bit charming in spots, it never cuts together the way I had hoped. Not enough time for creative thinking on the set – because I hadn't anticipated the problems with the dappled sunlight, the cumbersome outfit made the jabberwocky look awkward and clumsy, and mostly because I hadn't taken the time to write out a shot by shot shooting script.

Again, solid planning is always the key to success.

Neither *Duckling* nor *Jabberwock* enjoy the success of *Peter*. Though we finally find an educational distributor for both titles, they sell poorly. Except as part of the package of three that CBS and then Vestron Video buy. (Largely due to Bolger's name, I'm sure).[3]

---

[3] Although it took three years, our investors eventually recouped their money and even made a bit of profit on the two titles.

REELING THROUGH HOLLYWOOD

Helen and I produce two more short films in 1982. Unlike the tension and trauma that surrounds deal making in features, working with school and library distributors is a snap. Usually, we'll show up with an idea and talk to one person or maybe two. If they buy the idea they'll make a few suggestions (because they understand content and the whims of educators who purchase their titles.) After script approval it's just, "Prepare a budget." Then they'll check it over and call to say, "Looks good, let's do it." Done deal.

In producing Shire's eighteen films for the school and library market, nothing was ever dictated. No one ever said, "No, you can't do that." Creative freedom was the name of the game.

Today, educational titles are released on video or DVD and often shown on closed circuit. I came into the industry when films for schools and libraries were booming. Though several companies still distribute to this market, few of them fund outside producers. Most filmmakers raise their own cash, make the film, video or DVD then seek distribution. Pyramid Films, distributor of *Peter and the Wolf*, tells me that as of 2006 most of their titles continue to come from independent producers. It's still a viable way to break into the business.

While we are plugging away at the Bolger films, my father is still bombarding Hollywood with his old screenplays. Plus a new effort, based on his nightclub novel, *One For My Baby*. He sends it to Walter Matthau, who writes back to tell him it's wonderful but "too depressing for me." Not long after Pop's phone rings.

VOICE: Hello, it's Milton Berle, from Beverly Hills.

POP (ever the curmudgeon): I don't know any Milton Berle and if I did I would not like him.

BERLE: Why?

POP: Because I have seen him in the movies.

BERLE (pathetic): But I *am* Milton.

A Duck, a Jabberwock, and Uncle Milty

POP: If you are Milton, now that I have got off on the wrong foot with you, what can I do for you?

Berle then tells Pop that Matthau has told him about *One For My Baby* and that while Matthau has said "It's not right for me, but it would be great for you." So, after an exchange of humorous pleasantries, Pop agrees to send Berle the script. And does so. And Berle returns it with a note that says while he found it "tremendously interesting, very well written, funny and sad," he will pass. So Pop promptly sends it off to Woody Allen. Who also passes.

Unlike Pop, Helen and I have mostly given up on Hollywood. We don't live there (and don't want to), and my name is fading from the memory of most former industry contacts. Youth culture is rampant; twenty-year-olds are making million dollar deals for high concept screenplays. And I've just turned fifty. But thirteen films are now under our Shire Films belt. It's time to materialize our long held dream: to develop a feature length screenplay, raise production funds and make it.

A movie of our own. With me directing.

Lining up a shot. Cameraman Dave Espar (L), Helen, myself

My mother, Mary Burnett, with Harold Frisbie, whose tragic story we dramatized in *Hard Traveling*

THIRTY

hard traveling

I been a hittin' some hard travelin', I thought you knowed; I been a hittin' some hard travelin', way down the road . . .

Woody Guthrie

And it is *really* hard. Creating a feature film, that is, especially for a couple of small time producers with middling money connections. Producers who want to do so in a modest California town, with no high powered execs peeking over their shoulders, no budget-crunching accountants to answer to and nothing but their own best judgment to rely on.

Like all such ventures, making your own movie means taking a big chance. You might win, you might lose. You roll the dice (with some understanding of the odds, let's hope). And while William Goldman's adage that the only Hollywood constant is that "nobody knows anything" is so much hogwash, whether or not your venture will succeed sometimes does come down to an educated crapshoot.

Every film starts with an idea. During the previous few years I'd conjured up several. *Off the Ropes* (the woman wrestler script) is still on the list. In Los Angeles I meet with a legendary woman wrestler, who agrees to advise. A crusty Oakland promoter supplies photos of women working the circuit. Helen and I scout locations. I prepare a budget. But generating excitement around a movie dealing with this "arm pit of show business" is like selling tickets to watch my toenails grow.

By the time the recent Bolger films are in the can, we've expanded the list to include: *Soldier Boy*, a fine play (and screenplay) by Severo Perez; *Rapid Transit*, an original I've written, taking off from an actual bus strike in Santa Cruz; and the political thriller *The Hostages*, screenplay by my father while I was working in Hollywood. But this involves a big cast, New York City locations and filming at the United Nations. Too ambitious.

Though I'm initially dubious, Helen convinces me that the story we should tackle is one based on my own family, a true story that my father had novelized in 1941. The title, *Bread and a Stone*.[1]

Long story short, and without the pathos: Pennsylvania, 1940. My mother, now married to Harold, an itinerant farm hand, was struggling to make ends meet while raising brother David and me.

---

[1] The title is from Mathew VII, 9: "What man is there of you, whom if his son ask bread, will give him a stone?"

HARD TRAVELING

Harold borrowed a gun and set out one day to hold up a store to get money to pay Mom's mounting bills. Along the way he hitched a ride. Deciding to hijack the car in order to get where he was going faster, he pulled the gun and ordered the driver to pull over and get out. Instead, the driver grabbed for the weapon. It discharged (accidentally, said Harold), killing the man. Harold, terrified, hid the body then drove home with the car, a new Buick, lying to Mom that he'd been off trying to sell a (nonexistent) house he owned. The Buick, he said, belonged to his brother. The police showed up at our home within days and arrested Harold. He pled guilty before a three-judge panel, but in spite of an impassioned defense relying on testimony about his cruel and abusive upbringing he was sentenced to die in the electric chair. Appeals took almost a year, but were to no avail. Harold was executed on December 21, 1941.

More than a murder story, Pop's book tells a moving tale about a man who, though he tries desperately, is never able to overcome the terrible hand he's been dealt early in life.[2] Critically acclaimed, the *New York Times* called *Bread and a Stone* "A vivid, understanding portrayal of a man who could have been many things, but never had the chance to become anything." The Book-of-the-Month Club said, "Its emotional impact is comparable with Dreiser's [*An American Tragedy*, 1925]." Pop had tried for years to get it produced as a film. First in 1943, by handing a copy to his friend Bette Davis. Then sending one to Joanne Woodward and Paul Newman during the 1960s. A note from their secretary thanked "Miss Bessie" for sending it along. My father even wrote an outline for a modern version. It never got made, possibly because it was seen as a downer.

Any creative person with a sense of social responsibility faces a critical decision in terms of what they write, paint, perform, or produce. Will they go with their conscience, or opt for commercial success? Not that these are mutually exclusive; Dickens' writing was popular as soon as it appeared and he became wealthy, while at the same time framing the social fabric of his day in starkly realistic terms. Van Goghs not only sell in the millions, but also capture the

---

[2] See my family history, *Rare Birds*. Or to read the longer story, with the pathos, seek out *Bread and a Stone* itself

REELING THROUGH HOLLYWOOD

passion of what that tortured artist felt about nature and humanity surrounding him. (Though it took decades for the world to understand.) *Cabaret* was a critical and financial success as both a play and a film, while painting a moving portrait of individuals caught up in the march of Nazism. And it was wonderful entertainment.

In film, those who don't give a fig about social responsibility or about reflecting human values in their work are perhaps fortunate. They can cut directly to the commercial chase with little concern for content. The rest of us hope that by utilizing our skills and by following Shakespeare's admonition to be true to ourselves we can create something that will, if not rake in millions, at least not find us on welfare at the end of the day.

And this is what Helen and I are determined to do when we decide to base our feature on *Bread and a Stone*. We hope this story of a decent man driven by circumstance to kill someone will engage audiences as well as add a bit more insight into what kind of a society creates people such as Harold. John Ford did it with *The Grapes of Wrath* (1940). Sydney Pollack did it with *They Shoot Horses, Don't They?* (1969). And if you haven't seen the British masterpiece *Brassed Off* (1996), rush right out and rent a copy. We hope to turn out something half as good, make a statement, and entertain at the same time. Although we'll put everything we have into it, ultimately we know it's going to be a risky venture.

The first hurdle is my grumbly father, who wants to "negotiate." Early on, I suggest that he might want to write the screenplay; or maybe we'll write it together. A hassle develops. How much money is he going to get, he wants to know? How much creative control will he have?

"It's my novel the script will be based on, after all," he writes me, as if he's dealing with some avaricious mogul. I reply that while I'll certainly respect his ideas and honor the book, the only way to financially protect those from whom we'll seek investment is for Shire Films to have final approval of the screenplay and on what gets to the screen. Our letters fly back and forth. He's hurt, and

Hard Traveling

implies that I don't feel he can turn out an excellent script. Though I never say so, I'm not sure he can. His style is still circa 1945. But I'm willing to let him give it a whirl.

He also seems to believe that Helen and I have made a bundle off the Bolger films. Where he gets that from, I have no clue. Though he leavens his references with humor, he's serious. Eventually, I convince him that while we aren't panhandling, neither do we have a fat savings account. (In fact, we have none. And though we eventually make a fair profit on the series, this doesn't start coming in for another two years.) Finally, the negotiations became so wearing that I admit I'd prefer to write the screenplay myself. Then, after I remind Pop that I won't be taking a nickel for doing so, or for directing, and that neither will Helen get a producing fee, he decides that I should write the screenplay (with his input) and he'll be satisfied with a percentage. He too is worn out. It's been like pulling teeth. With me the dentist.

We also agree to raise enough investment money to advance him $5000 toward the rights to *Bread and a Stone* and enough extra to reprint the book as part of a pre-publicity campaign for the film. A campaign that will continue for two years, the time we anticipate it will take to write a screenplay, raise the money, choose a cast, find locations, hire a crew and get ready to shoot.

Bread and a Stone is told in flashback. Beginning (circa 1940) with the arrest of Ed Sloan (Pop's name for Harold in the book), the story cuts back in time to his meeting with Norah Gilbert (his name for my mother). From there, two dovetailing plot lines advance the story: Ed and Norah's courtship, marriage and increasingly hard times on the one hand, and Ed's trial, judgment and impending execution on the other. It works beautifully in the novel, and in spite of screenwriting gurus who rant against flashbacks, for this story I feel they are appropriate. Sections of the novel are discursive, framed in Ed and Norah's thoughts. But since this can seem hokey in film (without using a narrator) and since I follow Pop's structure, it only takes me a few weeks to write a first draft. And I've come up with a new title: *Hard Traveling*. Though Pop is adamant that *Bread and a Stone* is far better and argues with me about this until (and even beyond) the film's release. Two drafts and six months later, and with input from both Pop and Helen, we have a screenplay that we all feel is true to the book.

Simultaneously, we've begun seeking investors and locating principal cast. To begin, we figure a $625,000 budget; later increased to $800,000. Peanuts by Hollywood standards, but adequate, we believe, to pay a professional crew, hire SAG talent and have enough for everything else we'll need to produce a first class movie.

Ed and Norah are the key roles, and even before writing the script we've been thinking of Ellen Geer for Norah. Daughter of Will Geer (Grandpa, in *The Waltons*, 1972-81), Ellen heads the Will Geer Theatricum Botanicum, an outdoor performing space in Topanga Canyon near Los Angeles.[3] I've seen her there in everything from *Twelfth Night*, to *The Glass Menagerie* and have a good deal of admiration for her. Not only because of her acting ability, but also because, like me, Ellen "does her own thing," performing with a dedicated band of performers during the summer, and also introducing Shakespeare to inner city kids who are bussed to Topanga, where most of them quickly get into acting and all kinds of stagecraft. Ellen has, we believe, just the right mix of empathy and strength to portray Norah as the kind of woman my mom was. My very special mom, who, having given so many years of nurturing to everyone she knew, slipped into a gentle dementia and died in March of 1982.[4]

Others who come to mind are excluded mainly because Ellen seems so right. And even though Ellen generously offers to send the screenplay to Jane Alexander (*The Great White Hope*, 1970; *Brubaker*, 1980), after seeing her in *Testament* (1983) we decide that for our film Jane would come across as too cold.

---

[3] Ellen and I had become friends during the early 1970s, when I invited her to lunch one day after watching her (in the role of Sunshine Doré) fake *seppuku* in front of Bud Cort in *Harold and Maude* (1971).

[4] Mary Burnett, "Mom," also has a chapter in my book *Rare Birds*.

HARD TRAVELING

Ed is harder to cast. The actor needs to be highly intelligent, project a combination of inner warmth but outer danger, and convince viewers that he's a semi-literate farm hand. Early on, we set up a casting session in San Francisco. Comedian Bill Irwin, mostly known only to Bay Area audiences at the time, is a possibility. But he seems a bit too fuzzy warm. Not much of an "edge." Much more impressive is J.E. Freeman, whose film credits amount to a couple walk-ons. Tall and rangy, with a sad, angular face, it's clear from a single reading and with minimal coaching that Freeman has a grasp of the character. He's even quickly able to modify his thick Bronx accent. But he is also a nonentity in terms of name value, so the search continues.

Clint Eastwood is not on our list. (Though with hindsight, perhaps he should have been.) In May of 1983 we get a call from his company, Malpaso. Dirty Harry is coming to Santa Cruz to film *Sudden Impact* (1983) and they need five hundred extras. Though Helen and I are deep into fund raising efforts, we badly need a personal money fix. Rough waves have been pounding our monetary shore. Two recent short educational films, plus freelance animation, have been barely enough to keep us from being washed away.

Since we've already developed an extensive talent file, we're ahead of the game in finding extras. Helen takes on the job. Her press release and flyers attract a thousand hopefuls to a local community center for a "cattle call" (Hollywood lingo). Everyone brings a photo and fills out an info card. Over the next five weeks Helen selects folks Clint will need for all kinds of situations: fishermen, street extras, seniors riding in a shuttle van commandeered by the bad guy in the film. Even a group of Mafioso types for a wedding party.[5] She also hires talent for a few speaking roles. For these she contacts the San Francisco talent agent we'd used for *Peter and the Wolf* and who found us J.E. Freeman. "Be sure that whoever you cast can direct themselves," cautions the agent, "because Eastwood certainly isn't going to."

---

[5] With my counsel, at least one of the Mafia wedding party, Ralph Peduto, went on to get his SAG card and has been featured in films such as *Mrs. Doubtfire* (1993), *The Rock* (1996) and *Patch Adams* (1998).

And that's the impression I have as I watch him on the set. (Between gobbling down steak and lobster provided by Clint's catering service.) He doesn't seem to direct. Not on this film, anyhow. He just vaguely indicates what he wants to his cameraman and to his actors – prime among them, his girlfriend Sondra Locke. First A.D. David Valdes actually frames most shots, directs background action and keeps the show moving. I sidle up to David one afternoon while Clint is in the midst of showing Sondra how to aim a pistol (in the film, she's revenging a murdered sister). "This guy doesn't seem to be directing," I whisper. "I get the sense that you're doing most of it." David betrays a wry grin, but doesn't say a word.[6]

But however he does it, Eastwood has turned out some great films.

Helen, wondering which of the 500 extras she's cast that Clint Eastwood will want next

For five weeks of ten to twelve-hour days, Helen shuttles back and forth from locations – where she nudges Clint to decide what

---

[6] Actors I know who have worked with Eastwood on other projects have a different experience and say that he does indeed direct.

extras he'll need – to our home office, where she schedules talent and makes calls far into the night to line them up for the next day. The $6000 fee we earn provides a strong breakwater against our stormy financial sea and allows us to continue casting our own movie with much less fear of being swamped.

Clint probably wouldn't have taken the job anyhow.

Clint Eastwood on the set of *Sudden Impact*

So we consider Peter Fonda, Martin Sheen and John Ritter. (Years earlier, I had spent time in an acting class with Ritter and his then wife, Nancy Morgan.) But we try Sheen first. His secretary reads the script then calls, enthusiastic. But a week later she calls again. Sheen is booked for the next year. We approach other big names. Scott Glenn (*The Right Stuff*, 1983) passes. Ronnie Cox (*Deliverance*, 1972) reads the script and is eager for the role. Helen and I audition him for the part opposite Ellen. Something, we feel, is missing. We meet director Alan Rudolph (*Choose Me*, 1984; *Breakfast of Champions*, 1999) at a soiree where several filmmakers (including me) are directing portions of a documentary honoring Hollywood blacklistees. Jules Dassin (*Never on Sunday*, 1960) is present, among others. Afterward, Alan invites us to a shoot he's directing, starring Keith Carradine, another possibility. We watch Keith work, look at some of his films then decide he isn't right.

Later, in the midst of a party at our house at which Pop appears (and weirds out a couple potential investors with his politics) the phone rings. Helen is preparing snacks and I am schmoozing, so someone else picks up. "Jane Fonda is on the phone!" they shout. Well, what timing. Ears perk up. I had called Jane the previous day to ask her opinion of Levon Helm, drummer in The Band and with whom she's recently starred in *The Dollmaker* (1984). She thinks he'd be great for our movie. (Though she doesn't invest in the film.)

We send Levon the script. He calls back to tell us he really likes it. Weeks later we meet him north of San Francisco, where he's filming. Then, after screening *The Dollmaker* at Fonda's office in L.A., we decide that while Levon's "look" is perfect, he probably can't sustain the complex role of Ed Sloan for an hour and a half movie.

So San Francisco's J.E. Freeman it is, name value or not.

The third major role is Sloan's attorney. Ellen Geer calls Jason Robards and asks him to read the script. I send it, wait two weeks then phone him at home in Connecticut. He's bent out of shape because I have his private number; until I reminded him that he had told Ellen I could send the script. Then he turns into Mr. Nice. He likes the script but feels that "this isn't for me."

In May, Helen leaves for Santa Fe for a week to be with a dear friend dying of pancreatic cancer. I stay home and continue trying to locate someone for the attorney role. We get the script to Ned Beatty (*Deliverance*, 1972; *Superman*, 1978). I speak with him at a party in L.A. and he says he'll let me know in a couple weeks. Richard Dysart (*L.A. Law*) is also reading it.

In June, my father turns eighty. Helen and I take him and wife Sylviane to dinner in San Rafael. A tummy lined with a gourmet French meal does wonders to make him forget his grievances with me.

HARD TRAVELING

The search for investors, meanwhile, proceeds apace. With $30,000 in seed money from participants in our Bolger projects, we have hired a Santa Cruz attorney to draft a limited partnership agreement. At a minimum $20,000 a pop, it's no slam-dunk. For the next year and a half we meet with, write letters to, or phone close to two hundred fifty contacts. We end up with twenty-two investors and raise $275,000. Largely from local business people. Far short of our $800,000 goal.

Meanwhile, ever optimistic, we've begun to prep the film. In her best selling production book, *Before You Shoot*, written after we've made a bunch of films, Helen points out that "time can equal money."[7] The more time available to find locations, gather props and complete other tasks on your own, the less you'll have to hire these out later. So, all during the casting and investment-seeking period, we are also looking for places to film. By the spring of 1984 we've explored nearly every rural road in Santa Cruz and northern Monterey counties. We've identified a decaying farmhouse where much of the action will take place and have found almost every other major location. Many big bucks saved that can be applied to many other needs.

We've also advanced $500 to a wardrobe person, who has been haunting thrift stores for clothing she can adapt to an early 1940s look. By the time we film she's put together outfits for all the actors plus a hundred extras. Wardrobe costs will eventually double our estimate, but are still much cheaper than for any big studio shoot.

The same for props. While Helen is on the Eastwood film, the prop man needs a dozen battered garbage cans. "I'll find them," says Helen. Shrugging it off, the prop man buys six brand new cans and "distresses" them by tossing them around, rolling them in dirt and marking them up with spray paint. Couple hundred bucks in labor and materials down the tubes. That's how Hollywood works. We don't have the luxury, so all through pre-production we borrow props and store them in our backyard shed.

---

[7] *Before You Shoot: A Guide to Low Budget Film and Video Production*. Available from Shire Press, 644 Hester Creek Road, Los Gatos, CA 95033. $12.00, plus $2.00 postage and handling.

We also hire our crew on a standby basis. David Myers, cinematographer on the last two Bolger films, will shoot *Hard Traveling*. Despite the aggravation between us on those films, I feel he's right for the job.

And we have a fine composer: Ernie Sheldon. His credits include hit singles such as "Baby the Rain Must Fall," and lyrics for Elmer Bernstein in several films. As well as music and lyrics for Severo Perez's Mark Twain TV special.

Pre-production flows steadily ahead. Fund raising flows like molasses.

July 1984. We need to shoot that fall or wait until the following spring. By now, we realize we'll never reach $800,000. Helen juggles figures, calculates how much we can defer, and comes up with a rock bottom $450,000. Still $175,000 short of what we've raised. We send out letters offering a small percentage for short-term loans. No takers. Crunch time. We're sufficiently confident about *Hard Traveling* that we decide to mortgage our home for a loan. And Helen takes out another loan on a house she owns in San Francisco. Plus a third on remote land she has in Mendocino County, land where she's built a cabin to which we sometimes go to get away from it all. With these loans in hand, plus the investor's money, we can make the film.

HARD TRAVELING

> Don't put your own money into a movie, says conventional wisdom. But if you have a passion, sometimes there's no alternative. Being true to yourself, assessing possibilities as realistically as you can and then taking chances is part of what makes life interesting. And if it doesn't work, remember, if your bank account goes bust and you can't afford the BMW or the trip to Puerto Vallarta, you'll still be able to drive to a sunny beach in your ancient clunker, or stroll to the park and smell the roses. Point being, you've opted to go for the gold, but if you don't win the trophy, life goes on. Or, as I wrote in a progress letter to Pop, "The worst that can happen is that we'll have to live in Helen's Mendocino cabin and grow carrots."

Last minute details: Pop wants to play the judge who passes sentence on Ed Sloan. I decline. I'm worried that he'll ham it up. (Though I don't put it that way.) He is furious – as I discover after his death, in an unsent letter to me found among his correspondence. In truth, frazzled and overworked as I am, I haven't been as sensitive to him in relation to his help and input as I should be. After filming, I tell him this and apologize. He seems to understand.

We still haven't nailed down the lawyer. Ned Beatty's schedule conflicts. Richard Dysart accepts, but two weeks later signs on for a high paying gig in another Clint Eastwood film. We're two weeks from filming and minus a key actor. But Dysart calls a friend, the superb Dana Elcar (*McGyver*, 1985). Dana has been having trouble with his eyes and can't do it. So he calls *his* friend Barry Corbin (*War Games*, 1983; *Northern Exposure*, 1990-95). I overnight the script to Barry, who calls two days later and says he'll be happy to play the role. For SAG scale (the same as all the actors are getting), plus a tiny percentage. Big sigh of relief.

We sign character actors James Gammon and Jim Haynie as detectives. Our creature from the Bolger poetry film, Michael Griggs (sans jabberwock costume) will play a country bumpkin who finds the body of the murdered man.

Everything is in place. We're ready to rock and roll.

J.E. Freeman and Ellen Geer with the boys, Anthony Danna (on Freeman's shoulders) and T.J. Thompson

Hard Traveling

The family (above). Ed Sloan (Freeman) after the killing (below left). Barry Corbin

REELING THROUGH HOLLYWOOD

Attorney Frank Burton (Barry Corbin) defends Ed Sloan. Nora (Ellen Geer) visits Ed in Jail (below)

Hard Traveling

October 2, 1984. We begin to film. In spite of a standard ten-hour working day for the crew (eight for actors; fourteen or more for Helen and me), the pre-planning pays off. We keep to our schedule almost exactly. We have to, the budget won't allow for mistakes.

Ellen Geer and Barry Corbin are a delight to work with. Professional and innovative, they add bits of business that aren't in the script: After first meeting Ed (Freeman), Ellen coquettishly undoes her hair, in a bun until then, to look more attractive. When she meets Corbin to discuss Ed's case, he leads her up a long stairway to his office. He huffs and puffs then stops to mop his brow. Helen, sure that a heart attack is coming on, rushes to his aid. "Are you all right?" she anxiously asks.

Ellen Geer getting made up

"Oh, fine," says Barry, smiling. "I just thought the character ought to seem like he's out of shape."

Most of the time the shoot runs smoothly. With notable exceptions:

• Filming in Ed and Norah's bedroom in the farmhouse we've rented for two weeks, I have an entire morning (five hours) to shoot nine fairly elaborate shots. A luxury, since I'm usually well organized, precut in my head (animation training) and know exactly how much I can cover in a given period of time. Except that Dave Myers takes three and a half hours to light the room. Now I've got an hour and a half to get everything. Including time to let David

REELING THROUGH HOLLYWOOD

readjust between shots. So, sinking into my head for a few minutes, I boil the sequence down to two master shots, plus three quick close-ups for coverage. And when we finish, stalk out, stifling my anger. Oddly enough, the scene turns out to be one of the more tender in the film. (Thank you, J.E. and Ellen.)

• In the same bedroom, Ed plays a guitar in one shot. The PA who has supplied the guitar has been goofing off, exaggerating her importance to the show and badmouthing folks. So Helen, with my agreement, fires her. Miffed, she takes the guitar with her. No time to find a substitute guitar, so although I've planned to use it in a couple more shots I have to reconnoiter.[8]

• We've scheduled a day along the ocean, where Ed takes Norah (and her two boys) for a "honeymoon" ride after their wedding at a minister's home. When we get to location, tidal waves of fog are rolling in. Norah exits the car and gazes out to sea, contemplating her life ahead. We get the shots, but at rough-cut the scene is visually ridiculous and slows the pace. As do shots of Norah's sons running along the beach.

• Another scene features the brother of Norah's former husband (who had died in an accident). He brings a gun to the farmhouse; the gun Ed borrowed and that is used in the killing. As the brother-in-law demonstrates his shooting ability, his wife, the boys and Norah and Ed look on. Scott DeVenney plays the brother-in-law in such an egotistical manner that J.E.'s blood starts to boil. He gets so much into Ed's character that I have to remind him that Scott is simply playing a role, for I'm convinced Freeman is about to attack him.

• We've scheduled thirty-five days of filming. Six weeks, six days a week (less one day). On the next to last day, shooting the film's opening sequence along a country road, it starts to drizzle. We chance it for a time. Then rain. Then the gaffer pulls the lights so they won't explode. This sets us back half a day. Half a day on

---

[8]Our fired PA went on to work as a casting director on features such as *Evita* (1996) *Contact* (1997) and *Master and Commandeer; the Far Side of the World* (2003).

296

HARD TRAVELING

which we've planned to do our last shots with Freeman. He isn't on the set at the time and no one thinks to tell him he'll still be needed for the extra half day.

On this shoot, J.E. is something of a prima donna. Often, he won't like my suggestions, so when I want him to modify a piece of business I use Ellen (who he respects and who agrees with my directing) as a go between. Later, understanding that I mostly do know what I'm doing, he starts affectionately calling me "moose." (I have no idea why; I'm 5'9" and a bit, hardly a moose.)

On the scheduled last day, and even though his role has just found him killing the driver he has hitched a ride with, J.E. is in hog heaven. He's received his salary and, wearing a new black leather jacket, is taking off for Los Angeles the next day on a new Harley.

"Well, look," I remind him, "after we finish today we've still got a few more shots to pick up. We have --"

I never complete the sentence. Freeman is livid. He won't have it. He's planned this trip and he's "Sick of your fuckin' direction and telling me what to do and I'm splitting!" Not tomorrow, right now! And off he goes, striding down the long rural road toward the sea. Forget the extra half day; I still have two hour's worth of shots to finish in *this* sequence. And there goes Freeman.

I shout after him. No dice. Helen appeals to him. He turns and curses her. The crew stands around looking at their shoes. Helen and I confer. What to do? Then my friend Thom Smitham, up from L.A. to work as our production accountant, saves the day. He climbs into his car and takes off, catching up to Freeman two miles away. An hour later they're back. Freeman doesn't say a word to anyone, just completes the day's work then takes off for Tinseltown. But we manage to get him to return a week later for the shots needed to complete his role. At which time he's far more agreeable. But an apology? Forget it.[9]

---

[9] Freeman has since had major roles in films such as *Ruthless People* (1986), *Millers Crossing* (1990), and *Patriot Games* (1992). As of 2005, he was still a featured player in films and on TV.

Freeman isn't the only tense character. Time and money pressures, tantrums and temperaments, all these add to the stress of production. Nor am I immune. Some of my grumpiness gets to Helen, who is trying mightily to steer *Hard Traveling* clear of the financial reefs. So we argue more than necessary. Then too, Helen, highly organized, but whose style many see as pedantic, grates on the crew. Especially cameraman Dave Myers. Even though her counsel is right on much of the time, David can't take it. When he finally blurts out his feelings, others on the crew snicker. Nor am I as supportive as I could be.

Supportive? Shit, I sometimes want to strangle her! (And in all fairness, the feeling is probably mutual.)

Still, our relationship has mostly been solid, so my decades-long tendency to wheedle my way into an occasional adulterous bed is long over. And though I've been completely faithful, the pressures around the shoot do find me flirting. Mildly. But even this gets to Helen. And we have a film to complete, so the pot on our domestic stove just simmers.

But along with the frustrations are many delights:

• Screenwriter Tom Rickman (*Kansas City Bomber*, 1972; *Coal Miner's Daughter*, 1980) lives in Santa Cruz; Good sport that he is, I recruit him – for a twenty-five dollar fee – to play the foreman of a road crew, part of a montage in which Ed Sloan is looking for work.

• The boys I cast to represent my brother David and me have never acted, so we have them spend extra hours with Ellen and J.E. before the shoot. By the time their scenes are on tap, they feel like a real family. And can ad-lib business, too. In the scene in which Ed and Norah get married, my character starts picking his nose (wonder where he got that from?) His "brother" jerks his finger away. They both crack up. And it stays in the film.

• We need a variety of 1920s and 1930s automobiles. Two hundred fifty dollars a day to rent (in Hollywood; in 1985, that is). Twenty-five bucks each in Santa Cruz. Including drivers, who are

Hard Traveling

delighted to trot out their Model A or shiny new 1940 Buick just to be part of the show. One driver, wrongly informed about what cars are needed, appears on location miles from town in a 1915 Olds, complete with himself and his wife dressed in dusters and goggles. "No problem," he says when told of the mix-up. Smiling, they turn right around and head home.

• No problem too, when I discover, in a country store up the coast from Santa Cruz, a cache of period grocery items to stock Norah's cupboard. Rental charge? Not a penny. "Just don't forget to bring 'em back."

• Authentic license plates for the period cars? America is a collectors' paradise so we find all we need in a garage twenty miles from town. Ten bucks for all forty of them, for as long as we require.

• And no problem getting General Mills to ship us their single remaining box of circa 1940 Wheaties. Return postage is the only cost.

• Need an airplane? In nearby Gilroy, a huge restaurant, The Flying Lady (now demolished), features model aircraft flying around the dining room on an overhead trolley. Adjacent, a gigantic hanger shelters the TWA tri-motor used in *Raiders of the Lost Ark* (1981). But they don't have the Stearman biplane we need, so we're directed to a small flying museum in nearby Morgan Hill. We find the plane, hire it, and a friendly pilot lands it right on schedule at the small mountain airport (that we use gratis) and waits two hours while we film. Then, up in the air again and he touches down two more times to make sure we have the takeoff and landing shots. All for $200.

• Early on in *Hard Traveling* I recreate a scene from my childhood. A scene not included in *Bread and a Stone*, because Pop never knew about it. One night in Pennsylvania, David and I had hitched to town with Harold to see Charlie Chaplin in *The Gold Rush* (1925). We need a copy of the film and this, I assume, will cost an arm and a leg. Not so, as it turns out. Chaplin never bothered to renew copyright so the film is in public domain. In other words, all we have to do is find a print and pay the cost of duping the section we want. (In which Charlie cooks and eats his shoe.) Total cost, $150.

And so it goes. Thirty-six days work and the show is a wrap. Only one day over schedule (because of being rained out that night on the rural road). And because I've compromised and combined a number of shots. But then I've also filmed sequences that will never make it into the final cut. We've shot in a farmhouse, in a jail, in a cramped and sweltering courtroom recreated upstairs in the Veterans of Foreign Wars building. In a packing shed, a junior high vice-principal's office doubling for a police station, along a foggy beach, inside and outside an old movie house, in the basement of the same theater (doubling for a police interrogation room), along country roads and inside Ed Sloan's "home" – a tiny hovel inside a dilapidated barn.

We've printed dummy newspapers, found 1940s packs of Lucky Strike and Camels, old new-looking copies of *Life* and *Look*, and I've designed Wendell Willkie posters and had them silk-screened. (The murdered man, a Republican, is out tacking up posters for the 1940 presidential candidate when Ed hitches the ride.) We've manufactured artificial rain for a scene looking into Norah's window, and created a look for the film reminiscent of the 1930s pallet of painter John Stuart Curry.

We've employed a crew of twenty-five, including several interns. We have paid SAG wages to all the actors. The non-union crew has received the equivalent of scale.

By a few days into the shoot, editing has begun. Susan Heick, with tons of TV and short film experience but eager for a feature credit signs on for a flat rate. With one assistant and with a 35mm upright Moviola set up in our spare room, she has a rough cut within a week after we wrap. Overly long, but that's not unusual.

Music is next. With only a harmonica and a guitar, our friend and composer Ernie Sheldon creates a winning score. An original song, sung by Ellen and Freeman, adds extra emotion to the already poignant ending.

And Helen has brought the show in at $25,000 under budget. An amazing accomplishment.

It's been a long, hard, rock-strewn road. *Hard Traveling*. But we've navigated past the boulders. We know that we still have a way to go to complete the film, but we're eager to get our baby out there and introduce it to the world. We are confident peo-

Family Ties

In 1941, half a dozen years before his "unfriendly" appearance before the House Un-American Activities Commit-

Dan and Alvah Bessie in 1940.

tee and subsequent blacklisting, screenwriter Alvah Bessie (*Objective, Burma!*) wrote a prescient novel of Depression-era persecution called *Bread and a Stone*. Forty-four years later, his son, Daniel, has adapted the novel into a feature film called *Hard Traveling*. The familial connections do not end there, however. The story that both father and son have been moved to tell and retell is itself based on family history.

The protagonist, Ed Sloan—an unemployed man who is executed for a murder he commits during a desperate robbery—was Daniel's stepfather, whom his mother married after her divorce from Alvah. In the film, the couple's son is eight years old—Dan's age when the events occurred. Of his stepfather's arrest, Dan recalls, "I was told that Ed had been taken into the army." It was not until he read *Bread and a Stone* years later that he learned the truth.

Dan was trained as an animator in the fifties, cutting his teeth at MGM's cartoon studio drawing Tom and Jerry. He moved into commercials and children's films; then in ⟨?⟩ he coproduced *Executive ⟨Ac⟩tion*, the Burt Lanca⟨ster⟩–Robert Ryan film about ⟨the⟩ John F. Kennedy assassina⟨tion.⟩ "It was the first of a genr⟨e de⟩picting the fact that the go⟨vern⟩ment can and will lie to us⟨,"⟩ says. In 1980, he and f⟨ellow⟩ producer Helen Garvy fou⟨nded⟩ Shire Films in Santa Cruz ⟨To⟩gether they have written, ⟨pro⟩duced, directed, and edited ⟨doz⟩ens of short entertainment ⟨and⟩ educational films. Dan ac⟨knowledges⟩ that *Hard Traveling*, Sh⟨ire's⟩ first feature, is not "obvi⟨ously⟩ commercial," but says the⟨y de⟩cided to "do something clo⟨se to⟩ our hearts. I had made ⟨my⟩ peace years ago with the ⟨psy⟩chological barriers and res⟨erva⟩tions [against approaching ⟨the⟩ story]."

Alvah Bessie died at eighty-five last July, ⟨?⟩ months after the film was ⟨fin⟩ished. After spending a ye⟨ar in⟩ Texarkana State Prison fo⟨r re⟩fusing to "name names" b⟨efore⟩ HUAC, the Academy A⟨ward⟩ nominee moved to San F⟨ran⟩cisco, where he wrote bo⟨oks,⟩ edited a longshoreman un⟨ion⟩ newspaper, and worked ⟨for⟩ seven years as a stage manager at the Hungry "i" nightclub. Dan says, "He would have liked to go back to Hollywood, but he wasn't going to beg. He made his choices." Dan describes his own approach as "less didactic" than Alvah's, but adds, "We have the same world view—a humanistic outlook."

Dan and Helen consulted with Alvah during the making of *Hard Traveling* and showed him the work at various stages. Its premiere screening in Santa Cruz attracted 250 friends and crew members. According to Helen, she and Dan knew it might be the last opportunity for Alvah to be among his supporters and admirers. They hope that, in *Hard Traveling*, Alvah Bessie's spirit lives on.

—**Robert Aaronson**

ple will love it. Then too, we look forward to the reviews, the festivals, the parties and the schmoozing, the perks that come with distributing a successful movie.

What we do not realize is that we've completed only half the journey. Another road lies ahead, a road filled with even bigger boulders. To navigate around those will take another full year.

THIRTY-ONE

hard traveling II
the agony and the ecstasy

Between 1984 and 1986, while we are producing and seeking distribution for *Hard Traveling*, Hollywood releases a string of high concept pictures: *Alien, Ghost Busters, Three Amigos, Back to the Future, Indiana Jones and the Temple of Doom* and *Friday the 13th Part IV: Jason Lives* (among others). By the time each has completed filming, distribution is a done deal. Theaters have been lined up or are bidding to show these titles, basing offers on their anticipated box office take.

Even before a major studio film starts to shoot, huge publicity machines are cranking up, getting ready to turn out posters and press releases, arrange interviews and personal tours, everything that might guarantee success. And because their investment is in the millions, this is just as important if the movie turns out to be a stinker.

Hard Traveling is definitely low concept. And Helen and I don't have millions. Or thousands. We've spent it all getting the film into the can. But just like Hollywood, we jump-start publicity long before the shoot. Making a movie is glamorous, especially in a small town, so local press is eager for stories and interviews. We use these to generate advance interest, and as soon as we wrap create a mailing piece announcing the fact. Off this goes to distributors and key press people. And we contract (for a small percentage) Jeff Dowd, a highly regarded producer's rep, to help us guide *Hard Traveling* along the festival route and into theaters. Jeff sees the film in roughcut and thinks he can land a distributor.

Hard Traveling II: The Agony and the Ecstasy

My father views the film in rough-cut too, along with an audience of fifty, from whom we ask suggestions for improvement. Pop, sliding gradually downhill with a series of infirmities (he's 80), is in tears. And in tears again weeks later, when, after re-cutting, adding music and effects and striking an answer print, we screen it for cast, crew and investors in Santa Cruz.

Now begins the agony. Much of it for Helen. We haven't transferred to video yet, so she flies cross-country, schlepping two heavy cans with six reels of 35mm film. In and out of planes and taxies, trudging New York's frigid February to screen for the Cannes Film Festival's Director's Fortnight. Soon after returning she drives to L.A. to show *Hard Traveling* to Paramount, Goldwyn and others who have responded to our letter.

We don't make Cannes. And Paramount and Goldwyn both pass. (Distributors don't exactly say no, because if a film later shows signs that it might become successful, their previous "pass" (card game terminology) at least leaves the door open. Like all cash-poor independents, our task is now to demonstrate that our little gem is worthwhile to take on. Because distributors are, after all, in the business of making money. So on to the festivals.

Seattle is first. Jeff Dowd gets us the invite. When the film is screened (on June 1, 1985), after local radio interviews us, we arrive to find a surprising five hundred in attendance. More than half fill out evaluation cards, with an overwhelmingly positive response. Seattle genuinely likes the film. We use this information as part of a second letter to distributors who haven't previously responded, praying that this time they will.[1]

On June 4 my father celebrates his 81st birthday. We are driving back from Seattle and regrettably can't make it to the party. Later that month Helen is in New York again to screen for the Rotterdam, New York and Toronto festivals. (None of which invite us; a big downer.) In early July we send another mailer, and began work on

---

[1] The film was shown on Seattle's "Discovery Weekend," along with two others. The *Post-Intelligencer's* film critic reported that, "Except for Dan Bessie's *Hard Traveling*, the other films are absolute clinkers."

another short film to rustle some cash to live on. On July 20 Helen and I take off on a day trip north to Point Reyes. We stop by Pop and Sylvian's en route. To our shock and concern, an ambulance is parked outside. Pop has had difficulty breathing during the night and is suffering chest pains, so off he goes to the hospital. We follow and spend two hours with him, by which time he's become his old chipper, curmudgeonie self, joking and reminding us that in spite of his ailments – including a dose of bladder cancer his doctor has assured him is curable – he promised to live until the film was finished.

We return home that evening. Next morning the phone rings. My sister-in-law Carolee is on the line. My father, she sadly relates, suffered a massive heart attack that morning and has died in the hospital. David is too broken up to come to the phone. My tears start to flow, but just as I did when Mom died I soon find myself at the computer, typing out my feelings about Pop, who he was and what he's meant to me. My own form of release.

Hard Traveling II: The Agony and the Ecstasy

And he lived up to his promise; he hung on long enough to see *Hard Traveling* completed (if not distributed) and was immensely proud of what Helen and I had accomplished.

In September we screen at the Mill Valley festival, where editor Robert Dalva (*The Black Stallion*, 1979; *October Sky*, 1999) offers suggestions for shortening *Hard Traveling* to pick up the pace and intensify the drama. Soon after, Warners, Columbia and Fox call; they've read the superb *Variety* review we received after Mill Valley. So Helen is off to L.A. again. From studio to studio she lugs the heavy film cans. Everyone says they like the movie. But we feature no big stars and it isn't typical Hollywood fare, just a small, character-driven slice of life. "We don't know how to distribute it," runs the refrain.

In October we spend a week in New York, talking up the film at the Independent Feature Market. We attend a flock of parties (including a strange affair inside a converted church and another with at least two hundred crammed inside a tiny Greenwich Village loft). But we leave New York encouraged; three small distributors now want the film. (Though they have no money to advance.) Also, we're holding out for a biggie. Mini-major New World Pictures has also made nibbling noises, but no firm offer. Still, we score another plus, an invite to the Florence Film Festival, where only American independents are screened. By now, we've been with the movie for two and a half years and with the distribution effort six months. Helen and I are getting edgy with one another, so Europe should be a welcome break. With a small profit from a recently produced educational film, plus an unexpected gift from Helen's parents, off we go to Italy.

November in Florence. The festival hosts us in a charming old hotel on a street the width of two donkey carts. Exploring the city, I circle Michelangelo's *David* for nearly an hour and am stunned by Botticelli's *Birth of Venus* at the Uffizi. We hang out with animator Faith Hubley (*Cosmic Eye*, 1986)[2] and others, and take off on a

---

[2] While living in Santa Cruz I was privileged to have played a small part in a homage to Faith, organized by Les Goldman (see Chapter 14).

day trip to medieval Siena. Closing night we caravan to the village of Fiesole in the hills above Florence, where the festival director's high-school-age daughter and friends host a party in a restored Sixteenth Century villa. The temperature is in the low thirties. The daughter and her entourage are decked out in Renaissance finery: bare shoulders, no stockings, and sandals. Freezing their tootsies. (And everything else.) A hundred fifty, we are told, have been invited. Five hundred cram into the place. No room to move. And no one has had dinner. "Downstairs," says one of the hostesses, "when you hear the bell." We wait. Two hours. At eleven p.m. the long anticipated bell rights. The starving hordes crowd toward the cellar, flowing like molasses down a four-foot-wide stairway and into a long, narrow basement. Once downstairs, Helen and I begin weaving through the mob. (What if someone yells fire, I'm thinking.) The cellar is Coney Island on the Fourth of July, wall-to-wall bodies. And at the far end stands a life-size winged statue of Mercury, fashioned of cardboard and covered with tinfoil. Stuck into the foil are tiny slices of cheese and salami, olives and other condiments. Half an hour later, Helen and I have elbowed our way to the statue. By which time most of it has been picked clean. We quickly devour the few remaining sad-looking leaves of lettuce.

Bye, bye Florence. Now we're off to Helen's relatives in southern France, spend a week driving around the area then return home.

In November, *American Film* runs an article about *Hard Traveling*. And the highly respected *San Jose Mercury* reviewer Glenn Lovell writes an appreciative piece, especially praising Ellen Geer's "subdued and wonderfully textured performance."

In January 1986 we're accepted at Sundance – then still called the United States Film Festival. Arriving early, we head first to see Dinosaur National Monument, but call the festival just to be safe. "Oh," chirps a charming female someone, "you're supposed to be here. Bob is hosting a brunch for the filmmakers." "Bob" is Robert Redford, so we race forty miles back to the Sundance Institute. I get a smile and an "excuse me" from "Bob" as he edges past me in the buffet line. We schmooze with Bay Area friends, then, after

Hard Traveling II: The Agony and the Ecstasy

chow, head for the festival office to find out where we'll be lodged. Assignments are alphabetical, so we find ourselves in the middle level of a three-story condo, each level with a huge wardrobe and bath. Below our room is Duane Byrge of the *Hollywood Reporter*. Above, Brazilian director Hector Babenco (*Kiss of the Spider Woman*, 1985). A great guy and also one of the festival judges, Hector is constantly on the phone with Jack Nicholson or his agent, working out a deal for Jack's appearance in Hector's next film, *Ironweed* (1987).

Critic's Choice (*San Jose Mercury News*)

■ Film ■

FOR GOOD or ill, Hollywood's hopes for summer '86 — "Top Gun," "Karate Kid Part 2," "Aliens," etc — are already out there. The two weeks before Labor Day, and the arrival of the fall movie crop, traditionally have been a time when independent distributors dump everything that's left.

This Friday is no exception as such exploitation quickies as "Reform School Girls," "Bullies" and "Born American" open locally. "Reform School Girls" is a bad women-in-prison opus New World Pictures hopes to pawn off as high camp. "Bullies" looks to be a perverse love story that mixes elements from "Deliverance" and half a dozen vigilante-justice thrillers. And "Born American" has the distinction of starring Chuck Norris' son Mike in another red-baiting tale a la daddy's "Invasion USA."

My advice is to seek out the low-budget but deeply moving "**Hard Traveling**," which was shot in Santa Cruz County by Dan Bessie. Ellen Geer (Will's daughter) and J.E. Freeman co-star with many Bay Area actors in this autobiographical story about love and desperation during the Great Depression.

To his credit, Bessie, working from father Alvah Bessie's novel "Bread and a Stone," has combined the rich period look and harsh social criticisms of such disparate stories as "A Death in the Family" and "In Cold Blood."

"Hard Traveling" may be rough-hewn and amateurishly acted in places, but, like such recent independents as "On the Edge" and "Desert Bloom," it's a movie of undeniable compassion and integrity. ■

— Glenn Lovell

Norah (Ellen Geer) and Ed (J.E. Freeman) in Dan Bessie's 'Hard Traveling'

'Hard Traveling' doing some traveling on the festival road

By DUANE BYRGE

PARK CITY, Utah — "Hard Traveling" has been traveling the film festival circuit this year (Seattle, Mill Valley, Florence, here) and winning positive response, according to the film's director, Dan Bessie.

Set in a small town in the 1930s, "Hard Traveling" is based on an incident in Bessie's early life, which his father, Alvah Bessie (one of the blacklisted Hollywood 10), wrote about in his novel "Bread and Stone."

"It's a love story based on the investigation of a murder," Dan Bessie said about the story line for "Hard Traveling."

"Two stories merge — the love story and the investigation — with the backdrop being the Depression of the 1930s," he said.

In "Hard Traveling," J.E. Freeman (a San Francisco-based stage ac-

tor) is featured as a small-town handyman. He's considered by many to be shiftless and no-good, but a schoolteacher (Ellen Geer) falls in love with him. The emerging relationship is shattered when Freeman is booked for the murder of a prosperous local businessman.

Bette Davis expressed interest in playing the Geer role in 1944, Bessie noted, but wanted the film to have a more upbeat ending. "If you stick to your guns for 40 years, you can get your film made," Bessie said.

Financing for "Hard Traveling" was secured through a limited partnership and Bessie and the film's producer, Helen Garvy, raised the $425,000 for "Hard Traveling's" budget.

Actual filming began Oct. 15, 1984, and wrapped six weeks later. "We were on time and under budget," Bessie said. "This is remarkable since our filming was done entirely on location, but the secret to making an independent film is having a high level of organization," Helen

"If you stick to your guns for 40 years, you can get your film made."

Garvy is a superb producer, extremely organized."

The film's production was further assisted by the excellent cooperation of the local communities in Northern California, where film was shot. "One of the great advantages in filming in a small community," Bessie

said, "is that people in a small town are delighted to help. We had very few problems and in being very selective in our cast selections — Freeman was chosen, despite overtures from more well-known actors — we got tremendous performances."

"Hard Traveling's" director of photography David Myers' feature film credits include "Welcome to L.A.," "Zoot Suit" and "THX-1138," among others.

"Our production has the look of a $4 million film," Bessie said. "The support and cooperation we had from everyone involved made for that."

At present, producer Garvy and director Bessie are considering offers from distribution companies. "The festival reactions we had ... was tremendous and very positive," Bessie said.

Among other 1985-86 films, Wayne Wang's *Dim Sum* is a festival entry, along with *On Valentine's Day*, written by Horton Foote. *Hard Traveling* is shown twice, once at Park City's modestly rococo Egyptian Theater. After the screening, a creative team that worked on *The Trip to Bountiful* (starring Geraldine Page) crowds around, congratulating Helen and me and expressing amazement that we could turn out such outstanding work on our beer and pretzels budget.

We don't win the Jury Prize; that goes to *Smooth Talk*, starring Treat Williams and Laura Dern. And though Babenco later tells us (in confidence) that he's voted for us for Honorable Mention, we don't get that either. But soon after the festival we land something perhaps more important: a major distributor!

Ever since the Independent Feature Market the previous October, we've been shining on the small fish eager to handle the film but who have no front money. (Just like everyone else in the movie business, we can't afford to say no to anyone.) Then too, New World has continued to dangle a distribution carrot. We've met with them but so far no offer is on the table. And we're leery because their reputation includes such scintillating titles as *Slumber Party Massacre* (1982), *City of Blood* (1983), and *I Like to Hurt People* (1985). Though they've told us they want to "move in a different direction."

Another potential is Steve, a friendly New Yorker who has had a career booking films for Warner Brothers and is now eager to move into distribution. He sees *Hard Traveling* as his calling card. Finally, weeks after Sundance, and with a promise that he'll promote the dickens out of our movie, we agree to meet for lunch in L.A., along with his partner, and with our rep, Jeff Dowd. Over Sushi, we push Steve for an advance. He agrees to $50,000, spread over six months.

Hard Traveling II: The Agony and the Ecstasy

Not much, but at that point the best offer we have. Helen looks at me. I look at Helen. Jeff looks at us both. Then I excuse myself to make a call. (I'm late returning a message from New World.)

"Hi, Dan Bessie here," I say to our contact, Walter Calmette. "You called?"

"Yes," says Calmette, "we'd like to know how much you want for the film. As an advance."

Palpitations. I have no idea what they'll spring for. Should I ask for a million? Half a million? No way. New World certainly knows we didn't spend anything like that to make the movie. Let's see . . . Steve has offered $50,000. I'm thinking fast. (And maybe too fast.)

"Well . . . we'd like to get at least a hundred fifty thousand."

Long pause, then, "I think we can manage that."

I'm happy. But also cursing myself. Would he have sprung for twice that? No way to know. We've been at this a year and it's time to get our show on the road.

Back at the table I stall Steve and his partner, telling them we want to consider the offer. "But we'll get back to you." (The old Hollywood line.) After they leave I tell Helen and Jeff about the New World call.

Helen and I return home to weigh options. We like Steve, he seems like an honest guy. And we're still edgy about New World. But we have a responsibility to our investors; they need the best return we can negotiate and there are no more distributors to approach. So we call Steve to explain our position, trying to soften the blow. He is clearly pissed.

Steve doesn't have a deal. But we do.

New World adds another $25,000 to re-cut the film, so we can shave off ten minutes. Helen does the work, from suggestions made by Bob Dalva at the Mill Valley festival, and this is the print we screen at Sundance. The extra money not only pays for the new cut, but also for legal fees and Jeff Dowd's three percent of the advance.

We retain rights for China and the U.S.S.R., for which we work out a separate arrangement with International Films Exchange in New York. IFE negotiates a $25,000 deal with the Russians, this being added to the funds returned to our investors. China, we never sell to.

New World agrees to our publicity suggestions, changes their poster design to suit recommendations Helen makes while on an L.A. visit, gets ready to send us on a five city tour, and blows smoke up my ass about wanting to "finance your next film."

Well, at last the movie is traveling.

Helen and I, on the other hand, are not traveling so well. By early summer, maybe because of a dose of negativity on my part, or due to her own version of the "seven year itch," or coming out of the immense pressure on us those past three years, she wants to end our

HARD TRAVELING II: THE AGONY AND THE ECSTASY

relationship. I'm devastated. Protests avail me only an agreement to a "trial separation." Except that we can't afford separate digs. And New World is making plans for us to promote the film and be interviewed all over the U.S. as this fun, movie-making couple. (Gotta maintain the image.) So in August, off we go on tour.

Decent crowds show up at first run theaters in San Francisco, Toronto and Seattle. A disappointing twenty at the Embassy 72nd Street in New York. And the same at the Goldwyn Pavilion in L.A. We're limoed from hotels to movie houses, and to interviews with the *New York Post*, WMCA Radio, CNN, NPR, *San Francisco Chronicle* and a flock of others. Two weeks on the road. During all this time Helen and I are civil and friendly to one another, mostly sleeping in the same hotel bed (each huddling on his or her side, no body contact, thank you), and at the same time I am trying to talk her out of making the separation final. Except for the tension of being apart while together and though I often have to pop a Dalmane in order to sleep, the tour is great. Hobnobbing with media folk and talking to press and to audiences about the events behind the movie is a huge turn on.

And then the reviews arrive.

Hoping to hit a home run, big distributors spend millions in advertising. Reviews, word of mouth and box office take are the keys to success. But if a movie doesn't find what Hollywood calls "legs" within the first couple weeks, it's usually pulled. Advertising stops, losses are cut and the distributor may recoup at least some of their outlay through later TV and home video sale.

No home run for us. *Hard Traveling* doesn't get to first base. WOR-TV's Judith Crist calls it "tired, trite and tedious." No matter that the film is true to *Bread and a Stone* (which itself is true to the events from which the story's been drawn), the *New York Times'* Walter Goodman disgorges three columns of cynical ink about the social values in the story. It's "a true people's weepie," he writes, and "ideologically generated fiction." Goodman, I later find out, has had a long-standing hatred for my father. Why, I never learn. The *L.A. Times'* Kevin Thomas calls *Hard Traveling* "not worth the trip." (Critics are paid to be clever.) By the time we finish the tour the graceful swan we've nurtured for three years is pretty much a dead duck.

It makes little difference that later reviews are favorable. Even laudatory. A month into release who cares if the *San Francisco Chronicle* says that the film "has the feeling of an Andrew Wyeth painting," or that Charles Champlin of the *L.A. Times* (though he's no longer doing reviews) takes Helen and me to lunch then writes in a feature profile that *Hard Traveling* has a "quality . . . of unfeigned compassion that is as affecting as the events themselves". Doesn't matter that *Variety* hugs it to its bosom, as do *Billboard*, *The Boston Globe*, *The Christian Science Monitor*, *St. Louis Post-Dispatch*, *Seattle Post-Intelligencer* and a flock of others. And apparently not enough moviegoers watch *Sneak Previews* on PBS, whose Jeffrey Lyons ". . .won't forget this very relevant, powerful and deeply touching film. For an intelligent bit of Americana and drama, it is the movie to see." The box office is all that counts; when audiences vote with their wallets, that's the bottom line.

Still, New World deserves credit; they stick with us and with the film for the rest of the year and into 1987.

In September we're in Spain for the San Sebastian festival. The director has phoned us to come, since he feels we'll be a contender for top prize. (Forty thousand bucks is not to be sneezed at.) The Spanish press praises the film, interviews Helen and me, and at a Basque restaurant the patron recognizes us from news article photos and treats us to drinks. (Helen has lemonade.)

Hard Traveling is screened three times. On the premier night we arrive early to the venue, a turn of the century opera house, ionic columns, marble staircase and all. We're to meet the festival's director, but he hasn't arrived so we ascend to a balcony to watch the crowd. Soon after, he spots us and hurries to the landing. "You must make a grand entry," he whispers, as he spirits us down a back stairway. As we reenter, reporters take notes, flashbulbs pop and puzzled onlookers wonder if we are "somebody."

Hard Traveling II: The Agony and the Ecstasy

Seated in a box with the Spanish distributors, they greet us effusively. But soon after the picture begins they all seem puzzled. Whoops! New World must have sold it to them as a thriller.[3] As the picture ends the audience applauds wildly. Then the judges are introduced. Each is under thirty. All are drenched in black leather. We know that our hoped-for prize consideration has gone with the wind.

After the screening we descend the staircase under a bowed lattice of flowers held by teens. Half way down we stop while a company of young Basques execute an elegant folk dance in our honor. Helen, always taken aback by such pomp, feels like crawling into a hole.

On closing night we dine in an ancient church. Starting at midnight. (Well, you know the Spanish.) In a high balcony an unseen chorus belts out pop songs, while guests of honor Gregory Peck and Ali MacGraw hold center stage at a front table. At two a.m. desert is served and at three, cordials. But Helen is leaving the next morning in our rented car to visit her French relatives, while I'm heading for Barcelona on a bus to visit director friend Jaime Camino. So we turn in early (four a.m.).

Seven a.m. I've got a raging fever. But as Helen drops me at the bus station I tell her I'll be OK. Then off she drives toward France. My bus arrives, and for the next four hours, hot tea and aspirin at each rest stop sustain me. I even sleep through most

Being sick on the Barcelona-bound bus

---

[3] *Hard Traveling* was released in Spain as *Balada Para Un Condenado (Ballad for a Condemned Man)*.

313

of a Charles Bronson shoot-um-up on the bus's TV. In Barcelona I meet Camino and he takes me to his condo on the Mediterranean, where for three days I sweat out the fever until Helen arrives. A day late. Which has me in a panic, because I've been imagining the car upside down in some desolate ravine in the Pyrenees. (Actually she had the wrong address and had slept in the car overnight.) Overjoyed as I am to see her, we are still "separated."[4]

In October I'm in Portland, Oregon (alone) to open *Hard Traveling* and present a workshop on independent filmmaking – one of several panels and seminars Helen and/or I appear on during this period. For nearly six months I've also been trying to convince her that we can make our relationship work. Finally, this seems to sink in, for soon after I return from Portland we are a couple again.

In the spring of 1987, the doorbell buzzes. Our friendly neighborhood postman holds an express envelope from the U.S.S.R. (with a picture of Lenin on the front). We open the letter while he looks on. No Ruskie gold inside, nor any scheme to subvert the American Way of Life, just an unexpected invite to the Moscow Film Festival. By now, *Hard Traveling* is going nowhere in the U.S. But we still believe in the film and this is at least one more chance to promote it. We're also curious about the U.S.S.R. under Gorbachev. So, with a couple more educational films under our belt, we have enough in the bank to take flight to Mother Russia.

TWA from New York is an hour late to Charles de Gaulle. With Helen leading the charge, we race for our Air France connection – and arrive at the gate as the plane is taxiing. But we're quickly ticketed onto Aeroflot. In Moscow, nobody is there to greet us. We wander around until a young man from the festival, also wandering around, discovers us. He's been assigned to locate lost souls. He directs us to a taxi. Wary of rip-off rumors, we ask our rescuer how much the fare will be. "No fare," he replies, "No cost of anything. You are guest of festival."

---

[4] Before leaving Barcelona we took in Jaime's acclaimed *Dragon Rapid* (1986) a marvelously crafted feature detailing Francisco Franco's rise to power. Five months after it had opened, the theater was still two thirds full.

Hard Traveling II: The Agony and the Ecstasy

After stowing our luggage at the massive Russiya Hotel (3000 rooms, matrons built like Notre Dame fullbacks standing guard on each floor), we head for the festival office. There, we learn that we're supposed to have an interpreter. "Go to the office just down the hall," says an official. (Days later we find out that we're supposed to hang out with all the other Americans, who have two interpreters assigned to them as a group.)

"Hello," I greet another harried official (all Russian officials seemed harried), "we understand we're supposed to have an interpreter."

"Oh yes?" she replies. "And you don't have one?"

"No interpreter."

She scans a chart. And frets. Then, looking beyond us, she brightens. Scurrying down the hall is a perky young woman in her twenties. The official catches her arm, Russian flies back and forth. Then the official turns to us and says, "This young woman will be your interpreter." And so we meet Vicki Melnic. Charming, a bit intense, but, as we quickly discover, savvy about how "things get done" in Moscow. She also speaks excellent English. Vicki hangs with us for most of the next five days, sneaks us in to see Marcello Mastroianni in *Dark Eyes* (1987; *Ochi chyornye* in Russian – the audience cracks up over all kinds of in-jokes we don't get), finagles tickets to the famed and fabulous Moscow Circus, guides us through the Arbat district where Helen's father had lived as a boy, flags down "gypsy" cabs – private cars driving with lights on in the daytime – when legal ones race by packed with riders, and becomes a good enough friend that she visits us for a week the following year in Santa Cruz.

"Your film, it will be presented in a medium sized theater," apologizes another official. "Medium size" turns out to be thousand-person capacity. *Hard Traveling* is screened three times over seven hours and each show is packed. But without subtitles and undubbed, an announcer *narrates* from a booth, translating each character's dialogue as they speak. Must have done a good job, for the audience reactions are just like those we've witnessed in the States.

Between showings we lounge in the office of the theater's manager, a stocky and gracious but tense character who plies us with cookies, hot tea and a strong liqueur. After each screening we take the stage, with Vicki translating as the audience peppers us with questions. Then, after the last round, we are mobbed by a gaggle of middle-aged women, many in tears, who want to know "the fate of your mother." (What happened to Mom after the events described in the movie.) They nod appreciatively when I tell them that following the trauma of Harold's execution she had gone on to become a nursery school teacher, helping young children to get the start in life that Harold never had.

Answering questions in Moscow

Much praise for the film. Except from one young man who demands to know, "How you can say this movie is authentic? The men are all wearing blue jeans." He scoffs and walks off when I tell him that Levis have been a staple in America since the mid 1800s. To him, in 1987, jeans are one of the latest (and more expensive) mod statements for the fashion conscious young Russian.

On the last day, festival attendees are shuttled by train to Leningrad (St. Petersburg). Somehow, we aren't on the list. But once again Vicki comes through. On the train, we spend time with the *London Times* film critic and with the engaging David Jones, direc-

Hard Traveling II: The Agony and the Ecstasy

tor of *84 Charing Cross Road* (1987).[5] We arrive at the Leningrad station next morning to be greeted by a military band. Then onto busses for a tour: to the Smolny Institute, where political debates raged prior to the Soviet revolution; to a memorial for the eighteen million U.S.S.R. citizens killed during the Great Patriotic War (as they call World War II); and to the summer palace of Catherine the Great, a masterpiece of restoration down to gilded mirrors, marble, and gold leaf roofs, after being used as a barracks by Hitler's army. Finally, that night, a grand banquet and "entertainment." Ah, we think, Russian folk dances. Marvelous. The dinner is so-so; rubber chicken. But that's OK, great culture waits in the wings. As an overture concludes, curtains part and a long line of leggy chorus girls in colorfully plumed costumes parade out and proceed to wiggle their tails about. A Las Vegas style floorshow! Helen and I crack up.

With our translator, Vicky (next to Helen) and a press photographer (R)

To bed by midnight and it's still not dark. Leningrad's "white nights" are upon us. By three a.m. it's still twilight. By four, the sky has started to brighten. Back to Moscow we go. Then by train to Budapest. A few days wandering that Magyar metropolis, a waterlogged afternoon among corpulent and semi-naked Hungarians

---

[5] Several years later I sent David Jones a script idea, asking if he remembered me. "How could I possibly forget someone I met on a train between Moscow and Leningrad," he replied. (But he didn't bite on the idea.)

splashing about in the Art Nouveau-style Hotel Gellért's indoor and outdoor pools, then up the Danube by hydrofoil to Vienna, where we stay with a friend from Santa Cruz now living there. After that, by rented car to Helen's relatives in France, then home via Paris.

It's now late summer, 1987. We take stock of our hard (but often joyful) traveling:

• Helen has sold her San Francisco house in order to pay off loans we took out to complete the film's financing.

• A year of making more short films has let us return the money borrowed against her Mendocino land.

• Traveling with the film to Seattle, Portland, Mill Valley, Park City, New York, Toronto, San Francisco, Los Angeles, Italy, Spain and the U.S.S.R. has been a blast. And the film has journeyed without us to festivals in Denver, Boston and Karlovy-Vary in Czechoslovakia.

• We've met scores of interesting film folk, appreciative fans (and a few cynics), attended fabulous parties, exhausted ourselves and survived the near breakup of a basically good relationship.

• The film has screened in twenty-five American cities.

• Reviews have been eighty-five percent positive.

• Both HBO and Cinemax will later air the film.

• New World, attempting to escape their slasher image, will release *Hard Traveling* to home video, in company with a Sissy Spacek feature, a documentary on James Dean, and a kids' fantasy, *The Peanut Butter Solution* (1985). Our video will sell a few hundred copies then die. (To find one, go to e-bay, where a VHS is often promoted as "rare." Your winning bid will probably be about $1.86, plus postage.)[6]

---

[6] Through a series of complicated sales, buyouts, and transfers, *Hard Traveling* is now owned by Ted Turner's media empire.

Hard Traveling II: The Agony and the Ecstasy

• Though it's a box office flop, our movie has been seen and appreciated by thousands. (Perhaps millions, considering TV.)

• That Pop was moved by the film touched me deeply.

Finally, what I said to the *Hollywood Reporter* when interviewed at Park City proved true: "If you stick to your guns for forty years, you can get your film made." (It had been that long since Pop first tried to sell *Bread and a Stone* to Warners.)

More amazing is that even after losing a bundle, a few investors still eagerly want to know "what's your next project?" There won't be one. Not a feature at any rate. Helen is burned out. Let down by our inability to at least return all of our backer's money, she vows not to undertake that kind of risk again. Who can blame her?

And how about yours truly? Would I do it again? Write and develop and direct a feature I believe in, that is? In a flash. But I'd also try to walk more gingerly. Losing people their house or their money is a bummer, especially when you're confident you won't. And the stresses of making a movie can rupture even a strong and loving relationship. With that in mind, however, it's possible to approach the process with even more thoughtful planning than Helen and I felt we had brought to *Hard Traveling*.

If you really understand what you're doing, making movies can be joyful, uplifting and contagious. And perhaps the most powerful way to say what you feel about all the quirky, sad, exciting and wondrous permutations of that mysterious thing we call life. As Luis Bunuel says, "Cinema is a magnificent and perilous weapon when wielded by a free spirit." But becoming a free spirit doesn't simply mean, "doing your thing" without care and consideration.

With that in mind, making movies can be less a crapshoot and more a creative challenge.

THIRTY-TWO

the littlest moviemakers

> Garvy, 44, is a gray-haired, pleasant and decidedly upbeat writer and former teacher who has also worked as a family therapist. Her books include *Before You Shoot*, a how-to book put out by Shire Press, their own independent publishing firm.
>
> Bessie, 54, is a balding, bemused and grizzled veteran screenwriter, animator, director and producer who has toiled on feature films, kiddie cartoons and TV commercials in Hollywood.
>
> *San Jose Mercury News*, February 26, 1987

Balding, yes. But grizzled? Well, that aside, the article, headlining "The Littlest Movie Makers," and featuring a posed photo of Helen and me entwined in 16mm film, covers a lot of ground. Mostly, it describes what we've been up to and what we *will* be up to between 1987 and 1992. Even with four years of *Hard Traveling* winding down, projects are unfolding at a rapid clip. Part of this has to do with the need to keep the larder full, and part because creativity is the lifeblood of folks who get high on making movies, writing books, drawing cartoons and teaching others to do the same. We do all of the above. (Though I'm the cartoonist.)

Helen's *Before You Shoot* has been selling like hotcakes. This intro to film production is now into a third edition. Theater and film bookstores sell hundreds of copies a year. University classes

The Littlest Moviemakers

and film groups use it. Besides inking sketches for *Before You Shoot*, I illustrate her other titles, including *Coping With Illness* and *The Immune System: Your Magic Doctor*.

This book, developed from a twenty-minute animated film with the same title, is one of a series on physiology.[1] Chained to the drawing board for five months on *The Immune System*, I scribble over six thousand drawings before it's complete.

We script each new title as a mini drama and often break stereotypes – casting a male ballet dancer in one film, for example, or a

Scenes from *The Immune System*

---

[1] *The Immune System* was screened at L.A.'s Third Annual Animation Celebration and was a finalist in the Birmingham and American Film and Video festivals.

gutsy young gal sword fighting in another. Helen, an accomplished editor by now, cuts our films together in about a week, so making these little movies involves not too much effort. With local talent and worthy subject matter, they are not only enjoyable to work on, but add a few thousands bucks to our bank account.

> Admonition: if riches and fame are your goal, don't start making films for schools. But if you can finagle the money on your own (distributor budgets are minuscule these days), they're a great way to learn the craft

Next up is a condensed version of *David Copperfield*, produced for the University of California at Santa Cruz's Dickens Project. Kate Rickman, recently divorced from director Tom (*Coal Miner's Daughter*) turns out a fine adaptation that moves, in an hour, through David's schooling and young manhood to his marriage. Most of Dickens' key characters are included: the Murdstones, Peggoty, Wilkins McCawber, Agnes (the companion of David's youth), Dora (who becomes his wife) and the despicable Uriah Heep. The Project has $9000 available, for which we're to write the script, pay and feed the crew, design sets, shoot, edit, mix, add titles and turn in a master 3/4" video and one VHS cassette for the entire show. (The Dickens Project pays the actors separately.)

Directing Gene Lewis (L) and Robert Fenwick, as they record music for *David Copperfield*

THE LITTLEST MOVIEMAKERS

The Dickens Players, half a dozen local actors who perform at the Project's annual Christmas party (complete with old English carols, spice cake and mulled wine), comprise the talent. We add Kate's son as a young David and talented college students to play Dora and Agnes. The rest of the cast doubles up, with two of them playing three different characters.

The budget doesn't allow for fancy sets, nor for more than a single location, so we shoot on a UCSC stage, using borrowed props. Rearranging lights allows us to suggest time, place and mood. And we do it all with a crew of four. In three days. With my tight shooting script, and taping at a virtually one-to-one ratio, we finish on time and on budget. And after editing (using an apprentice, with Helen supervising), there is actually $2000 left for us. More amazing, even without name personalities the acting is so good and the staging so effective that the video almost has the feel of a modest episode of *Masterpiece Theater.*

A lesson here: ever wonder why so many budgets get blown, so many films run disastrously behind schedule? No mystery. A lot of folks out there don't pay attention to what they're doing. Foresight in developing a script, knowing exactly how much is available to spend, nailing down every cost in advance, wise pre-production planning, attention to detail, sufficient rehearsal and choosing the right people to act in and crew a film or video can make a beer budget shoot look like Chateaunuf du Pape.

Helen and I are no longer the only little filmmakers on the Santa Cruz scene. By now, talent abounds; camera and sound people, grips, production assistants and a slew of wannabes. Especially since we've made a point of apprenticing locals, many of whom go on to professional careers: a P.A. who casts major studio features; a grip who becomes our production manager then moves to L.A. to produce and direct; a camera store salesman who signs on as Frances Ford Coppola's videographer. (And the list goes on.) Students from UC Santa Cruz tell us that they learn more working with Shire Films for two months than they have in three years at the university's film department.

Among the locals is Todd Flinchbaugh, a film teacher at a nearby college, who becomes my friend and mentor. Working together over several years, we combine his uncanny sense of structure with my ability to add color, texture and dialogue, to make a fine screen-writing team. But being far from the "tit" (as Pop's fellow black-listee Dalton Trumbo called Hollywood) puts us at a disadvantage. Though I mail scripts, write letters – and drew bravos from AT & T for the fat phone bills I run up – since *Hard Traveling* has stumbled, and because I'm no longer a "player" (if I ever was), my industry contacts are now few and far between.

Sometimes Todd and I luck out, and one of our projects receives a hearing. After we develop a terrific period musical, *Nobody's Boy,* I phone a contact at Sundance. "How do I get this to Disney?" I ask. She gives me a name. I call Disney. Which asks to read the script. Two weeks later it comes back with a "good work, but we'll pass" note.

How do I know this guy has any power? I ruminate.

"Why don't you send it to Michael Eisner," suggests Helen. I guffaw. "All he can do is say no," she continues.

Sure, why not. So I write a friendly letter to Eisner, telling him that *Nobody's Boy* had been rejected, but "I don't know if the fellow who saw it has anything more than veto power with you folks." Then I forget about it. Two weeks later the phone rings. It's another Disney exec. "Hi, Dan Bessie? Michael Eisner asked me to call. We'd like to take another look at your script." I send it again. Another week. Another call from the same exec. "Really fine script," he says. "If this were 1960 we'd buy it in a flash, but it's not really what we're looking for right now." Later, I submit it to Disney's TV division. One more turn down. Still, the project does get a shot.

> So take chances. Go for the brass ring. Worst that can happen is that some high muckety-muck will say no. And he or she just might say yes.

Eddie Wilenski and the Junior Commandos also gets a shot. Todd and I cobble this together out of my experience "guarding" a huge pile of scrap iron that neighborhood friends and I have collected for the war effort back in 1943. We combine this with the memory of my visit (along with brother David) to Hollywood in 1944, and with my father's career. Out of these ingredients Todd and I spin a clever yarn for kids. In it, eleven-year-old Eddie travels to L.A. to visit his dad, who is writing a weekly movie serial featuring an *Our Gang*-like bunch of kids who track down Nazi spies. Our outline gets to *Wonderworks*, a PBS anthology series. Our contact cares deeply for the project and pushes it hard, but *Wonderworks* operates by committee and the concept is nixed. (As I write, the project, rewritten as a pre-teen novel, is being shopped to agents.)

The one project we create that does fly, a funny and original half hour teleplay for a Canadian animation producer, gets drastically altered. (What else is new in media?) Still, a few of the better elements remain, and Todd and I share a $3500 fee.

Our final effort, *Hocus*, takes off from a quirky original screenplay by my good friend Thom Smitham. It's about a man who keeps turning into a teddy bear.

I can hear you laughing. Believe me, it works!

Todd and I rewrite it, cast actors and present it as staged readings in Santa Cruz and San Francisco. Almost no one is ambivalent about *Hocus*; they love it or hate it. And though we realize it's a script that Hollywood will never produce, we feel that once made *Hocus* might get a lot of play simply because it is so off the wall. With audience reaction in hand, we look forward to a rewrite. But as with so much in life, fate has other plans. The victim of unsound medical advice for too many years, Todd develops colon cancer, and near Christmas in 1993 he dies a hard and lingering death.

A huge loss, because Todd had so much left to do, has been a great help to many others, and because he's been a close and supportive friend. Another in the legion of unsung creative people whose influence continues long after they've gone.

By 1990, Shire Films has turned out twenty-one titles. A credible ten years work. Also by now, educational films are harder to get funded. Other projects are making little or no headway (including a new *Peter and the Wolf* concept with an anti drug-use theme). And even though I keep busy developing ideas, I don't realize that Helen and I will be involved in only one more production together.

But it will be among our finest.

My Uncle Harry, one of the stars of our next production

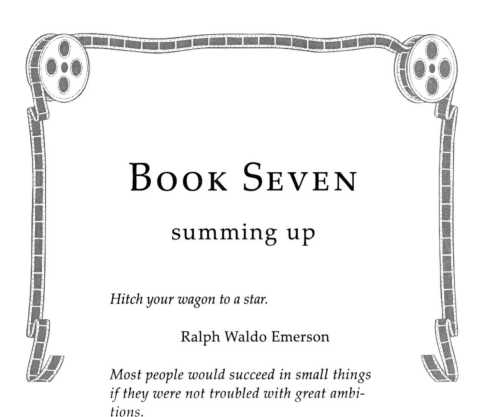

Book Seven

summing up

Hitch your wagon to a star.

Ralph Waldo Emerson

Most people would succeed in small things if they were not troubled with great ambitions.

Henry Wadsworth Longfellow

Turnabout Theater's opening number, with (L to R), Elsa Lanchester, Dorothy Neumann, Frances Osborne, Lotte Goslar, Forman Brown. Harry Burnett (with fiddle)

THIRTY-THREE

turnabout

I used to forge initials, on many a shady scheme,
To the post office officials, I was pinup boy supreme.
But my life of crime I quit it and I'm happy to admit it,
When I heard the magic word Turnabout . . .

This lyric, from the opening act in my puppeteering Uncle Harry's fabulous Turnabout Theater, might serve as metaphor for the point at which my forty-year film career begins to wind down. Still, the hour-long video that Helen and I create about Uncle Harry and his unique little Hollywood playhouse becomes the work I'll be proudest of.

Not that making movies is a "shady scheme," as the ditty might imply (though some producers make it seem that way). For me it's always been magic. If I never became a "pinup boy supreme" at least I got my mug on the calendar. And that's a damn site more rewarding than never having entered the contest.

When I was five, my restless and woolly-haired uncle Harry Burnett announced his arrivals by dropping nickels and pennies through the keyhole in our door. Then he'd pop in to dazzle us for half an hour with gregarious chatter and maybe a clever handkerchief trick. Then vanish like Houdini, until who knows when he'd show up again.

Harry usually showed up with his partners, Forman Brown (a second cousin) and the fussbudget Roddy Brandon. The Yale Puppeteers they called themselves, and they barnstormed America from the early 1920s until 1941, entertaining with songs and sketches and marionettes at colleges and women's clubs, in grand hotels and leaky sheds, from New York, New Hampshire and Pennsylvania to Iowa and Oklahoma. In 1941 they landed in California and established Turnabout Theater, a performing space with two stages that became world famous. Puppets at one end, a saucy adult review with live actors at the other. The seats in between had been salvaged from old streetcars. When the puppet show was finished patrons reversed the seat backs to face the review stage, so if you were in front for the puppets you were in back for the actors. "Turnabout is fair play," said Forman, hosting the whole shebang from his seat at the piano.

Until age twelve, on my first visit west, I didn't realize that Harry and his partners, in addition to being the toast of Hollywood, were also gay. (The term wasn't even current.) By high school and beyond I gradually got to know and appreciate Harry, Roddy and Forman and to love their enchanting hundred-sixty seat playhouse. I took heartthrobs there on dates, and until Turnabout closed in 1956 saw one or another of their shows a dozen times.[1]

Brother David (L) and me in front of Turnabout Theater. Summer of 1944

By 1987 Roddy had died. Harry and Forman were both eighty-six and still very much "with it" mentally. I'd been visiting them off and on for a decade, in the rambling two-story Hollywood home they had shared since a fan let them have it for a modest and never increasing rent. The walls were a congestion of photos, autographed by old time stars who had seen

[1] Much more on Turnabout Theater and the Yale Puppeteers can be found in *Rare Birds*.

them perform: Marlene Dietrich, Ramon Navarro and John Barrymore, everyone who was anyone. Half a dozen marionettes, lonely survivors of the more than six thousand Harry created during his career, peeped out from cobwebbed crannies. On a low stage at one end of the room, Harry and Forman dazzled visitors with their old routines. They also celebrated their January birthdays with a party I often managed to attend. Elsa Lanchester (*Bride of Frankenstein*, 1935), Turnabout's star attraction for twelve years, showed up regularly until her death in 1986.

Here, I decide, is an important slice of theater history that will soon slip into the mists of time. I have to get these guys down on film. So I approach them with the idea. But, says Forman, a video maker friend has already interviewed them and is planning to put together a show. "Great," I reply. This is no crusade; I simply want to see their story documented. So I forget about it. For three years.

Nineteen ninety. Helen's father has died two years earlier. With money from his estate, she's started building a house in the Santa Cruz Mountains. Most of my time, aside from kibitzing on her house plans, is spent writing *Panchostein*, a quirky screenplay taking off from an idea by comedian Paul Rodriguez. But Rodriguez doesn't understand the quirky humor I've integrated into the completed script, so one more for the bone yard.

On another L.A. visit, I check in with Harry and Forman. By now, Harry is spending most of his time in a favorite easy chair knitting little woolen caps, that he donates to a children's hospital. He's also getting a bit woolly in the head. I ask Forman about the video. No progress during the previous year. And Harry and Forman are now almost ninety. Time's a wastin'.

I make an appointment with the videographer (who is also a marionette collector). His home is floor to ceiling with puppets and paraphernalia. Narrow passages between hundreds of props and marionettes hanging helter-skelter allow him to thread his way from one room to the next. I fret; a fire will certainly incinerate decades of theatrical history. And he's run out of money and doesn't know when he'll be able to complete the show. But he's willing to let me see his footage. So he squeezes into a back room and soon emerges with a pile of boxes containing what's been shot so far.

Helen and I screen the cassettes. His interviews are fair, and he's videoed a number of Harry's puppets plus a few old photos. But there are no performances (because these had never been filmed). And the interviews cover nothing about Harry, Forman and Roddy as gay men, an aspect Helen and I deem crucial. How did they survive in a straight world when most every gay was in the closet, we'd like to know? Did being gay have an effect on their work? How did the three of them get along together for seventy years? (Fifty, in the case of Forman and Roddy, who were lovers.)

I make a proposal: if I can use the already shot footage I'll raise the money and complete the video. And if the show brings in a dime beyond expenses the videographer will receive a cut. Deal. But I know this is going to be a labor of love and that profit potential is slim, so approaching those who have invested in previous Shire Films projects seems like a dead issue. Still, I'm determined that Harry and Forman see the show before they sail away to join the great puppeteer in the clouds. Time to get cranking.

Of a hundred twenty-five films written, produced, directed, or animated during my career (not including TV spots and cartoon shows), *Turnabout: the Story of the Yale Puppeteers* will be only my second documentary. Budgets for the kind of hour-long show we anticipate creating often run to two or three hundred thousand. Helen isn't into fund raising and there is no way I can rustle up that kind of money myself. And even if that were possible, I don't believe the sales potential will justify a fat budget. So, without writing in salaries for either of us, I peg the production at $25,000.

Even raising that sum is no stroll in the park.

After acquiring non-profit sponsorship from San Francisco-based Film Arts Foundation, I labor for weeks writing grant proposals, mainly to documentary film funds and foundations supporting gay and lesbian causes. Each group has specialized requirements, so every application has to be agonized over and adjusted. Each potential funder wants a "statement of purpose" tailored to its particular mission. And none offer grants of more than a few thousand. Over the course of 1991 I pull in a total of $7000 from four different foundations. The rest is raised through letters to friends, family and sympathizers.

Ultimately, money comes in from thirty-six individuals (two dozen of these at a party in L.A., hosted by a Municipal Court judge). And none is investment; each donor makes a "non-guaranteed loan," one we don't have to return, but that will earn them back their contribution, plus up to fifty percent interest if and when costs are recouped. Total raised, a bit over $19,000. Which doesn't equal my budget, but is enough to get started.

After analyzing the footage already shot, it's clear that we need more. The interviews are static. Harry and Forman sit on a couch and talk, and that's it. Everything is in two-shots, no close-ups. And though Forman plays the piano and sings songs for guests at Turnabout House (their Hollywood abode) and though Harry still does funny sketches on their living room stage, none of these are included. Nor is there anything about the gay lifestyle.

So, over the next eight months we video Harry once and Forman three times. Always with a crew of four, all we require for a tightly confined show of this kind. Besides, we're cash poor. Because of his increasingly fuzzy memory, I'm especially anxious to get Harry nailed down. Right off, we tape his story about becoming interested in marionettes, how he'd seen a traveling puppeteer in his hometown of Ann Arbor, Michigan and got hooked. Like Ray Bolger with *Peter and the Wolf*, Harry rises to

Uncle Harry, making up as President Truman (Bill Balantine sketch)

Reeling Through Hollywood

Backstage after the show, Puppet Master Burnett lets the audience in on the puppets' intricate private lives.

Bill Ballantine drawing, for *Holiday*, September 1950

Turnabout

Harry created puppets of many famous people of his time, including Charlie Chaplin, Gary Cooper and Albert Einstein

the occasion, describing with animated joviality how he built his first puppet. Later, he manipulates his favorite, Simon Legree (from *Uncle Tom's Cabin*). Then, with Forman at the piano, he recreates a heartfelt routine in which an old vaudevillian recalls his melancholy career playing the hind end of a horse. Several minutes into it Harry stops cold, looks at me and says, "I can't remember the rest of it." Fortunately, Helen finds a way in editing to repeat one of the earlier verses, so that it seems as if he's concluded.

Forman is another story. Consistently engaging and with a memory like the Encyclopedia Britannica, he recalls the puppeteers early days, bumping from town to town in a Ford touring car, passing the hat for a fifteen dollar take at one show then finding but a few coins in it at the next, and performing for Amelia Earhart and her all women flying club and for a Gary Cooper fan club. As well as a private evening for Albert Einstein, featuring a marionette of the great scientist crafted by Harry for the occasion.

Forman sings too, playing his piano and drawing from his repertoire of songs that don't sound as if they should rhyme but somehow do. He has stories about Elsa Lanchester too, tells how he composed more than fifty songs for her, about the many acts featured at Turnabout and about those they rejected. (Liberace was turned down "because we already had a pianist.") He talks about comic dancer Lotte Goslar, and about Odetta, the shy sixteen-year-old daughter of Turnabout's cleaning woman. How they discovered Odetta's wonderful voice and how Harry paid for her singing lessons.

Later, we record Odetta's robust and tender memories of working at the theater. And then get into Harry, Forman and Roddy's gay lifestyle.

TURNABOUT

Though at ninety my uncle is still slightly taken aback when I ask about his experience as a gay man in deep-in-the-closet America, Forman is frank. He discusses writing his early gay novel, *Better Angel* (reprinted in 1987) about affirming his homosexuality when seduced by a young man he met on the way to Europe in 1928, and about falling in love with Roddy Brandon who became his life partner. Ever up to date, he concludes the session with a newly composed song, "You Won't Get Aids," helping to relieve young kids of their fear of the disease.

After taping three times (two and a half days all together) we have footage galore, including footage on me, as narrator, since I've decided to tell the story from a personal point of view. Now to gather the rest of the elements, because documentaries with nothing but talking heads can often trundle viewers off to the Land of Nod.

Fortunately, Turnabout House is a museum of Harry and Forman's life and work, housing the autographed movie star photos, old posters, boxes of snapshots, and the very hat they passed to collect money in their traveling days. All the blue covers from Turnabout's streetcar seats are there too, with names like "Pyramus n' Thisbe," "Vim n' Vigor," and "Betwixt n' Between," stitched on in white script. And though no footage of Turnabout performances seems to exist, rooting around in an upstairs trunk I discover a small can with a 16mm roll inside that turns out to be three minutes of black and white film taken backstage during the early 1940s. In it, Harry, Roddy and another puppeteer operate control sticks while marionettes dance on the stage below. Not much, but a beginning. Then Forman remembers a video they have, shot a decade earlier by an L.A. TV station. This features Harry operating his Simon Legree puppet. Harry's faculties were sharper then and the performance better than the one we've recorded. There is also a poignant clip with Harry making up as a sad-faced clown, talking to himself about this, his last show.

Then, as I get Forman to jog his memory further, he remembers that someone had taped a performance of Elsa Lanchester. Turns out to feature her appearance at a Hollywood nightclub. Though it wasn't on the Turnabout stage, she sings several numbers by Forman. I'm thrilled, especially since, even in her sixties, Elsa still had the same vivacious style she had when I saw her in my teens.

In a Turnabout House hallway I find stills from a couple of old films. Both include Harry, Forman and Roddy. Do these movies still exist, I wonder? Forman has no idea. After several calls I locate the only extant print of *I Am Suzanne* (1933), at the Museum of Modern Art in New York. I also learn that Columbia has recently transferred the other, *Whom The Gods Destroy* (1934) to video. Both had been produced nearly a decade before Turnabout Theater, but each one features Harry's marionettes. In *I Am Suzanne*, a puppet-size Lilian Harvey, star of the film, glides along a wire over the audience and lands on stage – which then fills with ice skating marionettes. Quite a chore to acquire the footage, because the Museum of Modern Art allows only a one-month window during which their rare films can be looked at and sections copied. For a fee, of course. Columbia wants $3000 for a minute of footage from *Whom The Gods Destroy*. But after I send them a letter explaining the labor of love nature of the project, they let us have several clips for transfer costs alone.

As I locate more items (a photo of Robert Frost, another of Carl Sandburg – Forman knew both men in his college days – an album of songs recorded at Turnabout Theater, a recording of Odetta singing "Water Boy"), I write letters to seek permission and square away legal issues. Details, always details. But since the budget is so tiny, someone has to do it. Once again, that's the essence of low budget movie making. But there's a lot of satisfaction in knowing that what you eventually see on screen is something you've put together yourself.

With all the elements assembled, I transcribe every snatch of interview dialogue to typed copy and, based on the best material, cobble together a script. Helen has scrounged enough out of the budget to buy a used off line editing system.

Finally, we're ready to put the show together.

Turnabout

During the past year Harry has suffered a series of small strokes, has been in and out of the hospital and is now in a convalescent home a mile from Turnabout House. Forman, frail himself, walks the mile there and back seven days a week to visit Harry and play piano for the residents. The pressure to complete the video seems urgent.

Helen works diligently. Within weeks we've got a rough cut. But it doesn't have quite the punch we want. So she cuts and snips, reverses the order of scenes, and after more long hours comes up with a fine cut that not only merges the stories of Harry, Forman and Roddy as gay men, but also their lives as entertainers. And does so seamlessly. By the time we go on line with the show we're confident we have a winner.

Our first audience is Harry and Forman. Forman loves it. We take it to the rest home. By now, Harry is losing it big time. He can't mentally focus on what he sees, his eyesight is shot and I'm not sure he even realizes that it's himself in the film. But when Forman explains it all he smiles and seems to understand.

Turnabout is now complete. Harry gets to see it (sort of). And 1992 is winding down. Time to introduce my uncle and his family to the world.

Harry Burnett (L) and Forman Brown at age 92

Marketing an independently made documentary is no piece of cake. Usually, by the time a "doc" airs on PBS, or gets released theatrically, it's been through the grant-funding mill of the National Endowment for the Arts, or received corporate grants, or has interested one or another PBS venue – which may even have sunk money into the production.

Even before completion I send out information packets to The Discovery Channel, Bravo, Lifetime, Cinamax, The UK's Channel Four, ZDF in Germany; to other cable channels and to PBS. Then, as soon as we have cassettes, off they go to everyone who has requested one. And many do.

American Experience feels that *Turnabout* is "a wonderful lively portrait of two talented artists, done with much humor and affection," but "doesn't venture beyond their private lives" to include a broader social or historical context. *Arts and Entertainment* can only support "the most highly visible projects." Polite but friendly turn downs too from *American Playhouse*, HBO, POV and several others.

But then, success! In May of 1993 the Retirement Research Foundation awards *Turnabout* the $1000 second prize in their documentary category and pays my expenses to Chicago to receive their National Media Owl Award, presented by sob sister Ann Landers and reviewer Gene Siskel. An event capped by a dessert reception open to anyone. In addition to celebrities and award winners, half of Dearborn Avenue's street people look forward to this annual muncharama. Kind of like at the Salvation Army, they have to sit through all the speeches first.

Then we make a sale to PBS station KQED in San Francisco and another to WNET in New York. This last via Pop's cousin, Mike Bessie, a WNET board member, who passes a cassette to those programming the station's gay pride week. "The only show I've ever been able to get them to buy," Mike tells me, with some pride.[2] Later, *Turnabout* is aired on PBS's Seattle/Tacoma affiliate.

---

[2] Simon Michael Bessie too has a chapter in *Rare Birds*.

TURNABOUT

Harry never gets to celebrate. After gradually sliding physically down hill he dies on May 27, 1993. A huge loss for me, but much more sad for Forman; the departure of his best friend since their college days, his workmate of seventy years, and the second third of his family.

Through the fall of 1993, *Turnabout* enjoys a modest theatrical release (we've struck two 16mm prints): weekend screenings in San Jose, Santa Cruz and Los Angeles.

Small crowds for the most part, but a wonderful reception each time. I appear at all three venues to answer questions.[3]

There are no "mixed" reviews. Not a mediocre one in the bunch. All raves. Even the L.A. Times' Kevin Thomas (who had slammed *Hard Traveling*) finds *Turnabout* "delightful," and promises his readers that the show "is a great deal more than how sophisticated live entertainment in Los Angeles actually could be forty or fifty years ago. It is the story of how three men, who happened to be gay at a time when being out was not a realistic possibility, managed to share their lives and their talents to forge remarkably creative accomplishments." To the *San Francisco Examiner*, it's "a heartwarming tale," and to the *Santa Cruz Good Times*, "engaging, upbeat and hugely entertaining." But since *Turnabout* makes little headway at the national level, most remaining reviews come from the gay press, which uniformly adores the show and writes article after article about it.

My biggest kick comes at the festivals. In June, a loud, enthusiastic reception for *Turnabout* and for Forman himself at the San Francisco International Lesbian and Gay Film Festival; five hundred in attendance at 5 p.m. on a Wednesday. At a bookstore reception following, fans keep him answering questions for an hour and a half.

---

[3] Forman submitted to a healthy lionization over *Turnabout* and was featured in articles in gay publications, with headlines such as "L.A.'s Oldest Living Fag."

Later, appreciative crowds at festivals in Los Angeles, Chicago, Washington, D.C., Minneapolis, Boston, Portland, Winnipeg and Connecticut. (Helen and I make L.A. and Connecticut.) Each festival celebrates gay and lesbian media. Although most who see *Turnabout* understand that it deals with universal questions around aging, friendship and creativity, the video rarely gets out of the "gay ghetto," and is programmed for TV only on shows celebrating that theme. Exceptions are the International Festival of Puppet Theater in Jerusalem, the American Film Festival (a finalist) and the National Educational Film and Video Festival, where *Turnabout* wins a Silver Apple award.

And then, along comes Leipzig.

When to my surprise *Turnabout* is invited to the Leipzig Documentary and Animation Festival, I'm stoked. And eager to attend, especially since they'll pay bed and board for three days. I'm a bit puzzled that Helen doesn't want to make the trip, but since she says I should go, and since we can afford the airfare, I leap at the chance.

In 1961 my father had traveled to Berlin, and while there had adapted his novel *The Un-Americans* (1957) for both radio and TV. His contacts were TV producer Klaus Wishnewski and his wife, Christa, producing for radio. And it's this engaging couple I meet the day I arrive in Leipzig. Quite possibly (though he denies it), *Turnabout* was invited because Klaus, one of the festival's directors, recognized the Bessie name.

Most films are in German, so I see only two. Though I'm somehow able to make sense of a long documentary about Hitler's favorite filmmaker, Leni Rifenstahl (*Triumph of the Will*, 1935), who "was never political" (so she claimed). I pal around with the one other American filmmaker, visit Papa Bach's grave, and Auerbach's Keller where Faust is supposed to have made his pact with the devil. Typical tourist stuff.

Turnabout is screened in the "Queer Doc" section. Shown at 11 p.m., an audience of forty dwindles to twenty. Unsurprising since *Turnabout's* wall-to-wall words, in English, is hard for most Germans to understand. Profuse apologies from Klaus and Christa. But they make it up by chauffeuring me, via Wittenberg where Martin Luther lived, to Berlin, where I marvel at the Ishtar gate from Babylon at the Pergamon museum (just like the Brits, Germans archeologists had been all over the middle east, swiping everything they could lay their hands on), drive by the site of Hitler's bunker – now covered by expensive high rise condos – and visit the ruined cellar of the former Gestapo headquarters, featuring a "Topography of Terrors" exhibit. At Checkpoint Charlie, former Russian GIs sell fur-lined hats and matrioshka dolls. And in the museum housing the magnificent work of Käthe Kollwitz, a sign in front of her sculp-

REELING THROUGH HOLLYWOOD

tures invites visitors to "Please Touch. Come in contact with the art."

Although the Germans are outgoing and friendly, and though instead of a Nazi oompah band parading down Unter den Linden, Bolivian flute players now pipe their pipes and peddle cassettes to the natives, for me, Berlin is eerie. As a child of the Second World War I half expect a squad of beefy storm troopers to round a corner, seize me and cart me off to Buchenwald.

June 1995. No more TV sales, no chance for more theatrical screenings. And I'm worn out trying to promote the video. We do, however, have a distributor for the VHS market, who advances $2000. But otherwise, *Turnabout* has run out of steam.[4]

So, apparently, has Helen's and my relationship. Though I won't know it for another three months.

By the time we return from the Honolulu Gay and Lesbian Film Festival in July, Helen has begun work on a video history of Students for a Democratic Society (SDS), the radical student group she belonged to during the 1960s. By September she decides to work on the project with an old SDS buddy. So off to Oregon she goes, to brainstorm ideas with him. By the time she returns she and her old buddy are in love. And she wants to end our relationship.

What, *again*? I am obviously pissed. We argue. I cajole, and for weeks wage a campaign to win her back, but to no avail. Her mind is made up. Then she's off again, on a cross-country trip to interview SDS friends and gather research material for her project. She wants me out by the time she returns a month later, so I start looking for new quarters. And though I make my peace with her decision fairly quickly (and am soon actually grateful for it – ain't hindsight grand?), I still never completely figure out why, in spite of my own faux pas, our deep commonalities and seventeen years of sharing a rich creative life couldn't have helped hold us together.

---

[4] In spite of wonderful reviews and decent publicity the video sold poorly. Perhaps there's simply a tiny market for a story about elderly gays. But there's still hope; I've recently brought it out on DVD.

Turnabout

Well, water over the dam. What can I say? People change. Before Helen returns, son Tim arrives with his Toyota pickup to help me transport my worldly possessions to a cute little cottage I've rented near downtown Santa Cruz. Helen and I will remain friends, but create no more movies together.

One door closes, another opens. Time to turn about.

Harry Burnett. New Hampshire, 1930's

THIRTY-FOUR

moving on

For Dan Bessie, with the hope that his life will be as rich and happy – his times as deep and exciting.

28 August 1948. From Alvah and Helen / Los Angeles, Cal.

This birthday dedication was written in the flyleaf of *Art Young, His Life and Times* (1939). If you've read this far you know that Alvah was my father. This particular Helen was Pop's second wife, Helen Clare Nelson. Combining as it does the story of early American socialism with the drive to become an artist, Art Young's memoir had a huge influence on me. At sixteen, I saw myself treading a similar path.

Young, one of America's great political cartoonists, was born into a conservative Wisconsin family in 1866. After reading a library book illustrated by Gustave Dore, he became so impressed that he became an illustrator. By seventeen, he was selling work to national magazines. After hearing a speech by a British socialist, he began to question his own politics. Then, after drawing an anti-immigration cartoon for *Life*, Young had second thoughts and returned the magazine's $100 check (no small potatoes in 1902). From then on he vowed to only draw pictures reflecting his own view of the world, and until his death in 1943 Art Young's work was so highly valued that even non-political mainstream publications accepted his cartoons attacking corporate greed and supporting causes he believed in. One cartoon so upset the Associated Press that he was indicted for criminal libel. Later, opposing America's entry into World War I, he was on trial again for producing material "undermining the war effort."

Moving On

I've never been privileged to stand trial for undermining America's involvement in any war, but I've carried signs and earned blisters while protesting every conflict from Korea to Vietnam to Gulf War II in Iraq (AKA "The Revenge of the Bush Leaguers"). Also like Young, I mixed art and politics for a lot of years. But his art and politics were based on firmer foundations than mine. Young thought deeply and changed his political views. I was a red diaper baby, and mine never changed (pun intended). He made art a serious study for years. I took classes for eight months, including two months of twice-weekly classes at the same school Young did, the Art Students League of New York.

And there, both the similarities and the differences end. Art Young was a master. I've been one of those who "get by." No bumbling novice mind you (except at the start), but in my heart of hearts I always knew I could have achieved more. Not fame and fortune, but by becoming a better cartoonist, writer and film director. Proud as I've been of several films, some artwork, and the books I've created, I could have done much better, earlier.

Self-disparagement? (Creative folk are supposed to be ego driven, right? Pump themselves up?) No, I don't put myself down. Rather this is an attempt at assessment. And designed to convince you, no matter what your ambition, that if you can look at yourself honestly early enough, the possibility of a rich and rewarding life are magnified tenfold. I wasn't terribly focused until my late forties, didn't set disciplined and achievable goals and go for them, let too many inanities and a restless mind bog me down in fruitless pursuits. Often, I just didn't see the woods for the trees.

Would I have been a major player if I had done it differently? Be able to point to directing credits on twenty blockbusters? Been a nationally recognized cartoonist? I don't know. For each of us, in one way or another, life interferes. We fall in love, have kids, and are victim to the way we've been raised. Some of us emulate parents; others flee from them and their values in disgust. Some overcome intense trauma and achieve greatness. Most of us blunder along the best we can.

REELING THROUGH HOLLYWOOD

But taking a hard look at yourself doesn't mean that if you realize you'll never win the lottery you need to stencil "F" on your internal report card. Far from it. I look on my life as a roaring success. A success because most of the time I've done what I've wanted to do. Because even recognizing that some of my labor involved churning out commercial pap, I've usually enjoyed the creative process. Because I've spent much of my career contributing something of real worth to the world. Because I've kept growing and learning. And because new ideas never stop percolating.

Thus far, I've made no more films or videos of my own after *Turnabout*. But I continued to animate for Albuquerque's Bandelier Films for another three years, until Alan Stevens' son Tim mastered the craft and swiped my job. I worked for a year on a TV show helping to mainstream sign language, helped establish the first ever Santa Cruz Film Festival, worked with my friend Severo (who bought Learning Garden from me) in producing two of his films, and directed a staged reading of another friend's prizewinning screenplay that's not yet been sold. As recently as July of 2004 I directed a half hour pilot for PuppARTry Place, a potential new TV series teaching art to children.

And when a former screenplay student and friend, Susana Herrera, returned from two years of Peace Corps service in Cameroon (Africa), I mentored her in using the letters she wrote home as she created *Mango Elephants in the Sun* (2000), a poignant and much acclaimed book about her experiences.

There were more trips to Los Angeles. After Forman Brown's death in January of 1996 (one day after his 95th birthday), the City Council honored his life with a moving tribute. The Public Library held a gala celebrating the puppeteers when they acquired Turnabout Theater's memorabilia. I appeared at UCLA when their Screenwriters' Showcase honored my father (among other blacklistees) with a Lifetime Achievement Award, attended an American Civil Liberties Union dinner celebrating the Hollywood Ten, and took in the opening of the Academy of Motion Picture Arts and Sciences' exhibit on "Reds and Blacklists in Hollywood." (By

Moving On

2000, having once been a Hollywood Red had become a badge of honor.) And in 2005, I screened my pop's 1945 film *Hotel Berlin* and appeared on another panel on the blacklist at the 25th annual San Francisco International Jewish Film Festival.

Teaching continued as well. I held screenwriting workshops in my home, through UC Santa Cruz and other colleges, and became modestly well known as a screenplay coach around Northern California. Until budget cuts axed the entire arts program, I also spent five years leading workshops on creative writing in the California prison system. Some of the most dedicated and thoughtful writers I worked with had been dopers, rapists, murderers, and white-collar thieves. Terrible crimes, but most of these men were trying to turn their lives around, and my time spent with them was more than satisfying.

I've also seen three books published (including this one), and have illustrated several others.

With a great-grandfather who arrived in America as a stowaway then served in an all black regiment during the Civil War, an uncle whose ad agency created a dozen icons of American advertising, my blacklisted father, my puppeteering Uncle Harry, a cousin who saw more birds than anyone alive, and another who published *The Alice B. Toklas Cookbook*, and Anwar Sadat's autobiography, I just had to write about them. I've referred to the title earlier: *Rare Birds, an American Family.* Reviewers cheered:

"Bessie portrays his relatives - both famous and not - as striking examples of American individuality, ingenuity and creativity. . . This heartfelt, warmly intelligent kaleidoscope of intimate portraits never glosses over the rough edges."

Publisher's Weekly

REELING THROUGH HOLLYWOOD

" . . .a fetching family history . . .Rare Birds is an extended curtain call for a highly original cast, with an enamored but clear-eyed descendant working the curtain."

San Francisco Chronicle

" . . .his breathless enthusiasm . . .and flair for irony inform the entire memoir, as do the splendid family snapshots he has painstakingly assembled."

New York Times

Rush right out and buy a copy. And pick up *Alvah Bessie's Spanish Civil War Notebooks* (2001) while you're at it.[1] This faithful record of Pop's year in Spain in 1938 is a work he always wanted to see published. I toured California giving book talks and signing copies of both titles, drew respectable audiences, drove to Kentucky for a book festival, and through it all had a great time. But Oprah never called, so in spite of uniformly excellent reviews, the sales for *Rare Birds* froze at twelve hundred copies. And mainly universities, along with a clutch of die-hard Spanish Civil War buffs, purchased Pop's notebooks.

The name of the game is give it your best shot and hope the book or the movie will fly. Above all, trust your heart and go with what you believe in.

One more thing: I fell in love again. Twice. (After a couple false starts.) The first time, with the effervescent owner of a folk arts boutique. I hung in for three years, mostly as close friends, because even though we cared deeply about one another, for her the magic never quite materialized.

---

[1] You'll find it on Amazon, or through our website, bluelupinpress.com

Moving On

Then, more sputtering sparks with those of the female persuasion. And finally, after escaping to the Sierra foothills and purchasing a small house, and after many long weekends fixing it up, I began surfing the net. After a year of cyberspace dead ends I discovered that rare and wonderfully synchronistic connection, a captivating woman in a tiny row house next to an interurban railroad in central England. After forgetting about the message I'd sent to an online singles site, ten days later I got a reply:

Hello Dan the Writerman,

What a pleasant surprise to get your e-mail. Well, California is rather a long way but it sounds a lot more inviting than a wet and cold Birmingham. Actually, I've just returned from a couple of weeks in Barcelona, but even that was a bit wet and cold. Let me know when California has a drought and I'll come over, because I'm obviously a rainmaker.

Jeanne (pronounced the French way) is warm and giving, wickedly funny, and, after decades as a teacher and counselor, finding her métier as a writer and artist. After a year's worth of back and forth visits, stacks of immigration forms, and silly lingering doubts on my part (that old commitment thing) we got married. Now we share a cozy little home among the deer and the daffodils, in a pine studded valley at the end of what had been the world's bumpiest road but which has recently been paved. She has a book out too (*Starlings in the Park*. Check it out). And together we take on assignments to edit other's work. We make a great creative team. Life is more than good. It's the way I always knew it could be. There are no bumps. Not a one.

My sons go on being the kind and gentle souls they've always been. Tim works as a computer programmer, depletes his savings traveling the world, and in 1996 cycled cross-country with Bike-Aid, developing support for environmental causes. He visits Jeanne and me in the hills now and then, and will, one day soon (I hope) find the great love of his life. Son Joe, married for many years, is the Academic Vice-President of a Midwestern university. And I'm a grandpa now, with two energetic twins, Katherine and Alexander.

Joe and I see one another infrequently, and try to resolve the angst he feels about growing up with me as his father. And I keep on loving both these great guys with all my heart.

Back to the year 2000, the year of my fiftieth high school reunion. I was half an hour early, so I cruised around Santa Monica. Past Samohi, where, as head cheerleader, I yelled myself hoarse rousing fans for our basketball team that came within three points of winning the federation championship. I passed the alley off Pico Boulevard where I lived with brother David and Mom, and where my first wife Rose and I held our post-wedding fling. I cruised down Broadway, past where Signs By Smith was located. Even though I knew the old sign shop wasn't there, and that dear old paint-flecked Smith was probably pushing up the daisies, I couldn't help being overcome by nostalgia. After all, in a way, he started it. He had dreams of becoming an artist but never did. Maybe just because he didn't get there, that set *me* off, determined to live my dream.

Did I make it? What do you think? Fame only shadowed my doorstep. It never rang the bell. But instead of contemplating my navel, I became a member of that little-sung legion of media makers who try their damnedest to do what they can the best way they know how. And I decided to write this book. To entertain, I hope, and help you understand that you can enjoy a rich and productive life by doing exactly what you love to do. So long as you don't let anyone convince you that you're worthless or no good or a "loser" (a word that ought to be banished) if your name is never featured in three-foot high letters on the silver screen.

And I hope I've provided a bit more insight into the crazy but wonderful world of movie making than you may have had before turning the first page. That's why folks write, I suppose. To amuse and enlighten and say what they feel about life. And perhaps, if they're fortunate, make a little money.

As Porky Pig said, at the end of those old Warner Brothers cartoons (but without the stutter), "That's all, folks!" For those into media, it's your turn to run with the ball. Passing on what we learn from both our triumphs and our failures (especially our failures) seems to me an important part of what existing on this planet is all about. And to anyone seeking a direction, whether they are in media or not, I can think of no better words than those of Art Young:

> I think of myself as a kind of sample of the human race; in some respects a poor sample, and different, if not peculiar. But my problems, I feel, have been in the main much like those of most men and women, at least in this regional habitat of the race, the United States of America.
>
> Every one of us is born with some kind of talent. In early manhood or womanhood each individual begins to see a path, though perhaps dimly, that beckons to him or her. All of us have this leaning toward, or desire for doing ably, a certain kind of work, and only want an opportunity to prove our capacity in that direction. These hunches, these signs of one's natural trend, are usually right, and are not to be thrust aside without regret in later life.

To Art Young's thoughts I can only add this: try to remember that the art of living is not only the possibility of realizing what might be, or what you wish for, but the enjoyment of what is.

With Jeanne Johnson, my wonder of a wife